KU-390-075

LUCK OF A LANCASTER

LUCK OF A LANCASTER

107 operations
240 crew, 103 of them killed in action

Gordon Thorburn

Pen & Sword
AVIATION

First Published in Great Britain in 2013 by
Pen & Sword Aviation
an imprint of
Pen & Sword Books Ltd
47 Church Street, Barnsley, South Yorkshire S70 2AS

Copyright © Gordon Thorburn, 2013

ISBN 978-1-78159-073-7

The right of Gordon Thorburn to be identified as author of this work
has been asserted by him in accordance with the Copyright,
Designs and Patents Act 1988.

A CIP catalogue record for this book is
available from the British Library.

All rights reserved. No part of this book may be reproduced or transmitted in
any form or by any means, electronic or mechanical including photocopying,
recording or by any information storage and retrieval system, without
permission from the Publisher in writing.

Typeset in 10/12pt Palatino by
Concept, Huddersfield

Printed and bound in England by
MPG Printgroup

Pen & Sword Books Ltd incorporates the Imprints of Pen & Sword
Aviation, Pen & Sword Family History, Pen & Sword Maritime, Pen & Sword
Military, Pen & Sword Discovery, Wharncliffe Local History, Wharncliffe
True Crime, Wharncliffe Transport, Pen & Sword Select, Pen & Sword
Military Classics, Leo Cooper, The Praetorian Press, Remember When,
Seaforth Publishing and Frontline Publishing.

For a complete list of Pen & Sword titles please contact
PEN & SWORD BOOKS LIMITED
47 Church Street, Barnsley, South Yorkshire, S70 2AS, England
E-mail: enquiries@pen-and-sword.co.uk
Website: www.pen-and-sword.co.uk

Contents

BRITANNIA SHALL RULE THE SKIES

THEY WHO LOOK AHEAD

ISSUED BY HELLIWELLS LIMITED WALSALL AIRPORT AND AT DUDLEY.

WORLD TRAVEL
by
AIR FRANCE

Two giant legs straddling the hemispheres – that's the map of the AIR FRANCE trunk services. East to China, west to Chile, south to Africa – to say nothing of a network of lines that link the cities of Europe – AIR FRANCE planes ride the skies swiftly, regularly, smoothly and safely.

The newest and most airworthy craft carry you, the smartest and most courteously efficient staff serves you, and the reputation of a great national organisation stands behind you, when you travel AIR FRANCE.

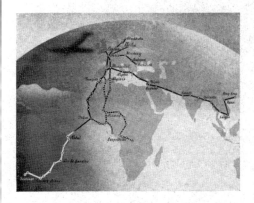

AIR FRANCE serves four of the earth's five continents, and throughout its history it has been continuously improving its planes, its services and its service – adding, extending and perfecting all the time.

Fascinating destinations are reached with ease by fast Dewoitines. Popular Bloch 220's speed you on short business or pleasure trips. Liore flying boats carry you over the seas. It's all luxury, and low-priced luxury at that.

Your travel agent will give you details of all AIR FRANCE Services. Or apply to:

AIR FRANCE

52, HAYMARKET, LONDON, S.W.1. Telephone: WHitehall 9671/4

Get into the air and *FIGHT!*

The Battle of Germany will be far fiercer than the Battle of Britain. It, too, must end in victory for the R.A.F. You with the fighting spirit, you too will want to be "in" — doing this grand job, full of adventure — getting the chance of a real crack at the enemy! Even if you are in a "reserved" job you can still volunteer for flying duties. And you who are being *de-reserved* and are thoroughly fit — even if you didn't express preference for R.A.F. flying duties when you registered for National Service with your age group — *you can volunteer now,* provided you are not yet posted to another Service. Men are wanted as Pilots (age under 31), Observers (age under 33). Pay, allowances and living conditions are good.

Volunteer for flying duties at the R.A.F. Section of your nearest Combined Recruiting Centre (address from any Employment Exchange), or post coupon for full details (unsealed envelope—1d. stamp).

Fly with the **RAF**

| To Air Ministry Information Bureau, Kingsway, London, W.C.2. *Please send* "*Flying Duties*" *leaflet.* |
| AGE.................. |
| NAME .... |
| ADDRESS |
| AKS/Mar. |

Coopers Y-fronts
ON THE AIR FRONT

A new conception in UNDERWEAR for active men.. and men on active service

Ask your Retailer or your own N.A.A.F.I. canteen for Y-Front Vests shorts, midways, longs

Coopers Y-front UNDERWEAR

Enquiries to
LYLE & SCOTT Ltd., Producers & Distributors **HAWICK, SCOTLAND**
or **IDEAL HOUSE, ARGYLL ST. OXFORD CIRCUS**

PARKERIZING
for
LUBRICATION

. . . . . A new principle of reducing wear on many parts has been discovered. This is a modification of the well-known "PARKERIZING" Rust-Proofing Process to give a non-metallic oil-retentive coating on engine components.

Pre-war this use of "PARKERIZING" for lubrication was only in the research and experimental stage. The necessity for making the best use of controlled raw materials to avoid rapid wear and to increase the length of life of working parts, has speeded up development to the extent that it is now being used in production.

In the public interest we felt that any development of value to the common effort should be released as soon as possible even though our technical investigations had not yet been finalised.

Pyrene
TRADE MARK

METAL FINISHING PROCESSES

PARKERIZED
Regd. Trade Mark

BONDERIZED
Regd. Trade Mark

SPRA-BONDERIZED
Regd. Trade Mark

Three words meaning rust-proofed with PYRENE Chemicals

THE PYRENE COMPANY, LIMITED
METAL FINISHING DIVISION
Great West Road, Brentford, Middlesex

"YOU *have been* LISTENING
to a RECORDING--"

In the 80's, "Punch" satirised "bottled music." To-day, gramophone reproductions of masterpieces of music, song, and oratory are scarcely distinguishable from the original performances. The "record" registering an illimitable number of sound gradations, in grooves measuring only one-hundredth of an inch, is one of the most marvellous examples of precision engineering.

Until war intervened, the British Salmson car was another product which owed its reputation to precision engineering, but the skilled craftsmanship which was put into it is now being devoted to war work.

PRECISION MACHINING OF ALL TYPES. FITTING AND SUB-ASSEMBLY WORK, ETC.
TOOL AND GAUGE MAKING: JIG BORING. SHEET METAL AND LIGHT PRESS WORK.

BRITISH SALMSON
AERO ENGINES LTD.
Precision Engineers
RAYNES PARK   LONDON. S.W.20

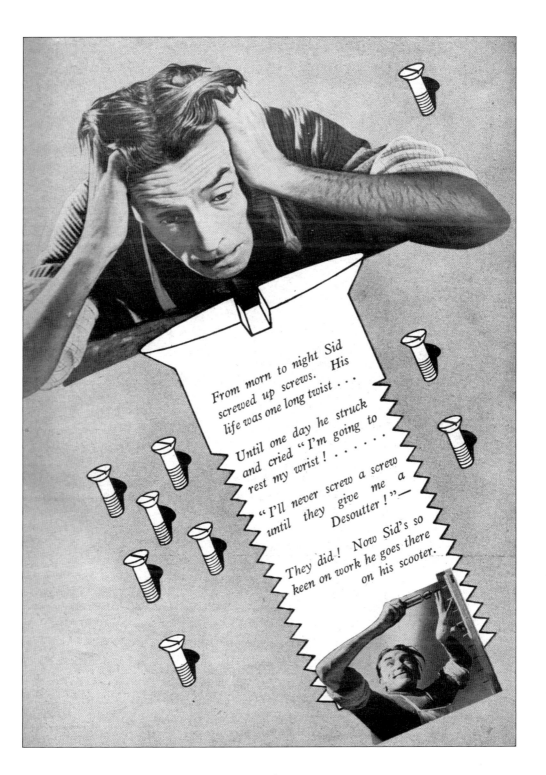

Book your seat for Berlin!

Not bombs alone. Not 'planes alone. Not guns alone will win this war—but *Men!* Men—under 33. Determined men. Men who know that they have a great cause to fight for. Men who know that team-work is the hardest work of all. Thousands of them are training to fly with the R.A.F. Thousands more are needed — to be ready for training when required. NOW is the time to reserve your place in Britain's Air Crew teams of the future.

MEN IN RESERVED OCCUPATIONS ARE FREE TO JOIN

Go to the R.A.F. Section of your Combined Recruiting Centre (address from Employment Exchange), tell them your trade and say you want to volunteer. You can be considered for acceptance as a Pilot if you are 17¼ but not yet 31. As Observers you may be accepted up to 33, or in certain special cases up to 41. The Recruiting Centre will give you all particulars. If you can't visit it, fill in the coupon. Take the first step NOW!

Fly with the

RAF

To Air Ministry Information Bureau, Kingsway, London, W.C.2. *Please send me latest leaflet, giving details of Flying Service in the R.A.F.*

AGE..............

NAME..............

ADDRESS

AKS/Nov.

Acknowledgements

Thanks to Stuart Watkins, Squadron Leader Dicky James, Jim Shortland, Terry Lintin.

Preface

Squadrons of the Royal Naval Air Service arrived in France at the end of August 1914, mainly to bolster the Royal Flying Corps of the army rather than to fulfil naval duties. No. 1 Squadron RNAS set up at Antwerp and attempted a truly daring feat on 22 September when four aircraft were sent on a bombing mission to the Zeppelin sheds at Düsseldorf and Cologne. The weather was very bad for flying but one did make it to the target, a Sopwith flown by Lieutenant C. H. Collet. After coming down through thick mist, he dropped three twenty-pounders, from the hand; the two that hit a shed proved to be duds.

The second attempt on 8 October was a triumph. Two RNAS Sopwith Tabloids set off from Antwerp.

The Tabloid had been built in 1913 for the civilian market as the aerial equivalent of a sports car. It could do 90mph; far more than standard service aircraft. A float-plane adaptation of it had won the second Schneider Trophy race in the April, at just under 87mph (the first race, in 1913, had been won at 45mph). It was said that, after seeing the Tabloid in practice, most of the other competitors didn't bother racing.

The RNAS pilots were in the single-seater version, unarmed at this point in the war, flying alone right into the Fatherland with nothing more than their service revolvers. It was a sensation. Here is an eye-witness report:

> 'I was in Düsseldorf when the English airman visited the town for the second time. It was a splendid feat – he took the Germans by surprise. The soldiers seeing the hostile aircraft high up in the air shot at it continually until suddenly the aeroplane started to glide lower and lower; the people were mad with joy and shouted 'hurrah'. The soldiers got ready to catch the aeroplane as it fell when suddenly from a height of between 100 and 200 metres the airman threw several bombs, one of which reached its goal –

the Zeppelin shed, in which there was the air-cruiser, the pride of Düsseldorf, which had received orders to join the army in France that afternoon. In spite of my being a good distance away, I heard the explosion, the smoke whirling high into the air, and I saw the airman escape in the common confusion.'

The German papers next day had 'Zeppelin shed slightly damaged' and failed to mention the four army officers killed or the heap of ashes that was the remains of airship Z9.

The English airman was Lieutenant Reginald L. G. Marix. While his aircraft was being hit five times by rifle shots and *mitrailleuse* (multi-barrelled machine gun), he dropped two twenty-pounders by hand from less than 600ft and changed the military outlook on bombing. As *The Times* said, under the headline 'The value of bomb-dropping':

'There has always been a little uncertainty about the value of bomb-dropping, for although it seemed possible that buildings might be set alight with incendiary explosives, it was another matter to make sure of hitting the right building. The naval pilots have now shown at Düsseldorf that this is possible.'

The other aircraft, flown by Squadron Commander D. A. Spenser-Grey, found Cologne but missed the Zeppelin base there, so bombed the railway station instead. Marix and Collet were both awarded the DSO; Spenser-Grey already had one.

The Admiralty pointed out that the importance of the Collet attack lay in the fact it showed that: 'In the event of further bombs being dropped into Antwerp and other Belgian towns, measures of reprisal can certainly be adopted, if desired, to almost any extent.' Charles Herbert Collet DSO would not live to see much in the way of reprisals. He was killed in action at Gallipoli in August 1915.

The Admiralty also said: 'The feat (by Marix) would appear to be in every respect remarkable, having regard to the distance – over a hundred miles – penetrated into country held by the enemy'.

The Times added a footnote: 'Demand for air risk insurance. There was again a very large amount of insurance effected in London yesterday against the risks of damage by aircraft and bombs and shells thrown therefrom; and underwriters hardened their rates. A premium of 2s 6d per cent is now regarded as the minimum.'

The Handley Page Heyford (above) was an improvement on the 1920s Vickers Virginia (below), pictured flying well within the speed limit with all her crew in the fresh air. The Heyford had a maximum speed of 142mph, a range of 920 miles, and a crew of four: two pilots, observer/navigator, wireless operator/air gunner. This was 9 Squadron's equipment from 1935 until early 1939. Note the huge, non-retractable undercarriage and the open cockpit. The possibility of such an aircraft penetrating into country held by the enemy was rather compromised by its armament – single Lewis guns in nose and mid-dorsal stations, and in the 'dustbin' turret hanging underneath.

With speed and range much reduced by a maximum bomb load of 3,500lb, 9 Squadron expected to be briefed to fly these sad-looking machines to the Ruhr, and to bail out over Holland coming home, out of petrol, if the Chamberlain/Hitler talks of 1938 had had a different outcome. Had they managed penetration, they would have been met by Messerschmitt Me109 fighters.

Penetrating into enemy country and making sure of hitting the right building: Bremen (A), Brunswick (B) and Essen (C) at the end of the Second World War.

CHAPTER 1

A Lancaster Called Jig

Every war has turning points and there are always disagreements about which were the turning points and what was the significance of each. For Bomber Command in the Second World War there were several in February 1942, which we shall come to shortly. Before that, there was a series of meetings in London at the end of July 1940 between an aircraft company executive and some government officials which resulted in possibly the most important single decision of the air war in Europe.

A. V. Roe Ltd, under chief designer Roy Chadwick and managing director Roy Dobson, designed and built a new bomber, answering Air Ministry specification P13/36, which demanded a twin-engined aircraft capable of carrying 8,000lb bomb loads. That seemed like a lot of work for two engines, so A. V. Roe and its rivals Handley Page selected the Rolls-Royce Vulture, a 24-cylinder, more powerful but novel successor to the Merlin.

One result, the Avro 679, the Manchester, first flew from Ringway on 25 July 1939. Plans were laid for mass production but development problems with the Vulture engine meant delays and confusion, among which Chadwick asked his team to look at the possibility of a four-engined Manchester, perhaps using the Bristol Hercules engine that would later make such an improvement to the Vickers Wellington.

Meanwhile, Handley Page had followed the same spec, resulting in a twin-engined Halifax with Vulture motors, but soon dropped the idea and switched to four Merlins.

By early 1940, it became clear that the troublesome Vulture was not the future, although development kept going until 1941, by which time some 200 Manchesters had entered service with a terrible reputation for engine breakdown and fires. A Manchester Mark III powered by four Merlins was being discussed. By April 1940, discussions had become designs but production priority for Merlin engines was unquestionably given to Fighter Command. It wasn't until early July 1940 that the Ministry told A. V. Roe to get on with its Manchester Mark III.

1

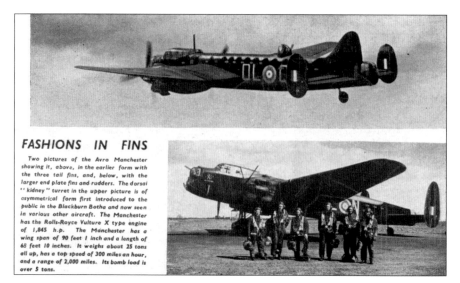

FASHIONS IN FINS

Two pictures of the Avro Manchester showing it, above, in the earlier form with the three tail fins, and, below, with the larger end plate fins and rudders. The dorsal "kidney" turret in the upper picture is of asymmetrical form first introduced to the public in the Blackburn Botha and now seen in various other aircraft. The Manchester has the Rolls-Royce Vulture X type engine of 1,845 h.p. The Manchester has a wing span of 90 feet 1 inch and a length of 68 feet 10 inches. It weighs about 25 tons all up, has a top speed of 300 miles an hour, and a range of 2,000 miles. Its bomb load is over 5 tons.

This picture appeared in the July 1942 issue of Aeronautics *magazine. Manchester L7522 OL/N had been already lost on 21 February in the sea off Stavanger. All seven crew were killed, including a second pilot. This was the first Manchester lost by 83 Squadron after re-equipping from Hampdens.*

Roy Dobson received the shock of his life on the 29th of that month. A letter from the Air Ministry told him to cancel the Mark III as his factory was going to build Halifaxes for Handley Page.

Frantic telephone calls, a trip to London and a presentation showing that the new bomber would be the performance equal of the Manchester Mark I,

What might have been ... the Handley Page Harrow, pictured here at 9 Squadron's then base at Stradishall, Suffolk, in 1938, was commissioned as a bomber but was obsolete as soon as it flew. Even so, five bomber squadrons were equipped with it but were grateful to have it replaced by the Wellington before matters got serious. The Harrow did have a minor role as a transport/ambulance in the war but could never do that job as well as the Douglas Dakota.

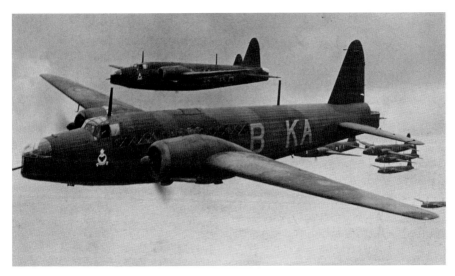

No. 9 Squadron Wellington bombers, shown in formation just before war broke out when squadron letters KA were changed to WS.

was enough for the approval of prototypes. They were to be built in one year. After many difficulties and frustrations, the new aircraft, renamed the Lancaster, flew on 9 January 1941 and the first production aircraft, L7527, flew on 31 October before going to a training unit. This aircraft eventually transferred to 15 Squadron on 3 March 1944 and was lost over Aachen on the night of 26 March, on the way to Essen. All crew were killed as she exploded in mid-air.

Production of the Lancaster, clearly a superior to the Manchester in every respect, was swiftly pushed to wartime pace and 44 Squadron took delivery of the first active-service Lancs on Christmas Eve 1941. As would be the case on all orthodox missions, they had a crew of seven, normally listed in order: pilot, flight engineer, navigator, bomb aimer, wireless operator, mid-upper-turret gunner, rear-turret gunner. The early Lancs also had a belly turret with twin machine guns but nobody designated to crew it. The belly turret was soon discontinued and later attempts to reinstate it were not a success (see page 113). The bomb aimer operated the twin machine guns in the front turret when required. Mid upper also had two guns; rear gunner had four.

Each aircraft had 120,000 parts. It took nearly half a million different manufacturing steps to build one Lancaster at an average cost per aircraft of about £59,000, not including certain kit such as guns, bombsight and wire-less, which equates to around £2 million in modern money. That sounds cheap compared with today's flying computers but the investment often didn't have time to pay back.

Wingspan was 102ft. The Lanc could do well over 250mph at anything up to 20,000ft. Normal cruising speed was around 200mph and in a dive it was specified to reach 360mph before pieces started falling off. With a 12,000lb bomb load, range was 1,730 miles but up to 2,500 miles with lighter loads.

The aircraft was unpressurised, to say the least. In fact, it was draughty and, at 20,000ft, the draughts were icy. Every man had oxygen and special clothing; gunners – exposed more than the others – had electrically-heated suits and slippers which usually worked but sometimes over-heated, so that burns and frostbite were equally likely.

The other highly successful British heavy bomber, the Halifax, was about the same size as the Lanc but was noted for difficult handling in severe manoeuvres. This was solved in later marks but it never quite matched the Lanc. The slightly earlier Short Stirling had a much bigger body but about the same wingspan. It couldn't get up to the heights needed later over Germany and so eventually was assigned other jobs. In training, as a bridge from two engines to four, it was regarded as harder to fly than a Lanc.

At school (conversion unit) for most aircrew the step from Wellington to Stirling was not a problem. The equipment was much the same as they were used to. For the pilots at this stage of training there were obvious challenges – four engines instead of two, a much larger machine altogether, and a poor reputation in taking off and landing. Also there was a lot of night flying and a great many aircraft doing circuits at any one time.

Bob Woolf was the Australian wireless operator in Doug Melrose's crew, in training at this point, eventually to become W4964 WS/J champions:

> 'We were returning from a cross-country one dark early morning when a Stirling, right behind ours but slightly higher, met another one head on. The sky filled with the red and yellow light of the massive explosion. It was a fireball, a huge fireball. There were pieces of blazing aircraft thrown in every direction. As if that wasn't enough of a shock, we had some gargled comments on the intercom when Dougie and Ted (flight engineer), and Ernie in the rear turret, by the light of the fire saw another Stirling pass directly underneath us, no more than thirty yards away. Our skipper was able to make a decent landing shortly afterwards, which was a tribute to him and his skill and discipline, but he was one silent and shaken captain, and so were we all as we handed in our parachutes and waited to find out which of our friends had perished in those flames.'

The other major Allied bombers, the B17 Flying Fortress and the B24 Liberator, again were much the same size as the Lanc but designed from a different point of view. Their crews of ten included four specialist gunners and two part-time gunners. They could fly higher but on missions over Germany could only carry smaller bomb loads, 5,000lb or so. American crews preferred the solid virtues of the Fortress to the more advanced Liberator.

The winter of 1941/42 brought matters to trial for Bomber Command. The charge was basically that it was heroic but useless. Funds, lives and materials could better be spent elsewhere. For evidence, call the *Scharnhorst*, the *Gneisenau* and the *Prinz Eugen*. These formidable warships had been at Brest for months, and more than a hundred aircraft had been lost dropping 3,000 tons of bombs with, as far as could be seen, little positive result.

This was unfavourably compared to the success of the Japanese at Pearl Harbor on 6 December 1941 and, four days afterwards, to their destruction of the *Repulse* and the *Prince of Wales*, the first capital ships ever sunk on the open sea by air power alone.

Hitler now made a decision that had at least one huge unforeseen consequence: it helped to force the changes that turned Bomber Command upside down and inside out. In fact, bomb damage to *Scharnhorst* and *Gneisenau* meant they were not fit for serious business in the Atlantic so Hitler ordered his ships home for repairs.

They set out on the morning of 12 February with navy and air escorts. Their route took them through the English Channel – our Channel, as the British public saw it. They sailed boldly up the Straits of Dover – our Straits, for goodness sake – where they met their first small problem. Six Fairey Swordfish of the Fleet Air Arm, slow and ancient biplanes with torpedoes, tried to get near but their few escorts could do nothing against the biggest flock of German fighters ever sent on navy duty. Swordfish leader Lieutenant Commander Esmonde was awarded the VC posthumously but the ships had been untroubled.

The Germans had purposely picked a bad-weather day and accidentally one on which almost all of Bomber Command was on a stand-down. There was a general order for every available means to be used to attack these ships so, once it was realised what was happening, a force of almost 250 aircraft was hurriedly launched into a filthy winter's afternoon. From 9 Squadron, only Sergeant Casey and his crew went in their Wellington, and they were one of the 200-plus who never saw a thing, briefed with a position wrong by 60 miles.

Operations Record Book, Sergeant Casey: 'To attack enemy battle cruisers off Dutch coast. Unable to locate target owing to heavy rain, snow and icing.'

It is believed that fewer than forty bombers got a reasonable sighting of the targets and, of these, fifteen Hampdens, Blenheims and Wellingtons were shot down into the sea. Almost all were lost without trace. The German ships took not one hit.

Where was Sir Francis Drake when you needed him? The fall of Singapore, symbol of Empire, was another disaster in a catastrophic week fully covered by the newspapers.

What the public didn't know was that matters in Bomber Command were actually worse than they appeared. Up to the end of February 1942, 13,614 tons of bombs had been dropped on German industry with results officially described as 'negligible'. Losses were just the opposite, with German defences greatly improved after an over-confident start. In round numbers, Bomber Command had lost over 2,500 aircraft in action, and 1,000 more from other causes, including training accidents and destroyed on the ground.

New technology was needed, new methods, better navigation, better target finding and marking, and bigger and better aircraft. Bomber Command was the only weapon the Allies had that could take the war to Germany but if they were to get all of these things and be able to use them properly, they also needed new leadership.

Air Marshal Arthur Harris arrived from his liaison post in Washington DC on 23 February 1942 to take up his new job as Commander-in-Chief, Bomber Command. A new aircraft, the Avro Lancaster, flew its first operation a week later and a new bombsight, the Mark 14, began trials. The new navigation technology, the Gee system, looked good, although not really as good as everyone hoped.

The strategy – destruction of factories, transport and cities – had been long laid down in a directive from the Air Ministry and it remained the same. Harris had been brought in because so far nobody had been able to do the job, but there was a difference. The air war was no longer a matter of saving Britain from invasion. Now was the time for aggression, to liberate Europe and win the war. Harris:

> 'The bomber force of which I assumed command on 23rd February 1942, although at that time very small, was a potentially decisive weapon. It was, indeed, the only means at the disposal of the Allies for striking at Germany itself and, as such, stood out as the central point in Allied offensive strategy.'

The total force at that moment was less than 400 aircraft of which only a small number were heavy bombers, all types of which were still in development. The four-engined Stirling and Halifax had made slow progress through their early problems. The twin-engined Manchester had made no progress at all and would shortly be withdrawn. Lancasters had been delivered to Nos 44 and 97 Squadrons, replacing Hampdens and Manchesters respectively, but they hadn't yet flown in anger. Harris had no more than seventy heavy bombers altogether. On any given night, perhaps 300 medium and heavy bombers were available for duty. Between them they were managing to drop a mere 2,000 tons of bombs on Germany in a month.

That there were any heavy bombers at all was fortunate. There had been a great deal of opposition to such machines, with arguments based on cost, complexity and relative size as a target for the enemy. Proponents pointed out that one heavy bomber with a crew of seven could carry the same bomb load as three Wellingtons or Whitleys with crews totalling fifteen to eighteen, and a hundred heavies could fly from ten aerodromes, whereas

300 medium bombers would need thirty. The big heavy could carry more ammunition – 'supply its gunners more lavishly' as it was put – for its turrets: 'The power-operated turret will go down in history as one of the great war inventions'. The greater speed of the four-engined aircraft would more than make up for its extra size as a target.

These arguments were held in the mid-1930s, of course, when everyone's idea of a bomber was a Handley Page Heyford biplane surging along at 120mph. Harris again:

> 'It is not too much to say that, owing to the small size of the force and the primitive methods then at our disposal, we could no more assail the enemy effectively by air than by land or sea. His defences were sufficient to prevent us from operating in daylight ... and by night we could not find our aiming points.'

The defences in question – a continuous belt called the Kammhuber Line made of ground radar stations controlling single night-fighters in a specified 'box' of sky – had been devised to combat Bomber Command tactics – the primitive methods – as they had been so far, with little co-ordination between bomber squadrons, no attempt to get masses of aircraft over a target at the same time, no technical aids, and captains instructed to fly around searching by eye for their aiming point until they found it or moved on to a secondary target or a Self-Evident Military Objective (Semo). The bombers, broadly speaking, flew as individuals and the Kammhuber Line picked them up. If they got through, they bombed what they believed to be the target but seldom was, and flew back through the Line.

Creature comforts were not a major part of the design brief for the Lancaster. Here we see the wireless operator's station (A), the bomb aimer's luxury couch (B), and the flight engineer's view (C).

No. 9 Squadron converted from the Wellington to the Lancaster in August 1942. W4964 was the seventeenth Lanc to arrive on squadron, in mid April 1943, and flew her first op on the 20th, by which time No. 9 had lost forty-one of their Lancs to enemy action and another five had been transferred to other squadrons and lost by them. A further thirteen of the seventy would

soon be lost by No. 9. All of the remaining eleven would be damaged, repaired, transferred to other squadrons or training units, and lost to enemy action or crashes except for three which, in some kind of retirement, would last long enough to be scrapped after the war.

The first of 9 Squadron's Lancs to be given the letter 'J' for 'Jig', W4197, turned out to be one of the three immortals. She flew eighteen ops before being damaged by flak over Duisburg on 20 December 1942. After repairs, she did duty with training units and was decommissioned in 1947.

The next 'J', ED490, achieved seven ops before Flight Lieutenant Jim Verran, on his second tour after thirty-five Whitley trips with 102 Squadron, took her to Berlin. He got there, was badly shot up and was three or four miles from home when J-Jig crashed at Heighington. Pieces of aircraft were scattered far and wide, three crew were dead and Verran was severely injured after being thrown through the canopy. He became a 'guinea pig', a patient of the legendary surgeon Sir Archibald McIndoe, and later joined 83 Squadron, pathfinders, where he was one of two survivors when his Lanc was shot down by a night-fighter. Again, he needed skin grafts and major surgery, but this time supplied by a German doctor.

The Linebook was kept in the officers' mess at No. 9 and many other squadrons. In it were noted remarks made by officers that were considered worthy of that old actors' expression, 'shooting the line'. They can seem rather poignant to modern eyes. Here is one by Flying Officer Albert Manning, a pilot who would fly in WS/J and be killed in another Lancaster.

Flying Officer Rushton, father of the writer Willy Rushton, was the Bardney adjutant. WAAF Nancy Bower was the barmaid in the officers' mess: 'Flying Officer Rushton drank pink gin. Well, I didn't know what it was and he obviously expected me to know, so the first time he just ordered it and said nothing. I got the gin and wondered how to make it pink and Rushton pointed to the bottle of Angostura bitters. I thought it must be like the Worcester sauce in a Bloody Mary so I poured it in. When he settled down, Rushton told me, four drops only. Ever after that he used to say, "four drops, Nancy, four drops".'

The third 'J', ED566, was lost without trace after nine ops on 9 April 1943, Duisburg, when three 9 Squadron Lancs FTR – failed to return, as they called it.

The letter 'J' was free again, ready for Lancaster Mark I W4964 newly delivered from Metropolitan Vickers. Her chances of setting a new endurance record did not look good.

CHAPTER 2

The First of Many

W4964 was slated for her first op on 20 April with a skipper only on his second as captain, Warrant Officer Wood, listed as W. E. although he was Herbert Edward, and her next would be with a debutant, Canadian Sergeant John Duncan, on 4 May. Her third, on 12 May, would be with Sergeant George Saxton, who at least had some experience. Even so, he and his crew were fated to be firsts of another kind, and very shortly.

Sergeant George Henry Saxton was from Carlisle, born in June 1915 so, at twenty-seven coming up twenty-eight, he was quite the old man. He and his all-sergeant crew had arrived at the end of March to find a squadron under a new CO which had managed a whole fortnight without losing an aircraft.

The practice at this time in the war was for a beginner 'sprog' pilot, before going on ops as captain of his own aircraft, to be sent out as a passenger with an experienced and well-regarded skipper – not necessarily a senior officer – to get the feel of flying over enemy territory. Whether this compulsory work experience proved useful rather depended on the skipper. Some regarded their extra load as a nuisance, a fly in the ointment of a well-practised crew. Some did try to help the new boy, passing on what tips they could.

The trips were called 'second Dickies' because earlier, in the days of Wellingtons and two pilots per aircraft, the novice went as second pilot to Dicky, the captain pilot, maybe half a dozen times or more, before collecting a crew of his own. In April 1943, Saxton and his like had two, or rarely three, such trips, usually standing behind the captain's seat. Very occasionally, the second Dicky trip found someone out, a pilot who seemed fine in every way but, once exposed to the German defences, lost his nerve. He would be quietly shipped off to a rather less glamorous job, out of sight. Sometimes, of course, the aircraft was shot down and Bomber Command lost a crew that had seen it all, plus a freshman whose training was thus entirely wasted, and now had to find work for a crew with no pilot.

Otherwise, the initiate would be able to tell his crew what it had been like over Essen or wherever, and they would have to hope that he had

11

learned enough to help him preserve their existence when they went out there together.

By 4 April, when Saxton was told he was on that night for his second Dicky, the atmosphere in the mess was solemn. Two Lancs had failed to return on the Essen raid, on the night of 3 April, one with a fairly inexperienced twenty-year-old skipper and one captained by a squadron leader, aged thirty-four, a pre-war veteran and flight commander, almost at the end of his second tour of ops. So, it was apparent to all the new boys that anybody could get the chop, go for a Burton, buy the farm, be killed.

Saxton's second Dicky was a highly unusual one, possibly unique, because most of his crew went with him. The captain was Wing Commander Kenneth Brooke Farley Smith DSO, the recently arrived 9 Squadron boss, a thirty-year-old regular from before the war, an Oxford graduate, married, and a man who took his responsibilities very seriously indeed. Officers commanding a squadron had no obligation to go on ops but many did to show solidarity and keep up morale and, sometimes, with a kind of addiction, because they needed to. Wing Commander Smith had already been on three trips as passenger since he'd arrived on 15 March; now he decided he was going to lead from the front.

He was not a Lancaster man. He had never captained a four-engined bomber over Germany. For his crew he took the squadron navigation leader, the gunnery leader in the mid-upper turret, novitiate Saxton as passenger, but the rest – engineer, bomb aimer, wireless operator and rear gunner – were all Saxton's virgin crew who had never been over Germany at all and, in training, had never teamed up in a Lanc with anyone other than Saxton. The Wing Commander must have been a very confident fellow.

They went to Kiel. It was a big raid – 577 bombers – but not a successful one. Smith reported 'results not observed'. Thick cloud and strong winds had affected the target marking and few bombs hit the town, but losses were light; only twelve went down; none from No. 9.

Five No. 9 Lancs went to Duisburg on 8 April. There were no losses, and next night it was Duisburg again, with Saxton going on an orthodox second Dicky with Pilot Officer Hale. In less hectic times, Hale would not have been thought experienced enough to take a second Dicky, but there were three novices to go that night so somebody had to do it.

Six bombers went from No. 9; the three with second Dickies came back. The other three did not (including J-Jig, ED566). All twenty-one men were killed.

At the next briefing, on 10 April for Frankfurt, the squadron could only muster seven crews. Wing Commander Smith said he was flying again to try to find out what was going wrong, with another scratch crew but including four who were usually together under their own skip and who had only a few ops to the end of their tour.

It was another big raid, five hundred plus, with no results in heavy cloud. Twenty-one bombers fell, including the Wing Commander's. That was six in ten days for 9 Squadron. The effect on Saxton and his men of such losses, of such a proportion of a squadron, can only be imagined, but there was nothing to be done, for them or the other new crews warming up, like Herbert Wood's and John Duncan's. The war had to go on, and they had to keep on climbing back into their Lancasters, which now included the new J-Jig, W4964, an aircraft that would figure in all of their lives.

The new CO, Wing Commander Burnett DFC, came from 5 Group HQ on 12 April, with the experience of a full tour over Germany with 44 Squadron. No. 9 moved from Waddington to a new aerodrome at Bardney on 13/14 April, meanwhile managing to send six aircraft from Waddington to Italy, to smash up the docks at La Spézia, and five for Stuttgart with four second Dickies including W/O Wood. Sergeant Saxton didn't take one because he was only skippering his first op himself.

It was the Škoda works next, at Pilsen (Plzeň, modern Czech Republic), which had become much more important to the German war effort since Krupp had recently taken quite a beating. Wood went for his part two on-the-job training and learned what it was like to take a flak hit that holed the port wing and removed the wireless aerial, and to be forced to land at another 'drome for bad weather.

At least they did get back to Blighty, unlike thirty-seven other Lancs and Halifaxes on that night of the full moon, more than one in every ten, and not a bomb fell on the Škoda factory while a mental hospital seven miles away was obliterated.

Italy again, on 18 April: four Lancasters took off within seven minutes of each other, just after nine in the evening (Double British Summer Time) to join five Halifaxes and 169 more Lancs on the long journey to La Spézia, to finish the job on the docks and to destroy naval barracks and two battle-ships that were supposed to be there. Last away at 21.10 was debut skipper WO Wood, and he was over the target at 02.20. The Halifaxes had dropped target indicators but the 9 Squadron bomb aimers could see what they wanted anyway, except for the battleships.

A lot of damage was done, only one of the 173 Lancs went down – caught off the French coast – and the boys were home soon after 06.00. That had been nine hours in the air, roughly the equivalent of a Berlin trip but a great deal less hazardous.

As if to show that there was no such thing as a trouble-free op, Wood's flight engineer Sergeant Clayton, anxiously watching his petrol gauges on the way back, told his captain that they didn't have enough to get home. Almost out of fuel over the Channel, they just made it to Manston, a fighter base a few miles in from the Kent coast where the ambulance crews and flight controllers were quite used to stray, shot-up or otherwise disabled bombers making forced landings on what had been a grass field but by this time had a long and broad runway.

Returning to Bardney the next day, Wood and his men saw there was nothing on that night but on 20 April they were listed for Stettin in the squadron's newest Lancaster, W4964.

REFERENCES.

Date	Aircraft Type & Number	Crew	Duty	Time Up	Time Down	Details of Sortie or Flight	References
20/4/43 (contd)	LANCASTER. ED. 654.	SGT. G.S. STOUT. SGT. J. GURNEY. SGT. J.H. BRYANT. SGT. K. GAVIN. SGT. H. NUTTALL. SGT. D. BURDEN. SGT. W. CORNISH-UNDERWOOD.	Bombing – STETTIN.	2144.	0520.	Primary attacked. 0120 hrs. 12,000 ft. NEUWERP not identified (west of track) but green T.I. seen. Oder River seen. Bombed concentration of 3 green T.I. Own bursts not seen. Concentration appeared good. Only twofires on outskirts. Fires seen for 100 miles.	
	LANCASTER. ED. 834.	SGT. J. EVANS. SGT. W.G. SMITH. SGT. R. BORTHWICK. SGT. F. ROBINSON. SGT. T. MYERSCOUGH. SGT. H. ASHDOWN. SGT. D.W. BROUGH.	Bombing – STETTIN.	2149.	0404.	No target attacked. Bombs jettisoned safe 55.37.N. 10.20E. 2359 hours. 200–300 ft. Port outer engine caught fire. Fire started in cockpit and under pilots seat. Port wing tip hit. Port side of fuselage hit. Fires extinguished. Explosion of jettisoned bombs caused severe damage to the aircraft.	
	LANCASTER. ED. 799.	F/L. W.A. MEYER. SGT. W.H. HUNTER. SGT. N.R. McCORKINDALE. SGT. D. WILEREE. SGT. S.H. SINCLAIR. SGT. A.D. HARP. SGT. T.W. JOHNSON.	Bombing – STETTIN.	2143.	0511.	Primary attacked. 0112 hours. 14,000 ft. Yellow markers seen at position "B". Timed run made from STOLZENBURG. white flares and very numerous red T.I. seen over target followed by green T.I. Green T.I. innaights. Own bursts not seen, but two others seen at time of bombing. Numerous fires well concentrated and a large red explosion in S.W. part of town lasting 4—5 seconds.	
	LANCASTER. W.4964.	W.O. WE WOOD. SGT. C CLAYTON. SGT. CHIPPERFIELD. P/O. T. MELLARD. SGT. T.N. GAINES. SGT. H.G. WATSON. SGT. N.Z. BAKER.	Bombing – STETTIN.	2147.	0524.	Primary attacked. 0119 hrs. 14,000 ft. Yellow markers seen at position "B" and timed run made from late near STOLZENBURG. Red T.I. and white flares seen over target when approaching and green T.I. seen over target. Outline of factory seen by flash and T.I. slightly to left of T.I. Own burst not seen. Numerous fires well concentrated were observed.	

An uneventful trip for Wood and W4964, but for John Evans, aged twenty, a Londoner on only his second op as captain and in a Lanc also on her second (ED589 WS/Z-Zebra), there was rather more excitement. They were hit by flak on the way out, about an hour from the target, which caused the fire under the pilot. No sooner had they extinguished that than they were hit again, losing the use of an engine and suffering various other damage, including the intercom going u/s (unserviceable). They turned back but, unaware of just how much height had been lost in the confusion, the bomb aimer, Sergeant Robinson, jettisoned the bombs on his own initiative and almost blew up his own aircraft. Somehow, twenty-year-old pilot Evans got them all home from a starting point a few hundred feet above the Baltic Sea, some miles north of Lübeck.

After the war, Stettin was ceded to Poland as Szczecin. When Wood was going, it was the port of Berlin, on the Oder, the capital city of the Prussian province of Pomerania, one of the main German ship-building centres and home to many sorts of industry.

Bomber Command had been there before but, because of the distance – 1,200 miles round trip – it had not been possible to give it the attention it warranted. A raid in September 1941 of 139 Wellingtons, Whitleys, Stirlings and Halifaxes did little damage for the loss of thirteen aircraft and Stettin had seen nothing since.

It was way beyond the range of the new target-finding system, Oboe, which was, like Gee, based on transmissions from ground stations in England but was highly accurate. It could guide an aircraft to within 300 yards of the target by calculations based on a radio signal sent back by the aircraft's transponder. The system's drawbacks made it unsuitable for general use in the bomber stream – night-fighters could home in on the radio signal and the ground stations could only handle a few aircraft at a time, flying them in a straight line – but it was a brilliant improvement for the target-marking pathfinders and, therefore, on general results.

Oboe was no use at Stettin, however, where the pathfinders had to mark the old-fashioned way, by looking. Of the 194 Lancasters – including only six from a much strained 9 Squadron – 134 Halifaxes and eleven Stirlings that went on the first of a short, irregular series of raids that would all but destroy the city, twenty-two went down but the prize was 100 acres of central industrial landscape, flattened. Fires were still burning two days later.

The next few nights were quiet for Bomber Command except for a mine-laying trip in the Bay of Biscay. Two Lancs went from 9 Squadron; only one came back, the crew having seen the other hit by flak and blowing up in the moonlight. These were the stories in the mess as another future W4964 pilot, Sergeant John Duncan of Saskatchewan, got ready for his first venture, as second Dicky to Duisburg, where 9 Squadron's eight Lancs were in the vanguard and so he may not have seen anything of the twenty-one aircraft lost, most of which fell to night-fighters over Holland. The squadron lost none and hit the target indicated but reconnaissance photographs later showed that the pathfinders had dropped wide.

Still, it seemed like a good show and Duncan could be satisfied with that. He is not shown as having another second Dicky but, in the clerical turmoil of war that does not mean he didn't. There would have been room for him on the next major raid, when ten went to Essen on 30 April, including Herbert Wood and crew, and George Saxton, but not in W4964. There seemed always to be cloud and industrial smog over the Ruhr and this was the case once more, but with Oboe to guide them the 305 bombers did reasonably well, hitting Krupp again.

Wood didn't hit anything. On route, the oxygen supply to the navigator, Sergeant Chipperfield, broke down, rendering him unconscious, so Wood turned back on a course that he hoped was the reverse of his journey up to now. Most of their bombs were jettisoned over the sea but six hundred 4lb incendiaries were hung up, to be with them when they landed, assuming they could find somewhere to land. With the help of positional fixes from the wireless operator, they did get home but that seems to have been the end of Chipperfield's flying career. The rest of them would be ready to go whenever the call came.

Nine Lancasters and crews were lost in action by 9 Squadron in the month of April 1943, plus one lost on an exercise, cause of crash unknown. Every man in every crew was killed, some with new captains, some with old hands. The effect on squadron morale can hardly be exaggerated. The most they had been able to send on any one op had been twelve Lancasters. Eleven new aircraft had been delivered in the month. We cannot tell exactly how many new crews turned up at the squadron in the thirty days of April because the records only show incoming officers, and most of the crews were sergeants, but it was about the same. (We know that Herbert Wood and crew arrived on 13 April because he had an officer bomb-aimer, Pilot Officer Mellard.)

Seven new captains flew their first second Dickies in the month and two experienced ones joined No. 9 from elsewhere. Of those, one was killed in the same month and five of the others would be killed, sooner or later.

Some bomber aircrew expected to die and accepted that as fact. They wrote letters home to be posted when it happened. Most, despite what they saw around them all the time, believed that it wouldn't be them who got the chop. They would last to the end of their tours of operations, thirty trips. How else, we must ask, could they have climbed into a Lancaster three times a week to fly over occupied Europe?

Bomber Command's senior management generally accepted losses of less than five per cent of sorties and of aircraft on a given raid as good; of more than five per cent, bad, which predicted an 'acceptable' life span for a Lancaster of nineteen ops. Over the whole war, average losses for all bombers were less than that, around three per cent of sorties flown, which sounds almost reasonable until you realise that such a rate of loss – three aircraft out of a hundred gone on every op – killed half of all the aircrew who flew in the war ('all the aircrew' includes those in training units). Add the wounded and the POWs, and the casualty rate becomes sixty per cent.

There were variations, obviously, according to the type of mission flown, the type of aircraft and the different stages of the air war. Of those types of aircraft employed in flying over 1,000 ops, much the worst machine to be in was the Manchester, with losses over five per cent, and much the best was the Mosquito – less than one per cent. The Lancaster was the best survivor of the heavies at just over two per cent of sorties and it was more exposed, flying as many ops as the Halifax, Wellington and Stirling put together. Ignoring work done and just looking at aircraft round numbers, 5,850 Lancs were delivered to RAF Bomber Command during this war. Some never saw action, but 3,380 were lost while flying with the active-service Groups.

Whatever you were flying, in the front-line, heavy-bomber squadrons in 1943 and 1944, the odds against doing a full first tour of thirty trips were much worse than even money – more like three or four to one against. Out of every five pilots, five flight engineers, five navigators, bomb aimers, wireless operators, mid-upper gunners and tail gunners who crewed an RAF heavy bomber, the maths said that one would live through it and four would die or, perhaps, become POWs.

No. 9 Squadron, one of many such front liners, lost an average of one Lancaster a week, from September 1942 to the end. By the time a lucky crew reached the goal of thirty ops, which took maybe four or five months, an entire squadron's worth of Lancasters and crews had disappeared and been replaced.

Night-fighters were the deadliest foe, unseen until (usually) too late, but some crews completed a tour and were never attacked by one. Flak (anti-aircraft artillery, abbreviated from *Fliegerabwehrkanonen*, flyer defence gun was always a danger, ever present, at every target, but at least you could see it – except, of course, for the flak that got you – and you had the defence of the fishes. There was a lot of you, so you might not be the one that was eaten by the shark.

Even so, the straight and level bombing run gave the flak gunners time to get your height, plus the extra time you had to fly after 'bombs gone', waiting for your photoflash bomb to explode and your camera to click.

A crew who strayed off track, over another city perhaps, would lose the defence of the shoal and become horribly obvious to the night-fighters' radar, or the sole occupation for flak gunners and searchlight crews who had not been busy that night.

Crashes on take-off and landing were often fatal, so too were mechanical failures in the air. Much rarer than at first imagined were mid-air collisions in the bomber stream and being hit by bombs dropped from above by a colleague. Both happened, but not as often as critics of Harris's tactics had predicted.

You could also fly into a stuffed cloud, one with a cliff or a hilltop inside it. You could be fired at by your friends who might be in a Royal Navy ship, or manning an English or Scottish coastal ack-ack gun, or flying an RAF fighter, or a bomber. All four types of friend executed bomber crews.

Whichever way the Germans got you, it was much more likely that you would be killed than become a prisoner of war. Everyone has heard of Stalag Luft 3 and seen the escape films. We can only point out that the numbers in the prison camps were a great deal smaller than the numbers in the cemeteries and on the Runnymede Memorial.

The month of May began quietly for No. 9 with two cancellations, so it was not until 4 May that J-Jig had her second outing, to Dortmund, with John Duncan and crew on their first op as part of a force of almost 600 bombers. It was the biggest raid so far, not counting the 'Thousand Plan' raids on Cologne, Essen and Bremen in 1942 which had included just about anything

Date	Aircraft Type & Number	Crew	Duty	Time Up	Time Down	Details of Sortie or Flight	References
4/5/43 (contd')	LANCASTER. W.4964.	SGT. J.D. DUNCAN. SGT. S.G. BLUNDEN. F/SGT. H.T. BROWN. SGT. G. BARTLEY. SGT. S. HUGHES. SGT. L.G. WARNER. SGT. D. McMILLAN.	Bombing. DORTMUND.	2202.	0410.	Primary attacked. 0155 hrs. 19,000'. Red T.I's seen also green T.I's but these had gone out on arrival. Red T.I's in sights. Fierce fires well concentrated with a few scattered bombs outside main area. Many bomb bursts seen in amongst fires. Smoke seen up to estimated height of 8,000'. Glow of fires reflected on the pall of smoke so that it could be seen from Dutch coast.	
	LANCASTER. ED. 551.	SGT. K.O. TURP.S SGT. D. BAILEY. F/O. H.A. CLARKE. SGT. W.F. FEERZE. SGT. J.W. PYM. SGT. S.E. SILVESTER SGT. T. SHELMERDINE.	Bombing. DORTMUND.	2157.	0336.	Primary attacked. 0127 hrs. 19,000 ft. Yellow track marker seen at posn. 'Y'. About 8 red T.I. seen over target, then four green. Green T.I. in sights. Green were in the centre of red concentration. Own burst not seen, but several others, well concentrated. Fires very numerous and well concentrated. 0113 hrs. Large orange explosion burned about '16 seconds. Flames to about 3,000 ft. followed by pall of smoke. Very large fire seen just after bombing.	
	LANCASTER. ED. 558.	W.O. W.E. WOOD. SGT. C. CLAYTON. SGT. B.L. CRAMP. P/O. T. MELLARD. SGT. G.T.M. GAINES. SGT. W.R. BARKER. SGT. H.G. WATSON.	Bombing. DORTMUND.	2150.	0330.	Primary attacked. 0132 hrs. 20,000 't. Identified by green and red T.I's. Yellow T.I. on track also seen. Green T.I. in bomb sights. Greater height should, if anything improve accuracy of bombing. Many big fires seen to be well concentrated. On run up on target a large explosion seen slightly to East of red T.I.	
	LANCASTER. ED. 499.	F/L.G. ROBERTSON. SGT. W. BROWN. P/O. R.H. SMITH. F/O. E.J. KNELL. F/SGT. K. GREENE. F/O. E.N. ARMSTRONG. SGT. A. KELLY.	Bombing. DORTMUND.	2138.	0250.	Primary attacked. 18,000 ft. 0106 hrs. Identified by red T.I's. Yellow T.Ids on track also seen. Concentration of red T.I's in bomb sights. Accuracy of bombing not affected by height. Results of own bombing not seen when leaving target, although early, bombing seemed confined to two concentrations.	

That's better. Fourteen of No. 9 went to Dortmund, fourteen came back, everybody bombed and thought well of it. Duncan and W4964 were last away and last home, ten minutes after George Saxton. The comments about height were due to a general shift upwards. Bombing heights of 14/15/16,000ft had been commonplace, but Lancasters could fly much higher. So they did. The force was roughly 45:55 Lancasters to others, but of the forty bombers lost to enemy action on this operation, twenty-eight were the lower flying Wellingtons, Stirlings and Halifaxes.

and everything that could fly and carry a bomb, from training units and wherever else they could be found.

Dortmund was the largest raid consisting entirely of squadrons in operational service, and the first major attack on that city even though it was an ideal target, being an important centre for iron and steel manufactures, a railway hub, one end of the Dortmund-Ems canal and the home of half a million people mostly employed in the war effort.

About half of the bombers hit within three miles of the aiming point. More than 3,000 buildings were destroyed or badly damaged, including many factories and dockyard services, and 700 people were killed – a record.

Duisburg on 12 May saw Saxton and crew in J-Jig. Twelve went, twelve came back. Everyone thought it a good show. Saxton bombed from 20,000ft, as did most of the rest, on pathfinder target indicators that had been perfectly placed. Duisburg suffered so much damage that it was a year before it came up again for a raid. Once more the force was approximately 45:55 Lancasters to others, but only ten of the thirty-four bombers lost were Lancs.

Next night it was Pilsen, and another unsuccessful attempt to hit the Škoda factories. This was a low-level attack with 156 Lancs going in around 10–12,000ft. No. 9 was among the first to bomb and claimed to have hit the markers but the pathfinders had erred to the north and most of the bombs fell in open country. W4964 was back with Herbert Wood. Saxton was given ED589 P-Peter and he and his crew became the first of J's crews to die.

There were no more major raids on Germany for ten days but everyone was talking about a small one, just nineteen Lancasters, on 16 May 1943. All were from a new, specially-formed squadron, No. 617, flying its first op from Scampton to the Ruhr dams. It busted two of the dams but only eleven Lancs came back. Of the eight crews, all were killed except three men.

For No. 9, the long gap ended with an order for a maximum effort, which meant sending every available aircraft and crew, including reserves and beginners. Results of the big raid on Dortmund on 4 May had not been good enough. The city was still functioning and so an even bigger raid was set for 23 May, which would be the largest of the whole sequence known as the Battle of the Ruhr with over 800 bombers. Seventeen went from No. 9, including five crews on their first op, only one skipper of which had had his second Dickies. Sergeant Tom Gill, assigned to W4964 for his first, hadn't had one but that was just too bad. There was a war on.

For a change, the visibility was good. The marking was very accurate, the bombing was spot on and 2,000 buildings were completely destroyed, including the massive Hoesch steelworks. The night-fighters were busy, accounting for most of the thirty-eight aircraft shot down (Heinz Vinke got another Tommy for his bag, a 10 Squadron Halifax), an 'acceptable' score of marginally less than five per cent, perhaps better than it might have been on such a clear night because of the sheer numbers of aircraft overwhelming the defences. For the next year, it was not thought necessary to attack Dortmund again.

DATE	AIRCRAFT TYPE & NUMBER	CREW	DUTY	TIME UP	TIME DOWN	DETAILS OF SORTIE OR FLIGHT	REFERENCES
13/5/43.	LANCASTER. ED.499.	F/L. G.F. ROBERTSON. SGT. W. BROWN. F/O. R.H. SMITH. F/O. E.J. KNELL. F/SGT. K. GREENE. F/O. E.N. ARMSTRONG. SGT. J. MOSELEY.	Bombing - PILSEN.	2126.	0440.	Primary attacked. 0120½ hrs. 12,000 ft. Identified by yellow and white T.I.'s on track and two red T.I's on target. One red T.I. in bomb sight. Bombing well concentrated around the red T.I.	
	LANCASTER. ED.589.	SGT. G.H SAXTON. SGT. D.C. FERRIS. SGT. W.G. McDONALD. SGT. R.M. MORRIS. SGT. J. REDDISH. SGT. J.C OWEN. SGT. J. BUNTIN.	Bombing - PILSEN.	2142.		Aircraft failed to return - no signals received.	
	LANCASTER. ED.654.	SGT. G.S. STOUT. SGT. J.R GURNEY. SGT. J.H. BRYANT. SGT. K. GAVIN. SGT. A. NUTTALL. SGT. D. BURDEN. SGT. V. CORNISH-UNDERWOOD.	Bombing - PILSEN.	2130.	0524.	Primary attacked, 0122 hrs. 12,000 ft. Identified by yellow and white T.I's on track and illuminating flares and red, and one red T.I. on target. One red T.I. in bombsights. Bombing well concentrated round the red T.I.	
	LANCASTER. ED.656.	SGT. J. EVANS. SGT. V.G.L. SMITH. SGT. R. BORTHWISK. SGT. P. ROBINSON. SGT. FIELDING. SGT. JEFFREY. SGT. H.I. ASHDOWN. SGT. D.W. BROUGH.	Bombing - PILSEN.	2133.	0548.	Primary attacked. 0120½ hrs. 14,500 ft. Yellow markers at "F". White at "B", red and green over target. Red T.I. in sights, only one seen. Others went down after bombing. Bombs seen to burst near T.I. - built up area seen. A few fires seen and several bursts - seemed well concentrated.	

This is how losses were recorded in the Operations Record Book. Unusually, the monthly summary does not mention Saxton's demise, which adds insult to death. What the Recorder of Operations could not know was that two hours after take-off, Oberfeldwebel Heinz Vinke spotted P-Peter as she crossed into Holland from the Waddensee. He shot her down near Sneek. The bodies of the two gunners, Sergeant John Owen and Sergeant James Buntin were found, but there was no trace of the others.

Vinke was about a quarter through his long career of over fifty confirmed victories, which would include a survived shooting-down but, eventually, death in February 1944. The Luftwaffe had no concept of a tour of operations. They kept going until they could go no more, for

Place	Date	Time	Summary of Events	References to Appendices
BARDNEY.	9/5. (contd)		were subsequently cancelled.	
	10/5.		Nothing of operational importance occurred. No flying was carried out.	
	11/5.		Several crews carried out bombing practice and aircraft were tested for operations which had been ordered for the night. Again, however, they were cancelled.	
	12/5.		The following aircraft and crews were detailed to carry out an attack against DUISBURG at night. "B" (F/O. BOCZAR); "D" (F/O. POX); "G" (F/O. HALE); "K" (F/L. WAKEFORD); "M" (S/L. HOBBS); "N" (F/L. MEYER); "T" (F/L. DERBYSHIRE); "X" (F/L. ROBERTSON); "W" (SGT. McCUBBIN); "Y" (SGT. EVANS); "J" (SGT. SAXTON); "U" (SGT. DUNCAN).	
			All aircraft took off and encountered good weather conditions on the way to the target. The attack was concentrated and considered by all crews to be very successful.	
	13/5.		Operations were again ordered, the following being detailed to attack PILSEN at night. "A" (F/O. HALE); "B" (F/O. BOCZAR); "D" (F/O. POX); "H" (S/L. HOBBS); "J" (W.O. WOOD); "M" (SGT. TURP); "N" (F/L. MEYER); "K" (F/L. WAKEFORD); "L" (F/O. WOODHOUSE); "O" (W/CDR. BURNETT); "T" (S/L. McFARLANE); "X" (F/L. ROBERTSON); "P" (SGT. SAXTON); "R" (SGT. STOUT); "Y" (SGT. EVANS); "U" (SGT. DUNCAN).	
			All aircraft took off, but "T" (S/L. McFARLANE) returned early as one engine caught fire. "H" (S/L. HOBBS) also returned early owing to inter-comm trouble. The remaining aircraft bombed the area marked by the P.F.F. and bombing was very concentrated. Doubt was expressed by several crews as to whether the pathfinders had, in fact, located the target.	
	14/5.		No operations were ordered for today and no flying took place.	
	15/5.		During the day bombing practice was carried out by many crews. During the night six crews undertook Bullseye exercises. There were no operations.	

J-Jig's sixth op, Düsseldorf on 25 May, was Tom Gill's crew's second. This picture of them with the aircraft was taken on that day. Standing from the left are: Bernard Devine, called Brian, bomb aimer; Tom Gill, pilot; Bill Morton, wireless op; Ray Gough, navigator. Kneeling, from left: Matt McPherson, flight engineer; Paddy McDonagh, mid-upper gunner; Bob McKee, rear gunner.

Düsseldorf on 25 May was almost as big a raid but with no significant results on a night of ten tenths cloud. The crews saw fires over a wide area and German reports later listed thirty people killed and less than 100 build-ings destroyed. Tom Gill in J-Jig reported incendiaries 'very scattered, some

Tom Gill and engineer Matt McPherson in the usual journalist's cockpit pose.

about 10 miles SE of target'. Losses were relatively light, less than four per cent, but they included a 77 Squadron Halifax, shot down by a night-fighter and exploding in the air with such force that two Stirlings went down with it, with all three crews killed.

Tom Gill, learning as he went along, went on his third to Essen in J. The squadron's fourteen were split into two groups, taking off with half an hour between them. Most of the losses that night, twenty-three from 518 raiders, seem to have been to fighters over Holland on the return journey. Those in the second wave bombed much later having followed a longer route and survived at a better rate.

Essen was not a successful raid, with thick cloud making marking very difficult, but the next one, 29 May, was the most effective of the war so far. Gill, Duncan and Wood all went – but not in J-Jig. She was having a night off, while over 700 bombers destroyed 1,000 acres of the Barmen half of Wuppertal, the ribbon city in a steep-sided valley where chemicals (Bayer, Bemberg), steel, textiles and other heavy industries made its destruction another severe blow to Germany's ability to sustain the war.

June began with a series of cancellations, scrubs, on the 2nd, 5th, 6th, 7th and 9th, with the squadron at varying degrees of readiness depending on the lateness of the cancellation. Some scrubs happened with the bombers on the perimeter track waiting their turn to take off, when a Very light fired from the control tower told the crews they wouldn't be killed tonight.

A cancellation was only a postponement. Tomorrow or the next day the target might be different but they would have to go through the same routines, the briefings, the tests and the build-up. A scrub was demoralising and exhausting; all that nervous energy wasted, and it brought on deep depression in some. For most of these young men, though, it triggered a more obvious response, and it was one tolerated, even encouraged, by the senior officers. As one aircrew member put it:

'For me and plenty of others, the mixed feelings of relief and disappointment (at a scrub) and the sudden escape of pressure had one result only: an irresistible urge to remove to the mess as fast as possible and get thoroughly hammered. It was generally the sort of carry on where you'd expect to get footprints on the ceiling. Leaping about like wild monkeys, getting thoroughly sloshed and singing extremely rude songs late into the night had not yet been classified by doctors of the mind but it clearly was an effective therapy. It came naturally and it worked.'

Five cancellations, with practice and training on the free days between, translated at last into the real thing on 11 June. Tom Gill and crew were off to Düsseldorf in WS/J, along with Wood, Duncan and sixteen more from the squadron – 783 altogether – on another maximum effort. Gill reported: 'Smoke up to 18,000ft prevented observation of detailed results.' The smoke was coming from almost 9,000 separate fires in an area of fifteen square miles, of which 130 acres were completely demolished. Losses were the standard five per cent; the squadron lost no-one but J-Jig suffered her first wound.

'Aircraft hit by flak over target while taking photo. Hydraulic pipeline fractured (gun turrets u/s). Bomb doors remained open. Bottle used for landing for undercarriage and flaps.'

This laconic description hides an incident that could very easily have been fatal. Gill had to fly home with the extra drag of open bomb doors, the knowledge that he was defenceless against the night-fighters, and the uncertainty of what might happen when he tried to land. The emergency compressed-air bottle, which acted as back-up should the main hydraulics fail, was rather like the spare tyre in the back of the car. It was not something you thought about until you needed it, and when you did, you hoped it had survived your neglect.

They got back to Bardney and were the last to land – probably kept up in the circuit in case of collapse on the runway – and J was fixed up and ready for the next night. Of course, no attempt was made to repair the jangled nerves of the crew. So, after the usual amount of self-counselling, Gill and his men were dropping bombs on Bochum twenty-one hours later.

The usual bomb load at this time was a 4,000lb 'cookie' plus incendiaries, usually in 250lb containers, plus a number of 500lb normal bombs called Medium Capacity (MC) because a large part of their weight was in the heavy steel casing to aid penetration. The cookie, also called the blockbuster, the 4,000lb HC (High Capacity), was not much more than a light metal drum packed full of explosive, a blast bomb rather than one that penetrated. The combination of the three sorts, perhaps a thousand or more of the four-pounders, the cookie and four 500lb MCs per aircraft, when dropped in concentrations, would overwhelm the German civil defences and fire brigades. Later in the war, two 4,000lb HCs were bolted together to make a double cookie, and towards the end of 1944 the triple cookie was also used. American aircraft couldn't carry cookies as their bomb bays were not big enough.

Over Bochum, J's cookie hung up but they managed to get rid of it near Münster. Another 9 Squadron Lanc had to return early with u/s hydraulics, another was hit by flak, another had an oxygen failure, but they all lived to fight another day, but not so Herbert Wood, first operational pilot of W4964.

For him, Bochum was the ultimate. Possibly he had gone off track because, at the same time that the rest were bombing Bochum, around 01.30, he was shot down by a night-fighter south-east of Arnhem. W/O Herbert Edward Wood, pilot, and his nineteen-year-old rear gunner, W/O 2 Herbert George Watson from Lethbridge, Alberta, were killed. The rest became prisoners.

Oberhausen on 14 June: of the original three W4964 captains, only Duncan was still flying. He and crew were in ED480 U-Uncle, which would do thirty-two ops. It was just another routine night for them, although possibly not for the new crew led by Sergeant J. A. Aldersley in W4964, another pilot who had been pressed into service without the benefit of a second Dicky. It was a Lancasters-only raid, not big, less than 200 of them, with Oboe-equipped Mosquitos to mark, in thick cloud but nevertheless accurately. The price was high, seventeen Lancs, 8.4 per cent, of which nine are known to have been shot down by fighters.

Seven Lancs took off in eight minutes from Bardney on 16 June, not including W4964 which was due for an overhaul after ten ops. The seven crews were briefed to be among the leaders of a 200-strong force headed for Cologne. It was yet another cloudy night, with marking by Halifaxes and Lancasters carrying the new H2S ground-scanning radar, still in early development and very temperamental as the bombers carrying it on this mission found. Fitted where the ventral turret had originally been was a Perspex dome with the radar scanning arm inside. This communicated with a box in the wireless operator's 'studio', which had a small screen with the classic clock-wipe signals showing on it. A drawback not realised at the time was that the Germans could pick up the H2S signal and home in on it.

Even when it worked, interpretation of what it showed had to be intuitive to say the least, and as a result, marking on this occasion was indecisive. Six of the 9 Squadron crews observed and commented on it as they bombed what seemed to be the best option at a few minutes after one o'clock. Behind them, the weather worsened and half the force turned back.

The seventh of the 9 Squadron Lancasters, flown by the fifth of J's crews, instead of being over Cologne, was going down near Antwerp, a hundred miles away, hitting the ground at 01.18, courtesy of Unteroffizier Hubatsch. The wireless operator, the bomb aimer and the pilot, Sergeant Aldersley, parachuted to become POWs. The other four died.

CHAPTER 3

A Great Escape

J-Jig had been on ten trips with five different crews, novices – or in Saxton's case, with only a little experience beforehand. Three of the five were gone, and all in a few weeks. There was nothing extraordinary about this. It was obvious to everyone on any bomber station that inexperienced crews were more likely to get the chop. The problem was how to get the experience. The pilot and the gunners clearly had a lot to do with that, but so did the navigator who was occupied throughout the flight keeping them on track and time, and the wireless operator, listening for messages from Group and for enemy wireless traffic and, later in the war, watching Monica, a radar system meant to detect incoming fighters. The flight engineer, with no help from any kind of computer or automated system, looked after the fuel, engines, hydraulics, oxygen, electrics, none of it perfectly reliable, governed by switches, gauges, cocks, meters and warning lights which were also fallible. He also had to assist the pilot during take-off and may have to fly the aircraft himself if the pilot was incapacitated or, indeed, killed.

The bomb aimer, too, helped with navigation by spotting landmarks and was, in effect, captain during the bombing run, the only time when there were conflicting tensions in the crew. Their objective, clearly, was to drop their bombs spot on the target, and the bomb aimer's primary job was to instruct the pilot, flying on instruments only, so that objective was achieved. Meanwhile, everybody else wanted to get the hell out before the flak gunners took advantage of their straight and level flight in the run up to 'bombs gone' and 'camera gone'.

They were unequal equals in pay. Assuming an all-sergeant crew: pilot, navigator and bomb aimer were on 13s 6d a day – in purchasing power, equivalent to about £24 today. A flight engineer got 12s, a wireless operator, with possibly the most technically difficult training, was on only 9s, while gunners, on whom everyone's life could depend, earned a mere 8s a day, or £14 in today's money, reflecting the brevity of the training course but not the increased danger as the fighter-pilot's first target.

So how was a crew put together that would last thirty ops, rather than two? Crews were not assembled at random and thrown in with a captain as had been the way at the start of the war. In those very early days, gunnery was not even recognised as a separate trade, and almost any aircraftman second class walking past a Wellington might find himself suddenly put behind a machine gun. One of the first Distinguished Flying Medals of the war was won by one such.

Neither were crews selected by any method that a modern human resources manager would recognise. The Americans were trying to develop psychological tests to help select pilots, but the British method was purely practical. If you wanted to be a pilot, and you could, you did. Some of the other crewmen began by wanting to be pilots but were diverted for various reasons. Navigators always said that they were the ones who could do reading, writing and arithmetic, whereas pilots were merely Drivers (Airframe) who would get jobs on the buses after the war. Wireless operators were often technical types. Gunnery was the shortest training time, six months, which attracted quite a few.

They were all volunteers for the most hazardous profession in the war apart, possibly, from U-boat crew and their colleagues in the Luftwaffe. Their success certainly depended to an extent on fortune, luck, chance, whatever you wish to call it, but professionalism, teamwork, trust, mutual regard, and retaining those virtues and more under extreme pressure were all important too, but how they came about in a group of seven individuals was also rather a matter of chance.

When pilots moved up in their training to the twin-engined bomber stage, to Wellingtons, they went to a party. It was rather a strange party, with no food or drink and all the guests were men who were part-trained aircrew. They would tend to assemble in their trade groups – bomb aimers together, navigators together, wireless operators together – although pairings might form, perhaps two Aussies might meet and chat, or two lads might have met before in the pub.

The pilots circulated, looking for they knew not what but hoping to recognise it when they saw it. Future crew members waited to be asked to dance, as it were, but, in view of the dance's serious nature, might well refuse. One pilot liked the look of this wireless operator but the w/op didn't reciprocate. Sorry, but another had a different opinion and said 'yes'. Gradually, settlements were made. Young men decided, some of them only eighteen or nineteen years old, using nothing but instinct and first impressions, on matters of life and death. Later, the gunners came in by the same route, and finally the flight engineer as they transferred to four engines.

John Duncan's crew had the same hopes as everyone on 4 May when they set out together for the first time in J-Jig, W4964. Sergeant Blunden, flight engineer; Flight Sergeant Brown, navigator; Sergeant Bartley, bomb aimer; Sergeant Hughes, wireless operator; Sergeant Warner, mid-upper; Sergeant McMillan, tail gunner. There was nothing to distinguish them from anyone else. Come 9 July, being briefed for Gelsenkirchen, they could look back over eleven ops together.

There had been Pilsen, when Saxton failed to return, Bochum, when Herbert Wood went down, and Mülheim on 22 June. They would never forget Mülheim. They bombed in a hurry at only 14,000ft, for a very good reason:

> 'Aircraft caught by searchlight and held at 18,500 ft. Considerable heavy flak directed at aircraft. 4,000 ft lost in evading. Aerial shot away and very bumpy as flak became more accurate. Bombs released approx. 3 miles from target, but bearing unknown.'

The squadron had been among the first in. The attack hadn't started when Duncan's men experienced that terrifying, blinding white-out that meant the searchlights had you. There were differing opinions about the pros and cons of being first in. It meant that there were fewer of you for the lights and flak to find before they were spoiled for choice, but neither were you silhouetted against the glow of fires for the fighters to see you from above.

In any case, if a light locked on to you, you generally had a few seconds before the flak gunners had your measure. In that desperate situation, it was all down to the pilot. Nobody else could help. Duncan threw his Lancaster

Mülheim, photographed from rather less than 14,000ft, was a tightly-packed Ruhr community of about 135,000 people centred around the Freidrich Wilhelm works. Shown here are the coke ovens and other features of the town's business – iron and steel.

around, trying everything he knew, while the flak exploded beside him and shrapnel rattled and banged on the bodywork like a crowd of madmen battering at a door.

It was the first and only major raid on the town; perhaps the flak gunners were not in practice. Duncan was in W4133 S-Sugar, one of the squadron's original equipment from September '42. He would be in the same aircraft again in six nights' time, over Cologne. Maybe she was a lucky one. She would do over forty ops before the luck was exhausted and she crashed in flames at Bardney after a night training exercise, killing all on board.

After S-Sugar left Mülheim, the rest of the force destroyed sixty per cent of the place, which made its living from iron and steel, and never had to go back again. For Duncan and crew there was Elberfeld two nights later, then

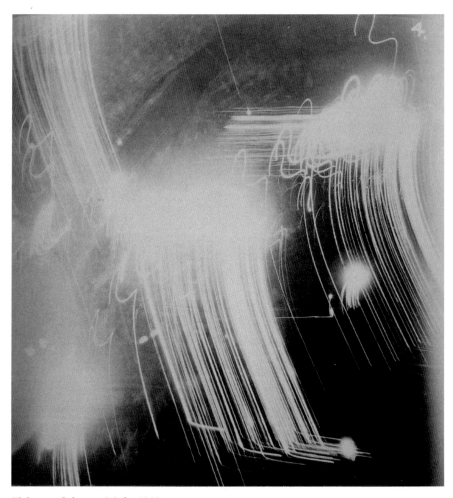

Flak over Cologne, 8 July 1943.

Cologne, and Cologne again last night, and tonight it was to be Gelsenkirchen, another town of mines, furnaces and factories pumping out essentials for the war but with the addition of a large synthetic-oil refinery that had long been on the wish list. There had been one big raid here since 1941, a fortnight before, although Gelsenkirchen had been regularly bombed when other towns were the target. On that raid on 25 June, the other towns took the punishment as Gelsenkirchen was largely missed because of cloud and malfunctioning Oboe sets, and bombs fell up to thirty miles away.

Now, on 9 July, the same thing happened. Oboes were not working, marking was hopeless, and the Germans thought the main target had been Bochum, which received far more hits than Gelsenkirchen. Losses were light, though, three per cent, but one of them was Duncan's ship.

After the straight and level bombing run, at around 01.30 they were hit by flak again, more seriously than 'very bumpy' though not so badly that they thought they were done for, at first, anyway. Sergeant Blunden, the flight engineer, had been wounded but not perilously so. They could make it.

As they flew home, the damage to fuel tanks forced a rethink. By the time they reached the Pas-de-Calais, at about 02.30, all hope and almost all the petrol had disappeared, so John Duncan gave the order: abracadabra, jump. The aircraft smashed into the earth near the village of Troisvilles. Sergeant Blunden and mid-upper Sergeant Warner were soon taken prisoner but the rest of the crew had a more interesting time.

The Canadian skipper landed in a cornfield east of Cambrai and changed nationalities:

'I immediately hid my parachute and Mae West. I walked south east across country till daybreak and then slept in a haystack till 11.00 hours. I continued across country, passing through a small town, where a boy gave me a loaf of bread and showed me on my map where I was. About 18.00 hours I went to a farmhouse near Cambrai and got food and shelter. I set off about 05.00 hours next day (11 July). About noon I stopped at a farmhouse and told the people I was English. They took me to another house, where I got food and shelter for the night. Next day I was taken by car to Chauny, where I was sheltered for eight days.'

Flight Sergeant Henry Brown, a milkman from Enfield, was the navigator:

'I landed in a tree near Pommereuil, about three miles NE of Le Cateau. I cut myself free and ran off. After about three miles I went into a wood and slept until 05.00 hours. I then took off my tunic and was in the middle of cutting off my sergeant's stripes when I heard German voices quite close to me. I hurriedly pushed my tunic into some undergrowth and ran off.

'After I had gone some way I stopped at a farmhouse, knocked on the door and asked for shelter. I do not speak French, but the farmer took me in and after much difficulty I eventually made him understand that I was English.'

Sergeant Gerard Bartley, a builder from Annfield Plain, was the bomb aimer:

'I came down in a potato field about half a mile due east of Cambrai. I hid my parachute, Irving jacket and mae west in a hedge and crawled a few hundred yards to a secluded spot, where I went to sleep. About 06.30 hours I went down a lane into a main road and walked into Cambrai. I got into the main street, still wearing my battle dress, from which I had torn all the badges. There were a large number of French people about on their way to work, and a youth told me to go back, as there was a German control on a toll gate.'

(The familiar sheepskin flying jacket, with zips and huge collar, is actually branded Irvin and, at the time of writing, can be bought new from the Imperial War Museum for £575.)

'I hid in a field watching for someone to approach. After a time, I shouted to a farmer. I told him I was English, and he hid me in the middle of a large cornfield. The farmer, his father and his sister brought me food, and said the Germans were making a house-to-house search.

About 14.30 hours, after asking the way to St Quentin, whence I wanted to get to Paris, I began walking, still in battle dress. I circled Cambrai to the south and reached the main St Quentin road. I followed the road all day, walking at first parallel to it and then on it. I saw no traffic except a few cars. I slept the night in a cornfield.'

Sergeant Sidney Hughes, from Darwen, a motor driver in civilian life, was the wireless operator:

'I landed several miles due north of Cambrai in a cornfield where I hid my parachute and mae west. I went through my pockets and tore up any papers with writing on them as well as £3 10s in notes. I lit a cigarette with another pound note. I then walked to the nearest farm and spent the night in a woodshed. About 08.30 hours I approached the farmer, who gave me some milk and showed me on my escape map where I was. I decided to make SE towards the Swiss frontier.

'After walking across country for a time I reached the main road to Guise, SE of Cambrai. I passed through several small villages and at one of them got food about midday. About 20.00 hours I was nearing Guise when a youth on a bicycle stopped and asked if I was English. He took me to his home in Guise where I was given a meal. As the police were looking for me, I was hidden in a hut in a wood. A gamekeeper kept the police in conversation while I was being hidden. After about an hour the gamekeeper, a postman and two other men brought me civilian clothes. I threw my battle dress into a well in the hut.'

David McMillan, a salesman from Ontario, was the rear gunner. He had the most exciting time of all:

'I landed at 03.00 hours in a large grass field about a mile SW of Le Cateau, spraining both ankles in doing so. I hid my flying clothing and equipment under brushwood in a clump of trees. My legs for a while were quite inert from the shock sustained on landing, but when I could move them freely, I started off in the direction of a clock chime which I heard some distance off. I thought that if, as was likely, the chime came from a church, I would try for help there.

I knew the crashed aircraft was not far away and thinking that if I walked too far, I should come up against the cordon which would be drawn round it by the Germans, I decided to hide somewhere quite near. Passing through the town, I heard whistling and scaled a low wall. In doing so I made a noise and found myself covered by a young armed German, who took me to a guardroom on the outskirts of the town, where I was searched by a sergeant, with my hands above my head.

He handed me back my escape box, purse and pencil with pencil clip, but removed my cigarettes, watch, a box of matches and a 10/– note. He did not find the round compass in my battle blouse. I wrote down my name, rank and number on a piece of paper. The sergeant telephoned, I think, for transport, but apparently none was available, and after a consultation between the two Germans I was marched off by the private.'

The escape kit was an imaginative assembly in the Boy Scout style. It had water sterilising tablets and razor blades, a snare for rabbits with instructions, a fishing line and hook, maps, matches and a magnifying glass for starting fires. Some aircrew remember a hacksaw blade, the main use for which was sawing off the tops of flying boots so they looked more like shoes. Later, much better kits also had sweets, tea, condensed milk and Elastoplast.

For a man with two sprained ankles, clearly doomed to become a prisoner of war, the lack of transport seemed disappointing. It turned out to be a stroke of good luck:

> 'My ankles were paining me considerably and after going a little way I sat down on a low stone wall, took off my flying boots, showed my swollen ankles to the German and started rubbing them. After a time he showed signs of impatience. In slewing round on the low wall to reach one of my boots I knocked it off. Feeling for it in the darkness, my hand came into contact with a large stone. I put the boot on, but reached back for the stone. I pretended by grunting and gestures to be in considerable pain and held out my left hand for the German to pull me, which he did, offering me his left hand. As he did so, I pulled him down towards me, and then crashed the stone, which I had kept all the time in my right hand, against the left side of his head. He dropped with a clatter. I tried to get the bayonet off his rifle but failed. I searched him hurriedly and recovered my cigarettes and watch, but found nothing else of use on him. He was quite senseless, bleeding a little from the nose, and I put him over the wall.'

Henry Brown:

> 'The farmer went off and returned in the afternoon with a man who spoke a little English. This man asked me if I knew anyone who could help me or if I wanted to give myself up to the Germans. I told him I had no friends in France, but that I intended to return to the UK. He went away and returned with a complete set of civilian clothes.
>
> A little later he came back again with a woman who spoke good English. She took down details such as my number, name, rank etc, took away my escape kit and RAF uniform, which she said the farmer would destroy, and took me by car to the house of a friend of hers.'

Gerard Bartley:

> 'Next morning (11 July) I walked to a small village and went into the church. I left after the service, and two youths followed me out of the village. They gave me food but no other help. At the next village I had to pass two German sentries but neither challenged me. That night a farmer sheltered me in a barn and gave me food and cognac. I walked all the next day, and at night again got shelter in a barn and food from the farmer.

'The courage of these French people was remarkable. The longer the airmen lasted, the longer and easier would be their trail for the Germans to follow back. The penalty for aiding the enemy was very likely to be the firing squad.'

Bartley:

'By midday on 13 July I was within a few miles of St Quentin, and while resting on a road bank was approached by a roadman who asked if I was English. He hid me on the other bank of the road, brought food, and arranged for another two men to come for me with a motor van at 18.00 hours. I was taken to Tugny, about 10 miles SW of St Quentin, where I was sheltered for two nights before being handed over to an organisation in Chauny.'

Sidney Hughes:

'I was taken to a house in Guise where a man who spoke a little English took my personal particulars and the names of the rest of the crew. That night I was moved by car to a small village near Guise. Three days later I was taken back to Guise, and a tailor measured me for a suit.'

David McMillan:

'I was feeling shaken and left the town at once. I nearly went back to get the German's boots but decided against it. I got onto a main road which took me roughly south. I avoided one motor cyclist by getting hurriedly into a ditch. I started walking at 04.30 hrs and at 09.00 hrs I reached Busigny on the Le Cateau–Cambrai road, and went to the station. There was an elderly Frenchman in the booking office. I said "Un, Paris" and put down four of the 50 franc notes from my purse. He gave me the ticket without comment and handed me back two of the notes with some small change. I asked him "Train, quelle heure?" and he wrote "4.30" on the back of the ticket.'

Sidney Hughes, in his new suit:

'The only thing my helpers could not provide was shoes, so I continued to wear my Service boots. I was then sent to another village east of Guise for three days. My helpers meanwhile got in touch with an organisation and one of them brought me a note from Sergeant Bartley and a form in which to fill up:- number of aircraft, personal number, name, Squadron, and the names of four non-flying members of my Squadron. Later I was sent via St Quentin to Chauny to join Sergeant Bartley.'

Sergeant McMillan never did catch that train. Looking for somewhere quiet where he could wait for it, three young Frenchmen in a farm cart hailed him in French, and then in English. He declared himself and was taken off to another hiding place, given food, advised against civilian clothes on the grounds that he would be shot if caught wearing them, and conveyed to Catillon in a covered cart.

Duncan, Hughes and Bartley journeyed through France and Spain to Gibraltar, handed on through the Resistance chain. They reached Gibraltar on 1 September and were back in England the next day. Sergeant Brown made the same journey, arriving Gib on 25 September. McMillan was not escorted all the way and took longer, arriving on 10 October.

Evaders generally could elect to be posted to a job out of the front line. For overseas personnel such as Canadians, it would have been standard practice to repatriate.

Duncan didn't want to do that. He still had more than half a tour to complete so he was supplied with a new crew and sent back to 9 Squadron.

CHAPTER 4

Operation Gomorrah

The last Gelsenkirchen raid on 9 July marked the end of the Battle of the Ruhr, a period of about five months during which two thirds of Bomber Command's efforts had been concentrated on that area, with many other raids elsewhere that prevented the Germans concentrating their defences exclusively. The Luftwaffe viewed the same period slightly differently but the general conclusions were the same. Extract from *The Luftwaffe War Diaries*:

'... the RAF's "Battle of the Ruhr" ended on the night of June 28th with a new attack by 540 aircraft on Cologne. Within a bare four months the inner cities of Essen, Duisburg and Düsseldorf were burnt out, and large areas of Wuppertal, Bochum and other towns lay in ruins.

The same four months saw the steadily increasing success of the German defence, both flak and night-fighters. The greater the distance the bombers had to fly to reach and return from their target, the greater was the chance of engaging them. In one raid alone – that of April 17th, on Pilsen in Czechoslovakia – thirty-six out of 327 bombers failed to return, and another fifty-seven were damaged. In other words 28.5 per cent had been put out of action.'

As we have seen with W4964 hit by flak over Düsseldorf and repaired for the next night, 'damaged' did not necessarily mean put out of action. Even so, the broad truth cannot be denied:

'The figures for the whole four-month period showed that of a total of 18,506 offensive sorties, 872 bombers had failed to return, and a further 2,126 had been damaged, some of them seriously.

But although the total loss of 872 bombers was an impressive number, it in fact represented only 4.7 per cent of the operating force.'

They mean 4.7 per cent of sorties ended in Failed To Return, rather than Bomber Command having 18,500 aircraft. Even so, if you look at that figure another way, ignoring new aircraft and crews replacing the losses and increasing the overall numbers, it actually represented rather more than the whole of the Bomber Command operating force at the start of the Battle. They had about 600 bombers then, but by the end of May could send 800 to Dortmund, of which 600 were four-engined heavies. Now a similar number was about to fly to a new target.

For Sergeant Charles Newton, a barrister in civilian life, Duncan's last op (as thought at the time) was his third. He and his crew had also flown the two Colognes, and he had had two second Dickies, also Cologne and Gelsenkirchen. After a spot of leave, on 24 July it would be W4964 and Hamburg, the largest seaport in continental Europe, Germany's second city and a greatly important industrial centre.

ED666 WS/G-Goofy, with Tom Gill in the cockpit, is about to take her fourteenth trip, the second Hamburg raid. The white bomb denoting her fifth is the shuttle raid on Friedrichshaven on 20 June 1943, when five specially trained crews flew on to Blida, Algeria, after hitting the target. On the way back on 23 June, they attacked La Spézia, Italy's chief naval base, hence the ice-cream cone. Goofy's spanner is presumably intended for throwing in the German works.

The city of Hamburg before the bombing.

The old town lay to the east of the river Alster and had recently become a low-lying maze of warehouses, canals and tenements. Beyond that, with the Alster dammed to form a lake, were harbour basins, the Elbe canalised river and a city of 1,700,000 people. Here, goods from all over the world were imported, making Hamburg the main distribution hub for middle Europe. Exported were all manner of machines and other manufactures from Hamburg's many, many factories and mills. In a single year, 15,000 ships would come and go, and more would be built there in yards able to cope with the largest types, for instance, the *Bismarck*. Latterly, the main ship-building business had been in naval surface vessels and some 200 U-boats.

The docks, railways, canals, factories and the vast population of workers, meant Hamburg was a life force for the Third Reich and, as Carthage for the Romans, had to be destroyed.

Once the Ruhr had been laid waste, Harris saw Hamburg as his next great target. Planning for Operation Gomorrah had begun in May, when Harris ordered his bomber group commanders to start preparations.

Hamburg had been meant to suffer the first of the Thousand Plan raids in 1942 but weather forced the switch to Cologne. Before and since, it had been bombed many times but not to any significant effect. Now there was going to be destruction and dislocation on a new scale. The aiming points were not on the shipyards and docks on the south side of the Elbe. The bombers would aim to the north, and the inevitable spread of explosions – the phenomenon recognised as 'creep', by which successive waves of bombers dropped short of the original marks – would devastate the residential areas as well as the industrial.

Hamburg was beyond the range of the UK-based navigation systems, Gee and Oboe, but was considered especially suitable for the airborne radar H2S because the geography around there was really distinctive. Rather than the usual puzzling fuzz of signals on the H2S screens which required inspirational interpretation by the operators, there would be a clearly identifiable coastline only 60 miles from the target, a wide river, harbour basins and various features that could hardly be missed.

The original idea with H2S had been to equip every aircraft with it, but it had proved impossible to make that number of sets. Only the pathfinders had it, and a small number of the main force aircraft, operated by the bomb aimers who sat behind the navigator's position rather than lying in their cold Perspex capsules.

Aiding and abetting for the first time was a new RCM – radar counter measure – called Window. That this laughably simple and very effective device had ever come into service must have been a triumph of persuasion for its advocates. It consisted of bundles of paper strips, 26.5cm long and 2cm wide – rough, thickish black paper – which had the equivalent of kitchen foil glued to one side. Paper? Foil? Ah yes, but, when dropped in the right quantities, at the right intervals and at the right height from an aircraft, the twirling black/shiny, absorbent/reflective surfaces of the strips utterly confused the radar of the time. Overwhelmed by false signals, the Würzburgs would be useless. As it turned out, the German early warning system, the Freya radar, operating on a longer wavelength, was also jammed although the operators could at least distinguish Window echoes from the real bomber stream without at first understanding the significance of what they were seeing.

Window had been tried and proved for over a year but not used until now, primarily because whoever made such decisions didn't want the Germans to find out about it and so produce the same thing themselves. Imagine King Harold saying: 'Put those long-bows away, lads. We don't want Duke William seeing we've got them'. What those Air Ministry decision-makers didn't know was that in a safe in Germany, belonging to General Wolfgang Martini, officer commanding signals, and kept secure under personal orders from Göring, were the research papers on Düppel, a similar RCM and similarly hidden for fear of discovery by the enemy.

What the Germans called 'chaff' had been tested over Düppel, a forest and neighbourhood south-west of Berlin, which was how it got its name. Göring would ensure that the Allies never got a whiff of this brilliant German idea and so locked it away and forbade any mention of it.

Window would be a great success. We can only speculate on the numbers of men who might have been saved from death, at the hands of radar-assisted fighter crews and flak gunners, in the year that it was held back.

In the darkness of the night of 24 July 1943, almost 800 bombers – in round numbers, 350 Lancasters, 250 Halifaxes, 125 Stirlings and 75 Wellingtons – set off on their long journey across the North Sea. Most went to a point fifteen miles north-east of Heligoland, where they would turn towards the German coast. In the aircraft with H2S, the bomb aimers watched their little radar screens as the radius 'minute hand' swept around and around, leaving behind a green trace for the coastline, gradually showing more clues until there was no mistaking what was up ahead: Hamburg.

Meanwhile, small groups of aircraft were dropping bundles of Window over Belgium and Holland and selling dummies with target indicators over the Ruhr.

As usual, the Luftwaffe commanders had known for hours that something was afoot; something big. A raid of this size could not be assembled in secret, although its possible destinations could not be guessed until it was well on the way.

In the British war films with scenes in Fighter Control, calls come in by telephone from radar stations and coast-watchers, WAAFs move model aircraft around on a table-map with long sticks, while senior officers watch anxiously and make more telephone calls to scramble the fighters. The Germans had something of the sort too, only ten times bigger and much more dramatic. Underground, at a place called Stade on the lower Elbe, was Second Air Division's ops room. Instead of the table and stick-pushers, there was a giant screen of frosted glass, with a map of Germany overlaid with a grid showing the 'cells', the three-dimensional boxes into which the sky was divided. Each cell had its Würzburg radar ground station and dedicated fighter, with the best crews – the 'Experten' – flying in the most fruitful cells (much to the frustration of the non-experts, the newer men who felt themselves at a disadvantage).

The German WAAFs sat behind the screen, about twenty of them, each with a telephone linking her to a coastal radar station. When a call came in, she would type the information into a machine – numbers of invading aircraft, height and course – and project it onto the grid location on the screen.

In front of the screen sat the fighter-control and air-raid warning officers, likewise connected to their units by telephone. More projectors showed the positions of airborne fighters. The same scene was repeated in four other ops rooms, near Arnhem, Metz, Berlin and Munich.

Just before midnight on 24 July, the first reports indicated a large formation of bombers over the sea, heading eastwards, and parallel with the coast off the northern Netherlands. Messerschmitt 110 stations were scrambled and crews took up their positions, waiting while new reports showed a formation of several hundred bombers to the north of the Elbe estuary. Where were they going?

The watchers noticed that the bombers were not moving. These great crowds of aircraft were stationary in mid-air. What was happening? Calls to radar stations all got the same answer: out of action by jamming. The Würzburg screens were showing an indecipherable snowstorm of echoes. Without precise information from the operators on enemy height and position, the fighters and flak gunners were blind.

Not so blind were the air-raid observer corps, but they could only report what the enemy let them see, which was a cascade of yellow flares near Meldorf, a town north of the Elbe estuary looking out across the Heligoland Bight. This, the German commanders rightly assumed, was a turning point for the bomber stream. More calls came in. The bombers could be heard. They were heading down the Elbe, straight for Hamburg, where fifty-four heavy and twenty-six light flak batteries awaited them, plus twenty-two searchlight batteries and three smokescreen installations.

The bombing started at about 01.00. The flak emplacements, with no radar guidance, sent up a guesswork barrage as 728 of the 791 starters began to reach the target, dropping 2,284 tons of bombs in fifty minutes. Only two bombers are known to have been downed by flak, a Wellington of 166 Squadron and a Lancaster of 460 Squadron. The other ten aircraft lost to enemy action were all confirmed/believed victims of night-fighters, or lost without trace which probably meant being shot down over the sea. Twelve aircraft and crews were lost out of 791 beginners: one-and-a-half per cent. Never had a major raid cost so little. It was a triumph for Window.

Such a small bag for the fighters, unable to receive any directions from their Würzburg controllers, was also because their airborne radar sets, their Lichtenstein apparatus, normally used in the final stages of an approach, were rendered useless by Window. One fighter pilot was Wilhelm Johnen, flying with wireless/radar operator Facius, a crew scrambled after the first warnings:

'I flew in the direction of Amsterdam. The ground stations kept calling the night-fighters … It was obvious that no one knew exactly where the enemy was or what his objective would be. Now the enemy was over Amsterdam and then suddenly west of Brussels, and a moment later they were reported far out to sea in Map Square 25. All the pilots were reporting pictures on their screens. I was no exception. At 15,000 feet my sparker (Facius) announced the first enemy machine in his Li(chtenstein). I was delighted. I swung round onto a bearing in the direction of the Ruhr. Facius proceeded to report three or four more pictures. I hoped I should have enough ammunition to deal with them. Then he suddenly shouted "Tommy flying towards us at great speed. Distance decreasing … 2,000 yards … 1,500 … 1,000 … 500 …"

I was speechless. Facius already had a new target. Perhaps the other had been one of ours. Facius shouted again: "Bomber coming for us at a hell of a speed. 2,000 … 1,000 … 500 … he's gone." "You're crackers, Facius" I said, jestingly, but I soon lost my sense of humour for this crazy performance was repeated a score of times.'

Wilhelm Johnen again, with a call from a ground station:

' "Hamburg, Hamburg. A thousand enemy bombers over Hamburg. Full speed for Hamburg."

I was speechless with rage. For half an hour I had been weaving about in a supposed bomber stream and the bombs were already falling on Germany's great port. (As we arrived) the city was blazing like a furnace. It was a horrifying sight. Too late!'

Pilots of the sixteen 9 Squadron Lancasters had noted how there seemed to be an absence of fighters and the ground defences were in disarray, with searchlights waving aimlessly about the sky and the flak bursting in confused patterns well below the main concentration. In the morning, millions of little strips of foil were found all over Holland, Belgium and northern Germany. People said they were meant to poison the cattle.

Most of the marking had been reasonably accurate and the bombing concentrated, with the predicted creep-back not mattering so much in such a big city. Large areas were demolished. Among the famous landmarks hit was the Nikolaikirche, designed by Sir George Gilbert Scott.

Over the next two days, the USAAF sent 252 Flying Fortresses in the hope of demolishing the U-boat yards and other industrial fixtures, but they complained they couldn't see their targets through the smoke. They didn't have Window, they were in daylight, and they lost aircraft and crews at the usual rate. After this first major joint effort with Bomber Command, they were not at all keen to follow again.

DATE	AIRCRAFT TYPE & NUMBER	CREW	DUTY	TIME Up	TIME Down	DETAILS OF SORTIE OR FLIGHT	REFERENCES
24/7/43. (contd)	LANCASTER. ED. 666.	SGT. T.H. GILL. SGT. HR. WALKUP. SGT. M. McPHERSON. SGT. R.V. GOUGH. F/SGT. B.P. DEVINE. SGT. W.A. MORFON. SGT. K. McDONAGH. SGT. R. McKEE.	Bombing – HAMBURG.	2232.	0338.	Primary attacked. 0109 hrs. 18,000 ft. Yellow T.I's on coast. Reds and greens over target. Ground detail seen. River identified. Red T.I. in sights. 1st red cascaded at 0102 hrs. Two others in quick succession followed by two greens. Many bursts seen. Very good fires well concentrated. Two large explosions 0108 hrs approx in immediate vicinity of T.I.	
	LANCASTER. JA. 869.	P/O. W.D. ERVINE. SGT. D. LEYSHON. P/O. H.J. MAY. SGT. A.B. GILES. SGT. P. LOMAX. SGT. J.C. DICKINSON. P/O. H.A. DICKINSON.	Bombing – HAMBURG.	2310.	0407.	Primary attacked. 0146 hrs. 21,000 ft. Yellow T.I. at coast. Reds and greens at target. Centre of concentration of five T.I's in sights. Reds had all extinguished on arrival. Greens were cascading frequently. Several bursts seen in run up. Thick column of black smoke up to 18,000 ft. Slightly S.W. of main concentration of fires. Town centre well ablaze.	
	LANCASTER. W. 4964.	SGT. C.P. NEWTON SGT. J. TURNER. SGT. P. HALL. SGT. E.J. DUCK. SGT. J. RYAN. SGT. W.J. WILKINSON. SGT. R. McFERRAN.	Bombing – HAMBURG.	2313.	0415.	Primary attacked. 0146 hrs. 18,400 ft. Yellow 0124 hrs. No reds seen at all. Green at 0144. Bombed concentration of greens, which were in sights. No results of own bombing observed. Too many fires seen to pick out anything definite.	
	LANCASTER. ED. 551.	F/SGT. G.E. HALL. SGT. L. FIELD. SGT. E.D. EVANS. SGT. E. COLBERT. SGT. O.J. OVERINGTON. SGT. K. CHORLEY. SGT. H.G. WILLIAMS.	Bombing – HAMBURG.	2235.	0336.	Primary attacked. 0112 hrs. 20,000 ft. Route markers yellow and red and green T.I's seen. River also seen. One red T.I. in bomb sights, seen to cascade at 0109 hrs. Bombing seemed to be well concentrated around T.I's. Explosion seen at 0108 hrs.	

Tom Gill's passenger Sergeant Walkup was one of four second Dicky pilots carried by 9 Squadron skippers this night. Charles Newton in W4964, bombing later, saw too many fires to pick out anything definite.

Meanwhile, another 700-plus raid was mounted on Essen the next night, in the hope of inflicting terminal damage while Window was still a surprise, and Krupp took its worst punishment yet. Dr Krupp himself had a stroke and, like his works, never recovered.

W4964 went with Flight Sergeant Gordon Graham, a Canadian on his second of a long but incomplete career. He had arrived on squadron on the 8th of the month and gone second Dicky the next night to Gelsenkirchen, and made his debut as captain on the first Hamburg. The Essen op, though, was a first for J to come back early with technical trouble. Intercom and electrical failures forced the return. Like recalls, such part-trips were noted as DNCO – Duty Not Carried Out – on a crewman's record, and so didn't count towards his tour, but were counted as operations for the aircraft for engineering/maintenance reasons.

Each aircraft had an aircraft manager, a sergeant who was usually the engine fitter/mechanic. In his dispersal hut he kept the much revered Form 700, the aircraft's maintenance log, which had to be signed by representatives of all the trades each time the aircraft was to fly, passing her over to the pilot and crew in serviceable order. DNCOs and recalls involved all aspects of a full op except the mileage, and so they went in the log and were represented on the nose-paint mission tally.

Graham had J again on the second Hamburg raid on 27 July. Tom Gill saw smoke up to 23,000ft. Graham said it reached 25,000. They could not have understood the meaning of such a sign – nobody could, unless they were there. A terrible firestorm had developed, not because (as is sometimes claimed) the bombers were carrying extra amounts of incendiaries. They had normal loads but the circumstances below were unusual. There had been no rain for weeks and it was a very warm, dry night. The bombing was especially concentrated, with most of the bombs falling in an area of only two square miles. The fire services were elsewhere, still damping down the fires lit in the first raid and unable to reach the new emergency through rubble-strewn streets. All of this added up to something the world had never seen before.

Here is part of the official report by the German 21st Army Group:

'... the fact (of another raid on Hamburg) in the night from July 27th to 28th was not surprising. Its magnitude and consequences, however, were far beyond all expectations. At least 800* planes attacked the city in several waves from all sides. The main weight of the attack was this time at the left shore of the Alster. Within half an hour the whole left side (of the city) was in a terrible situation by a bombardment of unimaginable density and almost complete annihilation of those town districts was achieved by the enemy in a very short time ... the alternative dropping of blockbusters, HEs and incendiaries made fire-fighting impossible, small fires united into conflagrations in the shortest possible time and these in turn led to fire-storms ... which went beyond all human imagination ... the overheated air stormed through the streets with immense force ... developing into a fire typhoon such as was never before witnessed, against which every human resistance was quite useless.'

* There actually were 787, including 353 Lancasters, the largest number so far on one raid, of which eleven were lost. Nineteen losses altogether, or 2.4 per cent, were mostly credited to night-fighters, including one at least to a certain Major Hajo Herrmann.

Earlier in the month, over Cologne, the Luftwaffe had introduced a new tactic that came to be known as 'Wilde Sau' (wild boar). Supplementing the radar-controlled two-man, two-engine fighters, mainly Me110 and Ju88, they put up Me109 and FW190 single-seaters with extra fuel tanks giving them two hours and more in the air. They would hunt by eye, looking for targets of opportunity in the midst of the bombing, rather than trying to infiltrate the bomber stream on the way in and out. The wild boars would watch for a Tommy lit by searchlights, flares or the glow of fires below. There would be an arrangement with the flak gunners – they wouldn't fire above a certain height – and it was hoped such an arrangement would work.

Major Hajo Herrmann was the progenitor of this scheme and, at Cologne, found himself in the thick of it. He came so close to a Lancaster that he could see the rear gunner in his turret, watching the burning city. Bomber crews would not have expected a fighter attack in among all this flak. Herrmann gave the Lanc a burst of cannon fire and down it went.

There were other victories too, for Herrmann and his small band of men. Twelve were claimed, the same number as claimed by the flak gunners. Whoever got how many of the thirty-two that went down that night – and it would seem that the boars got at least three – it was enough to encourage the formation of a new unit, JG300. Hermann was in the middle of organising this, on the day after the first Hamburg raid, when he had a telephone call from Göring. 'Hamburg, Hermann,' said the big chief. 'It has never been so bad. My entire night-fighter force was put out of action. You must start operations immediately, even if it is only small numbers.'

It would be some time before the RAF realised what was happening with the wild boars. Unable to appreciate the new danger, crews sometimes reported being fired on by their own. Later, in the fog, cloud and rain of winter, the Wilde Sau would suffer many losses, not from the bombers' guns but from the inability of the single-engined fighters to find home and land successfully in the dark. They had a radio homing beacon but even if that worked they would still have to approach an invisible field through cloud and mist and land blind. Crashes would be frequent. Pilots would prefer to bail out in bad weather, rather than risk coming down. In any case, a new Lichtenstein, the SN2, would come into service that was not fooled by Window. By March 1944, 30 Air Division of wild boars, grown from Hermann's JG300, would be disbanded.

In July 1943 Window had proved a great success and losses were well below what would have been expected without it, on the first Hamburg raid and the second, and no losses had been suffered by 9 Squadron.

Flight Sergeant Geoffrey Ward, a Yorkshire lad from Dewsbury, had gone on the first one (if he'd had the benefit of a second Dicky the Recorder of Operations missed it) and been to Essen. Being new, he possibly had yet to learn the art of laconic, understated reporting, without using words like 'enormous':

> 'Fires in target not fully visible owing to enormous pall of smoke which reached to higher level than aircraft. At 01.42 hours Lancaster had almost reached Dutch coast on return when an enormous explosion was seen back in target area which lit up the sky.'

Ward was at Hamburg again on the third attack on 29 July, in W4964 WS/J, one of seventeen from 9 Squadron:

> 'Fires appeared concentrated but not so numerous as other attacks. Large quantity of smoke but no column. 100 miles after leaving target fires appeared to flare up considerably.'

Losses on the third raid were up to almost 4 per cent, including one experienced crew from No. 9, and another fell on the final Hamburg raid, on the night of 2 August, when losses were up again, partly due to the foul weather. W4964 completed her hand of four Hamburgs with Newton, now a Pilot Officer, but the bombing was all over the place with very little hitting the target. They flew through severe icing conditions and electrical storms, only to find heavy cloud over the target up to 25,000ft. Like many that night, Newton bombed what he thought might be the aiming point, but towns many miles away had a few bombs each.

It did not matter. The bombers had already done their work. These are the words of Air Chief Marshal Harris:

> 'If the five months of The Battle of the Ruhr were months of severe trial for the enemy, the virtual annihilation of the second city of the Reich within six days at the end of July ... was incomparably more terrible.'

Hitler himself might have thought back to his words of 1940, speaking at a dinner in the Chancellery:

> 'Have you ever seen a map of London? It is so densely built that one fire alone would be enough to destroy the whole city, just as it did hundreds of years ago. Göring will start fires all over London, fires everywhere, with countless incendiary bombs of an entirely new

type. Thousands of fires. They will unite in one huge blaze over the whole area. Göring has the right idea: high explosives don't work, but we can do it with incendiaries; we can destroy London completely. What will their firemen be able to do once it's really burning.'

Back on the squadrons, there was little comprehension of what they, the bomber crews, had been able to do, but the Germans understood fully. Wilhelm Johnen:

'... 40,000 people were killed, a further 40,000 wounded and 900,000 were homeless or missing. This devastating raid on Hamburg had the effect of a red light on all the big German cities and on the whole German people. Everyone felt it was now high time to capitulate before any further damage was done, but the High Command insisted that the Total War should proceed.'

This was not a fireman talking, or a shopkeeper whose family and liveli-hood had disappeared, or a rescue worker who had found 300 dead bodies in an air-raid shelter, asphyxiated in the fire-storm. It was a fighter pilot's opinion, one who could have been expected not to recommend surrender. Accurate figures will never be known for the casualties in Hamburg. There could have been 50,000 dead. Certainly half of the city's buildings were nothing but rubble, and two thirds of the population, well over a million, fled elsewhere.

Germany's second city was hardly there any more and the other industrial centres were wrecks. The would-be conqueror was all but defeated. Wilhelm Johnen could see no way out. Neither could Albert Speer, Nazi party architect and armaments minister:

'The first heavy attack on Hamburg made an extraordinary impres-sion. We were of the opinion that a rapid repetition of this type of attack upon another six German towns would inevitably cripple the will to sustain armament manufacture and war production. It was I who first verbally reported to the Führer at that time that a continuation of these attacks might bring about a rapid end to the war.'

This echoed a speech in the House of Commons, made by a backbench MP called Simmonds in November 1942, with the Thousand Plan raids still fresh in everyone's mind:

'If each of the 25 principal German cities were in turn gutted as Cologne was the whole complexion of the war would change.'

Generalfeldmarschall Erhard Milch, deputy to Göring, and other senior officers of the Luftwaffe, realising that Hitler would never capitulate, saw that all they could do was defend. Every Luftwaffe resource had to be devoted to combating the bombers, day and night. Every aircraft built, every aspect of production and technical advance (such as a Window-proof radar), every moment of management planning and strategic thinking, had to be directed to air defence.

Hitler did not agree:

> 'The British will only be halted when their cities are destroyed. I can only win the war by dealing out more destruction to the enemy than he does to us.'

An 'Angriffsführer England' was appointed to deal out the destruction but he had virtually nothing with which to do it. The secret weapons programme that would lead to the V rockets was a long way from being operational. After conferences with his most senior aides, Göring issued the order. Defence was everything, regardless of Hitler. Stop the bombers or lose the war.

CHAPTER 5

Rocket Science

Hamburg and Essen had been well attended by J-Jig graduates and debutants – Newton, Graham, Ward, and Gill – and one skipper who had yet to have that privilege, Flight Sergeant Gilbert Hall, a married man from Appleton, near Oxford. There were two cancellations so they all had a few days off and, after five ops in a week, W4964 had a rest too. The last Hamburg, with Newton, had been J's fifteenth.

Graham went to Milan as one of ten who earned ice-creams on the noses of their aircraft, and Mannheim, which gave another future J pilot, Reg Knight, also married, from Carshalton, his second Dicky. Next up for J was Nürnburg, with Newton again, and Knight went too. It was a fairly successful raid with losses of only 2.5 per cent for the force of 653 aircraft, although one 9 Squadron crew had first-hand experience of the new wild-boar tactic but by a twin-engined fighter, a Ju88, which came at them during their bombing run. The mid-upper gunner was killed and the rear gunner badly wounded.

The short-term German reaction to Window and Hamburg had been to ditch the radar-guided system altogether and, from 1 August, deploy all night-fighters as wild boars.

'If we fail, we shall be overrun,' said Erhard Milch, the Luftwaffe chief of supply. Until they worked out a way of dealing with Window, they could not rely on their 'Himmelbett' (bed with a canopy, as in four-poster) system of radar-guided twin-engined aircraft flying in 'boxes' of sky, directed by ground controllers. No matter how many wild boars they scrambled, they still had the problem of finding the bombers in the dark, so some of the twin-engined fighters would seek out the bomber stream, sometimes guided by the Window droppings but, rather than go in among it, would fly beside it, giving a running commentary for the ground stations to study and, hopefully, deduce the target and direct the fighters there to wait for the target indicators to go down.

The British countered with spoof commentaries on the fighters' wavelength, for example telling the fighters to come home because of deteriorating weather. The Germans brought in women to relay instructions; the British had a woman broadcasting before the night was over.

Over the target area there was a different searchlight policy. The sky in general was lit, rather than trying to cone individual bombers for the flak, which could now be without radar guidance. This tactic worked especially well on cloud cover. To the fighter crews, looking down, the silhouetted bombers seemed – as one Luftwaffe pilot put it – like 'slow-moving insects crawling across a sheet'. There were also clusters of parachute flares dropped by the fighters, very bright but only of short duration. When a bomber crew saw some, they knew there was a bandit close by – unless they were spoof flares, dropped by Mosquito crews to attract the fighters well away from the target. After bombing, radar wasn't needed to work out where the enemy was going next.

The success of the new system depended absolutely on early identification of the target city, and so the response from Bomber Command was to deploy small diversionary raids which would send the fighters to the wrong place. This worked at first, notably at an upcoming raid on the secret weapons establishment at Peenemünde, for which 9 Squadron was already practising, doing what was called 'indirect bombing', timed runs from flares dropped away from the aiming point, and at low level. Before Peenemünde there was a different sort of diversion, a series of raids on Italian cities designed to hasten Italy out of the war, now that Mussolini was gone.

Geoff Ward, now a Pilot Officer, went to Milan on 12 August with Tom Gill (still a sergeant in his old faithful ED666 G-Goofy) and Reg Knight in W4964. Italian targets were always considered soft – softer, certainly, than German ones – and so here was a good opportunity to trial a raid-management system with its origins in the Dambusters op in May and the attack on the Zeppelin works at Friedrichshaven in June. As at Turin a few days earlier, one senior skipper (Group Captain Searby, 83 Squadron) was nominated as the Master of Ceremonies who would decide which markers were the most accurate and direct the bombers to them, ordering re-marking and generally managing the raid as it developed. As one 9 Squadron skipper reported: 'M/C heard giving orders to bomb green T/I straight and level. Very good fires burning in centre of town.'

At Milan there were no losses from the 504 that went. Four Lancs did go down over France, one due to engine trouble, and three more were in collisions at home.

During this night and two further raids, they hit Alfa-Romeo, the railway station and La Scala, and caused widespread damage to the city. Perhaps a thousand people died. Gilbert Hall was there on the last one on 15 August, in WS/J, listed as W4946. Since that aircraft had belonged to 467 Squadron, lost at Hamburg, we can be sure this was J-Jig's eighteenth. One 9 Squadron crew was attacked by a German night-fighter and seven other Lancs were

DATE	AIRCRAFT TYPE & NUMBER	CREW	DUTY	TIME Up	TIME Down	DETAILS OF SORTIE OR FLIGHT	REFERENCES.
17/8/43 (Contd)	LANCASTER. ED. 836.	P/O. R. WELLS. SGT. D.J. NUTMAN. SGT. A. DUNCAN. F/SGT. K. GARNETT. SGT. F. SMITH. SGT. W. GOUGH. F/SGT. S. MOSS.	Bombing - PEENEMUNDE.	2132.	0404.	Primary attacked. 0044 hrs. 6,000 ft. Ruden island seen from North end of which time and distance run was made. Green T.I's seen and through break in smoke road also seen. Centre of two green T.I's in bomb sights which were seen to cascade at 0043 hrs. Buildings in target area seen burning and big column of smoke also seen.	
	LANCASTER. R. 5744.	P/O. J.P. BILLING. SGT. F. HOPE. SGT. K.E. MORIARTY. P/O. K.N. GIBSON. F/SGT. J.M. CAMPBELL. SGT. J.B. FINDLAY. SGT. R.D. CURTIS.	Bombing - PEENEMUNDE.	2141.	0430.	Primary attacked. 0053 hrs. 6,000 ft. Red markers seen to go down ahead, but had burnt out by the time Ruden was reached. Green T.I's seen over target. Timed run from posn. "C", timed sections, and finally coincided with markers. Green T.I. markers in sights at time of bombing which were seen to cascade at 0051 hrs. Fires well concentrated around green T.I's, which were seen burning on sheds.	
	LANCASTER. ED. 666.	SGT. T.H. GILL. SGT. M. McPHERSON. SGT. R.V. GOUGH. F/SGT. B.P. DEVINE. SGT. W.A. MORTON. SGT. K. McDONAGH. SGT. R. McKEE.	Bombing - PEENEMUNDE.	2130.	0414.	Primary attacked. 0044 hrs. 6,000ft. Yellow and green T.I's seen on target. Green T.I. markers in sights at time of bombing, which were seen to cascade at 0042 hours. Fires well concentrated round green T.I's, which appeared to be very accurate.	
	LANCASTER. W. 4964.	P/O. C.P. NEWTON. SGT. J. TURNER. SGT. P. HALL. SGT. E.J. DUCK. SGT. J. RYAN. SGT. R. McFERRAN. SGT. W.J. WILKINSON	Bombing - PEENEMUNDE.	2124.	0451.	Primary attacked. 0057 hrs. 6,500 ft. No red markers seen. Green T.I's coincided exactly with timed run done from Ruden Island. Target identified visually. Green T.I's in sights at time of bombing. Fires well concentrated round green T.I. markers, and buildings seen to be hit.	

No. 9 Squadron, including W4964, skippered by Charles Newton, and Tom Gill in ED666, were flying their most important and technically most difficult operation so far.

lost to flak and fighters over France. Italy sued for peace at the end of the month.

If Commander-in-Chief Harris had had his way, J-Jig and the other 595 Lancasters, Halifaxes and Stirlings would never have gone at all, to Peenemünde. On a remote little peninsula on the Baltic coast, about two miles long, east of Greifswald and almost into Poland, was a research and development station. Nobody knew quite what was going on but reconnaissance photographs, plus intelligence reaching London from the forced labourers there, indicated something very odd.

What appeared to be a small aircraft with very short wings had no provision for a pilot or for a conventional engine. Rumours suggested that this machine, which people in the south-east of England would later know as the V1, was an automatically guided flying bomb. Launched from France, it could hit London at will. Further rumours suggested a missile that could hit New York (Wernher von Braun was there working on the rocket science that led to the V2 and, eventually, the Saturn rocket that took men to the moon).

Lord Cherwell, Paymaster General and scientific adviser to Churchill, said it was all poppycock. Harris said it was an unnecessary distraction from the real business of bombing Germany to defeat. The bomber commanders believed that heavy losses were inevitable on such a long trip in the full moon. The evidence suggested rockets, flying torpedoes, construction of launch sites and new anti-aircraft batteries in northern France, and what was this device, crashed on the Danish island of Bornholm? Details reaching London showed it to be the flying bomb of rumour.

Senior Nazis boasted publicly of new weapons that would win the war. That the Germans were engaged in a secret weapons programme was known and, possibly, this was it. So, whether the C-in-C liked it or not, Peenemünde would be attacked, and in the full moon. The three aiming points were: F, the houses where the research staff lived; B, the two big workshops and E, the development laboratories. To be avoided were the slave-labourers' quarters. This was indeed a question of 'hitting the right building'.

The three APs made a line with a small island to the north of Peenemünde called Ruden. To ensure greater accuracy than usual, as well as markers dropped at different stages on the various APs, there would be markers dropped on Ruden from which the bombers would make a timed run – indirect bombing. This would be especially valuable for the second and third waves who would have to bomb through smoke and fire.

Group Captain Searby had been practising his Master of Ceremonies role over Milan and Turin. This would be the first big performance, night of 17/18 August and, as the main force route would be more or less the same as if they were going to Berlin, the warm-up act was a dummy raid on the Big City.

Eight Mosquitos of 139 Squadron flew high over Denmark dropping great quantities of Window. German intelligence had already indicated a big raid on northern Germany. Radar showed a large force of bombers massing over the North Sea. It looked like Berlin, and when the 139 Squadron Mossies began dropping their pathfinder flares on the city, the population ran for the shelters and every Luftwaffe fighter was scrambled to defend the capital.

At more or less the same time, John Searby flew low over Peenemünde and wondered what could be down there that was so important. Well over 4,000 aircrew had been briefed that it was producing some kit that would revitalise the night-fighter force. Hit it tonight, or you will have to go back again until you do.

There was more cloud than had been forecast, but Searby judged which markers on the houses were right and called in the first wave of bombers, ordering them to bomb the accurate greens rather than the inaccurate reds. The next lot of markers were again a mixed bunch; some overshot. Searby broadcast his orders to the second wave: bomb the greens to the north, not the greens to the south.

There was chaos over Berlin with 200 aircraft in the sky, and the anti-aircraft batteries not knowing they were all German. The fighter pilots, reasoning that so many flak gunners could not be wrong, hunted desperately. Many claims were made for Mosquitos shot down; certainly there were some twin-engined aircraft destroyed that night but only one of them was a Mosquito.

There was an air raid going on but it wasn't on Berlin. The fighter pilots could see it, flares and bomb bursts and fires, way over to the north. Why the Tommies should be attacking the Baltic coast, nobody knew, but they could see it with their own eyes. Come on, it was only a hundred miles. The twin-engined fighters could get there in time.

Their controllers below would not release them. The Berlin all-clear had not been given. Until it was, they had to stay where they were, while Searby orbited the target again and again, trying to gauge the accuracy of his pathfinders while co-ordinating 600 bombers in three ten-minute waves.

The first wave started at 00.17 and finished at 00.27, going for aiming point F, the houses, while the pathfinders marked aiming point B, the factory. Newton, Tom Gill, Gilbert Hall and nine more of No. 9 were in the third wave, bombing between 00.44 and 00.57, at between 6,000 and 7,500ft, looking for aiming point E, the research and development shops.

Newton in J: 'Green T.I's coincided exactly with timed run done from Ruden Island.' Gill in G: 'Fires well concentrated around green T.I's, which appeared to be very accurate.' Hall in the long-serving ED551 M-Mother: 'Timed run from northern tip of peninsula coincided with green T.I. to the second, which Master of Ceremonies ordered to bomb. Three concentrations of fire at points F, B, and E. Fire at B being most impressive.'

Quite so. B included the assembly shops for the V2, and they were wrecked, but the final green TIs were in the wrong spot. The bombs hit the markers but not the R&D labs. Wernher von Braun was in there, sheltering, with his design drawings and calculations.

As the last bombers turned for home, the fighters arrived from Berlin. The area around Greifswald suddenly became a most dangerous a place to be, as bomber after bomber crashed to the earth there. Lancs and Halifaxes were picked off almost at will, silhouetted in the light of the moon and of the fires they had started, by the wild boars, some of them equipped with a new weapon, called *Schrägemusik*. This 'music on the slant', another term for jazz, was humorously named by its inventor, a sergeant armourer called Paul Mahle. It was a pair of upward-firing 20mm cannon, which Mahle mounted on a wooden platform behind the cockpit of a Me110 and which could be adjusted up to (a slant of) 72 degrees. The pilot fired them using a reflector sight in the cockpit roof, after positioning himself directly below the bomber, in the blind spot and without turbulence to spoil his aim. The standard, non-*Schrägemusik* approach was from below and behind but the pilot had to line up his aircraft with his target to fire his fixed guns, thus revealing himself to the bomber's freely movable guns. Now, thanks to Mahle, the fighters could attack in secret and without danger to themselves.

Mahle persuaded the sceptical airmen on his unit, II/NJG5 based at Parchim, roughly halfway between Hamburg and Berlin, to try it out. As it happened, the first opportunity came with the Berlin scramble followed by the rush in the opposite direction to Peenemünde.

One aircraft known to have fallen to this method was 467 Squadron's Lancaster ED764 PO/N, nicknamed 'Nuts' by the Nazis, which was shot down by Lieutenant Peter Erhardt, with five crew parachuting to prison. Erhardt claimed three more victories within half an hour. Corporal Hölker claimed two with his slanting cannon. With or without Schrägemusik, fourteen Halifaxes, twenty-two Lancasters and two Stirlings were lost to night-fighters, many of them near the target, the rest mainly when the wild boars found them again flying home over Denmark, while the flak got only three.

The combat report of Lieutenant Musset, pilot of a conventionally equipped Me110 with w/op Corporal Haffner, says it all:

'From the Berlin area I observed enemy activity to the north. I promptly flew in that direction and positioned myself at a height of 14,000 feet over the enemy's target. Against the glow of the burning target I saw from above numerous enemy aircraft flying over it in close formations of seven or eight. I went down and placed myself at 11,000 feet behind one enemy formation.

At 01.42 (local time) I attacked one of the enemy with two bursts of fire from direct astern, registering good strikes on the port inner engine which at once caught fire. E/A tipped over to port and went down. Enemy counter-fire from rear gunner was ineffective. Owing to an immediate second engagement I could only follow E/A's descent on fire as far as a layer of mist.

I make four claims as follows:

1. Attack at 01.45 on a 4-engined E/A at 8,500 feet from astern, range 30–40 yards. E/A at once burned brightly in both wings and fuselage. I observed it till it crashed in flames at 01.47.
2. At 01.50 I was already in position to attack another E/A from slightly above, starboard astern and range 60–70 yards. Strikes were seen in the starboard wing and E/A blew up. I observed burning fragments hit the ground at 01.52.
3. At 01.57 I attacked another 4-engined E/A at 6,000 feet from 100 yards astern. Heavy counter-fire from rear gunner scored hits in both wings of own aircraft. Burning brightly in both wings and fuselage E/A went into a vertical dive. After its crash I saw the wreckage burning at 01.58.
4. At 01.59 I was ready to attack again. E/A took strong evasive action by weaving. Enemy counter-fire was ineffective. While E/A was in a turn to port I got in a burst from port astern and range 40–50 yards which set the port wing on fire. E/A plunged to the ground burning brightly and I observed the crash at 02.01.

A few minutes later I attacked another E/A which took violent evasive action by weaving. On the first attack my cannon went out of action owing to burst barrels. I then made three further attacks with machine guns and observed good strikes on starboard wing without setting it on fire. Owing to heavy counter-fire from rear gunner I suffered hits in port engine. At the same time I came under attack from enemy aircraft on the starboard beam which wounded my wireless operator in the left shoulder and set my port engine on fire. I broke off the action, cut my port engine and flew westwards away from target area. No radio contact with the ground could be established. As I was constantly losing height, at 6,000 feet I gave the order to bail out. As I did so I struck the tail unit with both legs thereby breaking my right thigh and left shin bone. After normal landings by parachute my wireless operator and I were taken to the reserve military hospital at Güstrow. At 02.50 my aircraft crashed on the northern perimeter of Güstrow.'

A German force of about thirty aircraft shot down more than their own number of Lancs and Halifaxes. The total score of forty-one included twenty-nine of the third wave. Somehow, Newton, Gill, Hall and the others of No. 9 missed all this. Had the whole 200 fighters that had been waiting over Berlin, instead waited over Peenemünde for the tightly packed waves of bombers flying at low level, and had they shot down a similar share, the

The ground crew looking after ED666 WS/G-Goofy pose with her after the Peenemünde raid, the aircraft's twenty-third and Tom Gill's sixteenth. Often having to improvise spares and tools, groundcrews' motto was 'Ubendum Wemendum'. A fitter looked after the engines and a rigger kept the aircraft tidy and fully equipped. These two belonged to one aircraft and one aircraft belonged to them. The other trades – signals, electrician, and armourer – worked across a flight, usually half, sometimes a third of a squadron, with a Flight Sergeant in charge of each trade and each flight, who was known as Chiefy.

The Chiefy here is A-Flight Flight Sergeant Tav Taverner, in the overalls. The others are known only as (from the left) Joe, Jack, Smudge, Lofty and Tich.

RAF would have lost an unbearable number, perhaps half the force. Those eight Mosquitos with their Window and target indicators had saved Bomber Command from utter disaster – or, turned a precision moonlight attack from a horrific gamble into a success.

Group Captain John Searby DSO, DFC, one-day Air Commodore, began the war as a sergeant pilot, rising to command 106 Squadron, then 83 Squadron Pathfinders.

The raid was thus classified, despite losses of seven per cent. A marking error on aiming point F meant that the bombs largely missed the scientists' houses and instead levelled the workers' village, including the shacks where the Polish slave labourers lived, but they did smash a hundred buildings, including laboratories and workshops. The troubled V2 project had to remove elsewhere, delaying matters by months, not that the V2 ever did play much of a material part in the war.

But what of Schrägemusik? The rest of Mahle's unit soon had it fitted and the commander was able to write: '2 October. To date II/NJG5, using the experimental oblique armament, has achieved eighteen victories without loss or damage to themselves.' Mahle said: 'I soon had many well-known night-fighters among my clients, all wanting me to fit Schrägemusik to their kites.'

It was not long before the Air Ministry took over the idea, giving Mahle 500 Deutschmarks and a diploma. *Luftwaffe War Diaries*:

> 'By 1944 there were few night-fighters still flying without the weapon, and the tally of enemy bombers that suddenly burst into flames without their crews knowing what had hit them constantly mounted.'

The tactic was to aim for the wings and the fuel tanks rather than directly up into the bomb bay whence the explosion might catch the fighter too. Even so, the bomber would often blow up in the sky, rather than show the usual slow tumble to earth. When RAF Intelligence realised what was happening, an official rumour was put about regarding a new German comedy weapon called 'Scarecrow,' a huge but harmless oil-filled flare which made a blinding flash in an attempt to frighten bomber crews. That Scarecrow flares were Ministry moonshine became obvious as bomber crews observed Schrägemusik missing, coloured loops of tracer going over their own kite and a fighter then being revealed, or hitting another but causing the normal kind of downfall.

Gilbert Graham and Reg Knight were on for Leverkusen on 22 August, but J-Jig didn't go, and the next night Graham, Gill, Newton and Ward all went to the opening raid of the Battle of Berlin, but W4964 stayed at home. By the time she came back on duty, three of those five captains would no longer be available.

CHAPTER 6

So Far But No Further

A tiny event of little significance occurred on 30 August. A trainee pilot called Philip Plowright and his learner crew, still a way off conversion to heavy bombers, were pulled out of training to go in Wellington X3818 to bomb a German ammunition dump in the Forêt d'Éperleques. Although OTUs (Operational Training Units) had sometimes supplied aircraft and crews for main force raids earlier in the war, particularly in the Thousand Plan raids, it had not been done in 1943. It was not unusual to send them 'nickelling', that is leaflet dropping, but this was the first of a new practice, using them to bomb German targets in northern France. Two Wellingtons were lost; one man was saved from a dinghy in the Channel. Plowright and his men came home undamaged and would eventually join No. 9, fly in W4964, and show themselves to be very good at that essential art of homecoming.

Mönchengladbach, named the Gladbach of the monks after its ancient Benedictine monastery, was mainly a textile town before the war, population 130,000 or so, but its railway yards, oil depot and airfield made it a target for Bomber Command, if a small one. Next door, in the town of Rheydt (population 77,000) textiles also were made but there were various other factories producing machinery and goods for the war effort. If a raid on one or the other seemed hardly worth it, a double raid taking them both looked a more reasonable proposition for the first major attack on either, night of 30/31 August.

The pathfinders marked Mönchengladbach first, and then switched to Rheydt, which was where 9 Squadron was going with fifteen Lancasters. The Bardney runway was in need of repair so they flew from Woodhall Spa, home of 617 Squadron, the Dambusters, a unit that would figure significantly at the end of WS/J's career.

There were 660 bombers altogether and, with excellent Oboe marking on a clear night, half of each town's built-up area was destroyed – over 2,300 buildings. Combined losses for the whole raid were 4.5 per cent: seven Lancs, twelve Halifaxes – including three that struggled home with fighter damage but crashed on arrival – five Stirlings, and six Wellingtons including two that collided on the outward journey and fell near Goole, all crew killed.

One of the Lancasters lost was ED551 WS/M, only four short of her half-century of ops, on squadron since February, with Gilbert Hall and his men, J's tenth crew, on squadron since May. Hall was twenty-three but they were quite an elderly lot – five of them were aged between twenty-six and thirty-one.

Hall went down on his eighteenth, his thirteenth in ED551, and likewise for the rest of the crew except mid-upper gunner Bob Chorley, who missed four trips over eight days in June (possibly on leave – he was married, to Joan). It could have been twenty-one and fourteen but three of the first four trips were DNCO because of engine failure and getting lost in the cloud. Being lost and alone at 21,000ft and unable to find Düsseldorf had all the attributes of an op but for the crew it didn't count. Phil Plowright, with his little trip to France, would have one already chalked up when he came on squadron. Hall and his men did four soon after they arrived but only one of those got a tick.

Not that it mattered in the end. They did all four Hamburgs, and the Essen raid in between – five major ops in the space of nine days – and Peenemünde. Their one trip in W4964, to Milan, must have seemed like the fabled piece of cake in comparison, with the added excitement of the moonlit view over the Alps.

On their last, they had with them an extra navigator attached from 1654 Conversion Unit at RAF Wigsley, Pilot Officer Clarence Anderson, who had a wife, Edith, at home in Calgary, Alberta. Otherwise it was the original crew, all sergeants: Leon Field, Bill Evans, Ed Colbert, Oliver Overington, Bob Chorley, and Henry Williams. Every man was lost without trace.

The last of the month for No. 9 was thirteen Lancs to Berlin – Tom Gill and Reg Knight went but Gill had to come back with a dead engine – the middle raid of a series of three that finished with thirteen again, including Charles Newton and Gordon Graham, on 3 September. There were no losses for 9 Squadron but well over 1,600 sorties on these three Berlins resulted in an appalling 125 crews failing to return.

Berlin was the target of targets for Arthur Harris. Instead of doing what Speer and the other senior Nazis feared – reducing half a dozen 'easier' cities to a Hamburg-style nothing and forcing a revolution – he believed the same thing could be achieved by reducing the capital city, the best defended place in the world. He was going to 'wreck Berlin from end to end'.

Berlin could not be attacked in the summer months because the hours of darkness were too short for the long overland journey. Come the autumn, that stricture no longer applied. Unfortunately, the very length of the trip meant that Window lost its effectiveness. Although the Würzburgs were still rendered useless, the Germans had plenty of time to identify by other methods where 600 bombers were going and to assemble their fighters over

Date	Aircraft Type & Number	Crew	Duty	Time Up	Time Down	Details of Sortie or Flight	References
30/8/43 (contd)	LANCASTER. R. 5744.	P/SGT. G.A. GRAHAM.	Bombing – MUNCHEN GLADBACH	0013.	0457.	RHEYDT attacked. 0240 hrs. 18,000 ft. Red T.I's seen to cascade far ahead at 0218 hrs. Fires burning on arrival at target. Green T.I's seen to cascade at 0220 hours and 0234 hours. Reds had burnt out. Bombed centre of concentration on of 3 - 4 clusters of greens. A good concentration of T.I's and fires were seen, but there was also a certain amount of scattered bombing outside the concentration.	
		SGT. W. STATHAM.					
		P/O. D. McDONALD.					
		SGT. R.M. INNESS.					
		SGT. A.F. WILLIAMSON.					
		SGT. H. ALTUS.					
		SGT. K. MELLOR.					
	LANCASTER. ED. 666.	P/O. F. JAMES.	Bombing – MUNCHEN GLADBACH	0011.	0453.	RHEYDT attacked. 0261 hrs. 18,500 ft. Ran up on greens but just as about to bomb saw red T.I. on ground through break in clouds. This red T.I. in sights. Fires at Munchen Gladbach appeared to have got well hold. At Rheydt had hardly started, but good glow seen after leaving. Could see the two distinct concentrations.	
		SGT. G. TOMLINSON.					
		P/O. G.E. LOCKEY.					
		SGT. A.H. HOWIE.					
		SGT. R.W. BURKE.					
		SGT. N.W. CHIVERS.					
		SGT. H. CROXON.					
	LANCASTER. JA. 869.	P/O. C.P. NEWTON.	Bombing – MUNCHEN GLADBACH	0015.	0515.	RHEYDT attacked. 0244 hrs. 19,000 ft. Red T.I. seen at 0243 hrs. No green seen at all. Bombed red T.I. No results of own bombing. Bursts seen of other bombs at time.	
		SGT. J. TURNER.					
		SGT. P. HALL.					
		SGT. T.J. DUCK.					
		SGT. J. RYAN.					
		SGT. CRADDOCK.					
		SGT. W.J. WILKINSON.					
	LANCASTER. ED. 551.	P/SGT. G.E. HALL.	Bombing – MUNCHEN GLADBACH	0008.		Aircraft missing. No signals received.	
		SGT. L.J.G. FIELD.					
		SGT. W.D. SWANS.					
		SGT. E. COLBERT.					
		SGT. O.J. OVERINGTON.					
		SGT. N.A. CHORLEY.					
		SGT. H.G. WILLIAMS.					

Hall was an exact contemporary of Tom Gill. They'd flown the same first op – Dortmund, on 23 May, when Gill had been in W4964 – and set off on the same next five. Neither appears to have had a second Dicky.

the Big City, knowing that this time it would not be Peenemünde. The second of the three raids was also the first time that fighter flares were used, as part of the wild boars' answer to Window.

One 9 Squadron crew mentioned: 'Long string of white-green flares seen burning at height of aircraft'. They didn't know that Ju88s and Me110s were flying above them, watching their silhouettes against the cloud and dropping their parachute floodlights, all the better to see them with. Add Berlin's unrivalled number of searchlights and the bombers may as well have been operating by day, but without daytime defensive formations. Huge numbers were shot down by fighters charging around, their pilots unable to believe their good fortune, making it clear that, for the time being anyway, the Luftwaffe was still a mighty force.

Even so, Göbbels, the Gauleiter of Berlin, ordered all children and non-essential workers to be evacuated, while Harris withdrew from Berlin for the moment, instead sending 600-plus to Mannheim and Ludwigshafen (ports opposite each other on the Rhine) on 5 September. Mannheim had about 30 miles of quayside and was a smaller version of Hamburg, as the trading and distribution centre of southern Germany for imported goods.

The raid was highly successful – on a clear night with first-rate pathfinder marking. German records describe it as 'a catastrophe'. It was catastrophe too for R5744 WS/E, Reg Knight and crew, and for ED666 WS/G, Tom Gill and crew. All were killed as they fell to earth on the Ludwigshafen side of the Rhine.

Both skippers were married men, as was Knight's engineer, Thomas Bradford, and Gill's wireless operator Bill Morton. Apart from Bradford, aged thirty-one, Knight's crew were aged between twenty and twenty-four. Gill's were even younger.

Reg Knight knew Mannheim. How could he forget it? He'd been there on his one second Dicky less than a month before, when his mentor noted that a good many of the fires were on the Ludwigshafen side of the river.

His own first had been Nürnburg, with the same crew who died with him except for the mid-upper gunner. Knight never had a settled gunning partnership; the Scot Bob Nelson was always in the tail, but over seven ops he had five different mid-uppers: Sergeant Norman Adams, later killed at Berlin; Richard Jones who flew with Knight in W4964, and was killed in a crash at home after Berlin; Leslie Collins, killed at Stuttgart; Chester Davis, killed with Knight; and Sergeant W. H. Mullett.

From the *London Gazette*, 5 November 1943:

Distinguished Flying Medal

Sergeant Wallis Harry Mullett, who has taken part in numerous sorties, is an exceptionally keen and determined air gunner. One night in October, 1943, he was a member of a crew of an aircraft which attacked Kassel. Whilst over the target, the bomber was hit by a burst of machine gun fire from a fighter and the mid-upper gunner was killed, while the oxygen and electrical heating apparatus connections to the rear of the aircraft were severed. Sergeant Mullett engaged the attacker, however, and shot it down. Afterwards he lost consciousness owing to lack of oxygen and heat and did not recover for some time. This airman displayed great resolution and devotion to duty.

That same Les Collins flew twice with Tom Gill. Chester Davis flew with him three times when Paddy McDonagh was unavailable for some reason.

SECRET *No. 9 Squadron Combat Report*

Date: 22nd/23rd June 1943. Pos. Noordwjk area. Target Mülheim. Lancaster 'E' Captain Sergeant Gill.

T/E E/A sighted starboard beam slightly down, range 500 yards, firing with cannon and machine guns as it approached. The Lancaster was weaving systematically at the time and the enemy fire appeared to pass above. The MU gunner told the pilot to commence a diving turn to starboard and at the same time gave the enemy three accurate bursts. Tracers appeared to enter the E/A which broke off the attack at 400 yards and took up a position on the starboard beam flying parallel to the Lancaster. Our crew now observed that the E/A was on fire as a red glow was seen in its nose. Both rear and MU gunners now opened fire on the E/A which went into a dive obviously in flames The captain, bomb aimer and flight engineer then saw the E/A explode in the air. This aircraft is claimed as destroyed.

Comment
It is probable that the systematic weaving of the Lancaster in the first place prevented the enemy fighter getting any shots on target. The accurate shooting of the gunners, particularly the mid-upper, and the correct defensive manoeuvre being employed at the right moment, did the rest.

MU gunner Sergeant Davis 250 rounds
Rear gunner Sergeant McKee 100 rounds.

Spare bods could be around the squadron for several reasons, the most usual being that their crew had finished a tour while they had missed a few ops and so had to stay on to complete, or they might have come in with a skipper who was killed on his second Dicky. They might find a permanent slot, replacing a wounded (or dead) man possibly, drift from crew to crew until the fates caught up, or they might even get out of it alive.

Tom Gill did Essen, Bochum, Wuppertall, two Düsselldorfs, two Colognes, two Hamburgs, and two Berlins – all the usual grind of the bomber crews at this time of the war, with the unexpected release of some of the tension by flying to Italy twice. Practically two-thirds of the way through the tour, like Gilbert Hall's men, Gill and co might have thought the worst was over and they had a good chance of making it.

Gill's mid-upper gunner Kevin McDonagh, known as Paddy, was from Limerick, Republic of Ireland.

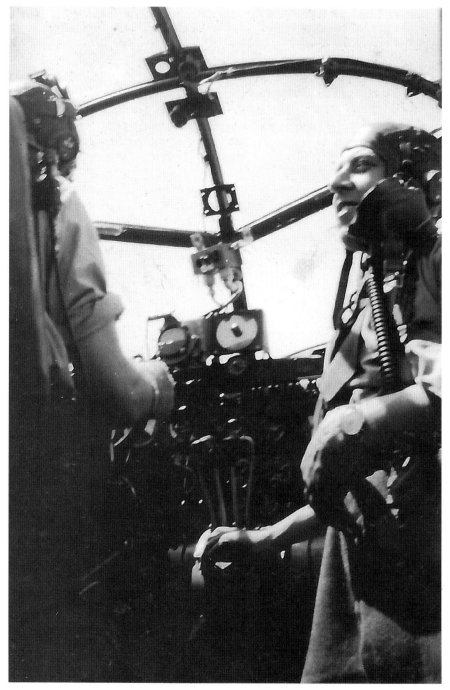

Ray Gough, navigator, is out of his curtained compartment for a chat with his skipper Tom Gill – a picture staged for the newspapers.

The averages were not known to aircrew, but they knew that most crews didn't get through. A few crews were lost on their first trip, therefore, logically, another few would have the luck to survive the thirty, while the rest went down in between. Or you could take it one op at a time. Each time you went, you were one of hundreds and, despite heavy losses, the great majority of the hundreds did come home on any given night. Cricket players noted that if you were batting and got to eighteen not out, you were more likely to score thirty than you had been when you'd just come in.

Michael Varley has calculated that for a crew to have had a fifty-fifty chance of surviving a tour of thirty ops, the loss rate must not have exceeded 2.3 per cent.

Out of Tom Gill's opening six ops, five were in W4964, and he had the distinction of bringing her home wounded for the first time from Düsseldorf on 11 June, when he'd had to lower the undercart on the gas bottle. Like his colleague Gilbert Hall, he went down on his eighteenth. He'd had two DNCOs and, unlike Hall, he'd taken two second Dickies, to Cologne and Hamburg.

Gill's wife, Mollie, was pregnant with their only child, a daughter, who would be born on 26 November and named Jane.

With Knight and Gill gone, the members of the J club left were Newton, Ward, Graham and crews. Newton and Ward went to Munich the night after Mannheim and Graham was admitted to the officers' mess but, after a couple of cancellations, for ten days in the middle of the month the squadron was stood down from ops and concentrated on training instead. Despite this learning off the job, the squadron lost three more Lancasters when it returned to duty, two new crews killed, and one experienced skipper with a second Dicky on board, ditching in fog with a faulty altimeter. Two men drowned. To illustrate the attitude and pressures of the time, note that second Dicky, Flying Officer Comans. After nine hours in a dinghy off Mablethorpe, he was captaining his own crew over Germany for the first time, two days later.

W4964 had had six weeks off but came back at the start of October with three ops in four days, with Charles Newton and his original crew from early July. They had all been sergeants then, Turner, Hall, Duck, Ryan, Wilkinson, McFerran; pilot and his navigator Hall were now officers. First of the three was Hagen – a Ruhr iron and steel town with railway and river junctions and a population of 150,000. It had not been seriously attacked before and, due to the success of this raid, would not reappear on the orders until late in 1944. About half of the industrial firms of Hagen were destroyed or damaged, one of which was a prime supplier of batteries for U-boats. Of course, the bombing was indiscriminate, in that it wasn't precisely targeted on any particular factory complex, but such knock-on effects were all part of the project. Bomb Hagen, make 30,000 people homeless, smash a small percentage of German heavy industry and, as a bonus, slow down U-boat production considerably.

Hagen was J-Jig's twentieth, and the next four followed in quick succession – Munich, Frankfurt and Stuttgart with Newton, and Hannover with Geoff Ward on 8 October. Results were mixed. On a night of light losses, two of the four Lancs going down at Stuttgart were from No. 9 meaning neither crew made double figures of ops.

According to the Recorder of Operations, Ward and crew went to Hannover on 18 October in W4963. As that Lanc was a trials aircraft at the Aeroplane and Armament Experimental Establishment at Boscombe Down, which the next day was doing take-off, climb and level speed performance tests at 63,000lb, the maximum take-off weight specified at that time, we can safely assume a WAAF typing error and count it as number 25 for J-Jig.

It was a punishing night of eighteen Lancs lost, 5 per cent, including one 9 Squadron crew on their first. Coming home safely were Ward, of course, and two second Dickies: Flying Officer Albert Manning, a married man from Ipswich, and Flight Sergeant John Syme, an Australian who had volunteered from his job as a plantation manager in New Guinea. Both would join the band of J-Jig brothers and, one sooner, one later, go the way of so many.

Both flew their first ops next time, Leipzig, on 20 October, with W4964 in the charge of Geoff Ward. Like the previous Hannover, this was an all-Lanc raid with 'acceptable' losses, and to a more distant target than had been usual – not as far as Berlin but still a round trip of about seven hours. None of the crews saw any worthwhile target marking or any bombing results through the cloud, although some noticed the diversionary raid on Berlin by twenty-eight Mosquitos. Leipzig, as a commercial centre ranked third in Germany behind Berlin and Hamburg, had a population of around 700,000, many engaged in the printing industry. There were other industries too and one of the greatest railway stations in the world. None of it suffered much damage on this night.

Flight Sergeant John Syme was 26 years old and from Adelaide, South Australia. He'd arrived on 24 September, been to Hannover as a second Dicky and to Leipzig as captain, but that was the extent of it so far. Now he was in the safest aircraft on the squadron, not that he knew it, W4964, for Kassell.

He reported two large red fires west of the river. Bill Read, another will-be skipper of J-Jig, noted: 'Very good concentration of fire – resembled one large fire over a mile square' and he was right. Nothing like it had been seen since Hamburg. More than half of the city was laid waste, and more than half of the population of 220,000 were made homeless.

Kassell had an old town and a new. The old, on the west bank of the river Fulda, was largely seventeenth-century winding, narrow streets and ancient houses – ideal for a firestorm. Elsewhere, factories making engines, railway carriages and scientific instruments were devastated and the three Henschel aircraft works, building V1 buzz bombs at a frantic rate, were set back months.

In bombing terms it was a massive success, but the cost was high. Of the 322 Lancasters setting out, eighteen were shot down; of the 247 Halifaxes, twenty-five. Six more bombers crashed at home, some as a result of German damage, making 8.6 per cent losses overall. No. 434 Squadron had four Halifaxes failing to return. Almost joining them in the flames and explosions were Albert Manning and his crew, on their second operation.

SECRET *No. 9 Squadron Combat Report*

22/23rd October 1943, Kassel. F/O Manning in WS/B.

MU and RG both sighted a Dornier 217, 300 yards starboard quarter up. RG ordered corkscrew starboard. Both gunners and E/A opened fire. As the E/A's fire passed above our A/C, the navigator, standing in the astrodome, sighted a second E/A port quarter up at 400 yards. As he warned the gunners the E/A opened fire and hit the Lanc all along the port side, killing the MU, disabling the RG and slightly injuring the navigator (F/O Hearn). As those two E/As broke away, the navigator saw two Ju88s closing in, one on either beam down. They fired but missed. Pilot continued to corkscrew throughout these attacks which happened almost simultaneously. Hydraulic pipes below pilot's seat severed. Visibility hampered by reflection of searchlights on Perspex. MU Sergeant Provis. Rear gunner Sergeant Birkinshaw.

Or, as summarised by the Recorder of Operations: 'There was considerable fighter activity and 'B' was attacked, resulting in the death of the mid-upper gunner.' This economical style of the squadron diarist had developed over the years of blood and mayhem, from the rather sporty, pre-war, 'jolly-good-show' attitude prevailing when hostilities began. Then, you might find a captain arriving home with his Wellington, Whitley or Hampden 'freely peppered'. In the ghastly reality of the modern war, only the Line Book in the officers' mess kept up that kind of spirit.

The corkscrew was a standard sequence of violent evasive aerobatics taught to all bomber pilots. When a fighter was seen, usually coming from behind or the side, it was almost invariably one of the gunners who spotted it and he, for the moment, was in command of the ship. In training, it went something like: 'Rear gunner to pilot. Yes, rear gunner. Rear gunner to pilot, enemy aircraft approaching starboard down. Prepare to corkscrew starboard. Corkscrew starboard.'

In reality, the first the pilot knew about it was a gunner screaming into the intercom, 'Dive starboard!' or 'Corkscrew port!', and if the pilot did not react on the instant, a volley of cannon shells would rip through his aircraft.

Into the direction of the attack, the pilot stood the aircraft on her left (or right) wingtip, dived and turned to the left (or right) at the same time, then rolled her back, climbed and did it the other way. Diving turns and climbing turns combined with half rolls, flown at the limits of the Lancaster's performance – often with a full bomb load – might get the Lanc out of trouble and, if the gunners were top notch, allow some return fire, bearing in mind that the Lancaster only had machine guns being aimed by men on the hairiest white-knuckle ride of their lives, trying to hit an object moving very fast in three dimensions.

A novice fighter pilot might try to follow the Lanc through the 'winding match', making a slightly easier target for the rear gunner. Experienced Luftwaffe men might sit and watch while the bomber pilot tried to imitate a mobbed sparrow hawk and, at the moment she was at her slowest between climb and dive, let loose the cannon shells.

The small advantage the bomber had was manoeuvrable guns that could follow the attacker's moves. The fighter's standard guns were fixed and so the pilot had to fly along his own line of fire. With the element of surprise, this was not a problem but a fighter pilot who fiddled about, showing himself to his enemy through innocence or over-confidence, could come off worst.

Manning and his men had been on squadron eleven days. There were no more ops in October for No. 9, although there was a cancellation on the 30th. We can't know if Manning was listed for that, but he was flying again on 3 November with two new gunners and James Hearn, his slightly injured navigator, on board.

John Syme didn't fly again with 9 Squadron. He was posted on 15 November, with crew, to a new squadron being formed down the road at East Kirkby, No. 630. That squadron's first op was Berlin on 18 November. Their first loss was on 23 November, Berlin; their second, 26 November, Berlin; their third, 2 December, Berlin. Their fourth lost Lancaster on 3 December, Berlin, had Pilot Officer John Syme in it with four of his 9 Squadron crew. The wireless operator, Sergeant Cattley, got out but the rest didn't.

W4964 was off to Düsseldorf with Newton on 3 November – up at 16.54, bombing at 19.45 from 22,000ft and home at 21.20. Bombing seemed to be concentrated around the markers. You couldn't ask for any more than that, Manning and Gordon Graham agreed.

Next up was something completely different – a trip to France. Today an Alpine holiday resort one hour from Turin on the TGV, Modane was then of interest to the bombers because of its railway station. Lying in the steep-sided valley of the river Maurienne, it was no orthodox target, requiring precise flying and very precise bombing to avoid killing French people. The only previous attack, on 16/17 September, in which five USAAF B17s joined the Lancs, Halifaxes and Stirlings, had not been a success. Now, German troop trains were assembling in the marshalling yards, ready to move into Italy (which had already surrendered) to confront the Allies moving up the mainland. The railway line for Italy went into the Fréjus tunnel so there were two things to do: smash up the station and the trains, and block the tunnel entrance.

This time it was all Lancasters – 313 of them – for an eight-hour journey there and back, but the bombing was not as accurate as it might have been with fifty-eight French people killed in two raids. Crews estimated that 70 per cent of the bombs fell on the yards and the tunnel entrance, and certainly the damage was severe. The German trains were clearly visible and men were seen running for shelter, although none had been provided in a town not expecting to be part of the bombing war.

W4964 was in the hands of F/O Bill Reid, a skipper who would finish his tour. Geoff Ward, now quite the old hand, had to come back early with an over-heating engine. Manning had the TIs in the bombsight but couldn't be sure he'd hit. Still, it was a remarkable raid, considering what was to follow. No opposition at the target and no aircraft lost on the mission was a description which could not be applied to any of the raids in the next few months.

CHAPTER 7

The Battle of Berlin

Just as Göring's and Hitler's preoccupation with London had meant missed opportunity for Germany early in the war, so was Harris's with Berlin for the Allies. The Big City was better defended than any other and it was very large, very spread out, its streets not at all likely to turn into a Hamburg-style firestorm. It was a long way for the bombers – which meant more fuel to carry, so fewer bombs – and, no matter how the routes were varied, the Germans would often guess the destination of the bomber stream in plenty of time.

Excerpt from *The Luftwaffe War Diaries*:

'With the advent of autumn weather, the number of clear and cloudless nights became progressively less. Furthermore, British Bomber Command chose to operate in bad weather, knowing that this would hinder the defence. Even so, the Wilde Sau went on taking off in conditions that previously would have been considered impossible for single-engined fighter missions.

Herrmann (wild sow commander) said in retrospect: "We were obliged to continue harassing Bomber Command in the weather conditions which we had imposed on us. Had we failed to do so, the RAF would have dominated Berlin from the air."'

Excerpt from *The Bomber Command War Diaries*:

'The unknown mass of more junior German crews did not regard Window as a setback; to these men, Window was the liberating force which gave them as much chance of finding and shooting down RAF bombers as the Experten. (Window) forced the Germans to send their fighters "freelancing" on the bomber routes ... each crew using its own initiative.'

They got better and better at it and, with the help of developing techniques, such as the running commentary, use of flares, new radar sets that were not inconvenienced by Window and better navaids, the *Zahme Sau* (the reorganised Tame Boars) took an increasingly terrible toll. The slower and lower flying Stirlings and early marks of Halifax suffered losses way beyond the 'acceptable'. After 23 November, all Stirling squadrons were withdrawn from the battle; in fact, they flew no more German bombing missions. By January 1944, Halifax losses also became unbearable, with some squadrons losing aircraft and crews at fifteen to twenty per cent of sorties.

The fighter pilot's view was that the Halifax was slower and less manoeuvrable than the Lancaster, notably in the corkscrew, and the crew's fields of vision were not as good, but the aircraft was somewhat tougher. The Lanc was harder to hit but more easily set on fire.

After the particularly bad experience at Leipzig on 19/20 February, Harris decided he could no longer order men to their deaths in his way and withdrew the Mark II and Mark V Halifaxes from the main force, gradually replacing them with the better-performing Mark III but losing a large part of his capability meanwhile.

The Battle of Berlin is said to run from 18 November 1943 to 31 March 1944, when Harris was forced to desist by the lack of payback for his losses, and by the need to soften up targets closer to home, ready for the D-Day invasion. The main struggle for Berlin was up to the end of January when the fighters were having their best times, and Bomber Command, out of range for Oboe target marking, was in danger of spiritual fragmentation. Aircrew believed their bombing was poor. If the marking was scattered, so was the attack. In fact, they were inflicting more damage than it looked from 22,000ft, but the fires, smoke and explosions they could see did not appear to compensate for the many, many flaming torches falling to earth.

The temptation to bomb anyhow and get the hell out was becoming too strong for some. Faults in the aircraft on the way there could be rationalised into an excuse to turn back. Naturally, the great majority continued to press on as ever, no matter how many died in the attempt, but everyone knew it was bloody, horribly bloody, out there. Harris:

'If the USAAF will come in on it (Berlin), it will cost between us 400–500 aircraft. It will cost Germany the war.'

Well, he was right about the aircraft. Including the three August/ September Berlin raids, losses were just over 500 and that was without the Americans who refused to come in on it. Otherwise, these were four-and-a-half months largely wasted in strategic terms. At the end of the time, contrary to Harris's original belief, Hitler was no nearer to surrendering than he had been before.

Apart from the physical destruction of such a large tranche of the bomber force, the morale in the squadrons could not but reflect the losses everyone saw, in return for gains that were not at all obvious. At the start of it, the attitude could not have been better. We were going to Hitler's capital, to pay him back for the London Blitz.

In a speech to the House of Commons on 21 September, Churchill said there was a possibility of saturating the German defences both on the ground and in the air, and 'if a certain degree of saturation could be reached, reactions of a very far-reaching character would be produced. We should have created conditions in which, with very small loss to ourselves, the accurate, methodical destruction by night and by day of every building of military significance in the widest sense would become possible.'

The German press and radio were saying that the Allies would have to abandon their raids as they could hardly sustain such heavy losses as suffered during the first week in September, when they claimed 218 British and American aeroplanes entailing a loss of over 1,800 trained airmen. Generalfeldmarschall Milch, Göring's number two, reinforced this view with his calculation that over 60,000 Allied aircraft had been destroyed so far in the war with 300,000 aircrew killed or taken prisoner.

The figures given by the British Secretary of State for Air, in reply to a parliamentary question, were 193 British and 92 American bombers lost over Germany in the whole of September. British official figures for bomber losses were accurately given out. Subsequent research by the indefatigable Bill Chorley discovered some minor variations, usually one or two that had not been counted on some occasions, but the Ministry did not attempt to cover up the awful truth.

Also, there was another way of looking at the fighter menace. The Secretary of State for Dominion Affairs, Viscount Cranborne, followed the King's speech at the opening of Parliament on 24 November, by pointing out that Bomber Command and the USAAF, in prosecuting the air offensive against Germany, were holding on the Western Front the great bulk of the German fighter aeroplanes that were urgently needed in the East. 'It is the measure of the fear and panic inspired by our air offensive that only one fifth of the first-line fighter strength of Germany could at present be spared to assist the hard-pressed German armies in Russia.'

How very comforting for the chaps that must have been, to read milord's comments in the newspaper as they sat in the mess looking at empty chairs. 'Never mind, you fellows. We're keeping Jerry busy so the Ivans don't have so much on their plates.'

W4964 went to Berlin seven times in 1943, between 18 November and 29 December, five of them with Newton, but Bill Reid took her there on 18 November, the first 'official' night of the Battle of Berlin, and the night that two Lancs of 9 Squadron failed to return. Only the rear gunner was killed in one of them, which had a mid-air collision with another bomber, identity unknown. In the second No. 9 Lanc were Gordon Graham and his crew, the same men who'd flown together on their first ops back in August, with an addition – Pilot Officer John McComb, a Belfast novice pilot on

DATE	AIRCRAFT TYPE & NUMBER	CREW	DUTY	TIME Up	TIME Down	DETAILS OF SORTIE OR FLIGHT	REFERENCES
18/11/43 (contd)	LANCASTER. DV.334.	S/L. J.N. DERBYSHIRE. SGT. T. SULLIVAN. P/O. K. GILL. F/SGT. F. OVEREND. F/SGT. OAKES. F/SGT. E.G. COLT. F/SGT. T. PARSONS.	Bombing – BERLIN.	1713.	0040.	Primary attacked. 2101 hrs. 22,500 ft. Identified by red and green T.I's and Wanganui flares. 1 "Wanganui glare" seen at approx zero – 5. Whilst getting into position for this 1 red T.I. seen to cascade into cloud a little to North. At 2100 hrs. glow from this red T.I. was in sights. Carried on for 1 minute and bombed. Immediately after bombing some green T.I's cascaded in the area. 2 or red T.I. was seen.	
	LANCASTER. DV. 332.	F/L. W.D. ERVINE. SGT. D. LEYSHON. P/O. H.J. MAY. SGT. A.B. GILES. SGT. P. LOMAX. P/O. H.A. DICKINSON. F/SGT. J.C. DICKINSON.	Bombing – BERLIN.	1710.	0129.	Primary attacked 2111 hrs. 21,500 ft. M.P.I. of two green T.I's seen to cascade at 2109 hrs. Yellow flares, red and green T.I's seen before bombing. Cloud prevented assessment of fires and effect of attack. P.F.F. concentration very poor. Route markers seen a position "V". Only a few route markers seen at position "Z" and they appeared to be inaccurate.	
	LANCASTER. DV. 284.	P/O. G.A. GRAHAM. F/SGT. McCOMB. SGT. W. STATHAM. P/O. D. McDONALD. SGT. R.M. ENNESS. S.M. A.F. WILLIAMSON. F/SGT. H. ALTUS. SGT. K. MELLOR.	Bombing – BERLIN.	1725.		Aircraft missing. No signals received.	
	LANCASTER. W. 4964.	P/O. W.M. REID. SGT. S.W. RICHARDS. P/O. R.D.H. PAETER. Sgt. D.G. MOIR. SGT. B. HARTHILL. SGT. C.J. WILHELM. SGT. G. BROWN.	Bombing – BERLIN	1742.	0152.	Primary attacked. 2106 hrs. 22,100 ft. M.P.I. of further of 3 green T.I's cascaded at 2104 hrs. Red T.I. seen forming very wide rough triangle with greens inside. Concentration fair only but many other aircraft bombed in same vicinity. Glow on cloud indicated three distinct circular fires covering estimated area of seven square miles. Big explosion (orange) at 2114 hrs approx.	

This was Graham's crew's fourteenth, plus one DNCO to Essen in J and an early recall from the last Hamburg, plus a second Dicky for the skipper – halfway there, you might say.

his second learner trip. They were all killed, shot down by flak. Judging by the bombing times of the ones who did come home, they were hit well after bombing, perhaps 45 minutes after, crashing near Weissenfels at 21.55, which makes it look as if they had strayed over the formidable flak emplacements of Leipzig.

They'd arrived at Bardney on 8 July; nineteen weeks later they had seen the squadron lose thirteen Lancasters (seventy-eight men killed). Tonight made fifteen, which was better than the all-war squadron average of one a week, but the Battle of Berlin had only just started.

Losses overall on this raid were light – nine out of 440 – as those fighters able to take off in the bad weather had not been able to find the bomber stream. Marking was scattered, cloud was ten-tenths and no results could be properly identified by Bill Read, Geoff Ward, Charles Newton or anybody else, including two future J captains who were rather different. Sergeant Denis Froud was a twenty-two-year-old novitiate from Leyton, flying second Dicky, and the new squadron CO was Wing Commander Edward Porter DFC, aged 32, an economics graduate who had volunteered after his sister was killed in one of the first London air raids. He had earned his Distinguished Flying Cross while completing his first tour of ops with 207 Squadron, had spent a while as an instructor at 1654 Conversion Unit and joined 9 Squadron four days before this raid, on which he took a scratch crew.

The next Berlin on 22 November, with Newton back in W4964, was a similar show, in that losses were fairly light – fighters once again largely absent because of the weather – and results could not be observed. It was the largest raid on Berlin so far, with 764 bombers setting out, and hindsight proved it to be the most effective of all. Although some important industrial sites were destroyed, including five Siemens factories, most of the damage was in residential areas, forcing a small army of soldiers to be brought in to help clear up.

Around 2,000 people were killed, including 500 in one shelter that took a direct hit, and another 105 in a shelter next to a gasworks, the massive explosion there being possibly what they saw in the Lanc carrying second Dicky and future J-man, Sergeant Phil Plowright: 'At 20.22 hrs very violent red explosion lit up whole sky and lasted 12 seconds, dying out very gradually.' Bill Read saw it too; he thought it lasted 20 seconds. That he got there at all says a great deal for his nerve and skill as a pilot: 'During action taken to avoid another Lancaster on outward journey, 20,000 feet 18.53 hours' (two hours after take-off) 'aircraft went into a spin for 30 to 40 seconds down to 13,000 feet when recovery was effected. All gyro instruments toppled.' Geoff Ward, his abilities in effecting recoveries untested on this trip, thought the raid 'a considerable improvement on the last attack.'

On the two raids on 18 and 22 November, just short of 4,000 tons of bombs were dropped. The German press reported that the Führer had conceived a sensational plan to bomb America in 1944 with a seven-motor aircraft, and that the morale of the Luftwaffe was higher than any other air force because officers and men ate the same food, went to the same restaurants and often shared the same table. This was unlike the practice in the plutocratic air forces, such as in Britain, where men were not allowed to enter a restaurant if officers were eating within.

No. 9 Squadron sent thirteen to Berlin on the third attack on 23 November. There had not been very much fighter activity on the previous two; perhaps in over-confidence, perhaps in a double bluff, orders sent the bomber stream on the same route as before. Luftwaffe controllers predicted this and, though the weather was not much better, the wild sows were up and waiting over the capital as the bombers rolled in. While the three hundred or so Lancs that reached the target increased last night's damage by almost as much again, often aiming at the glow of fires which were still burning, the defences knocked down nineteen Lancasters and five more crashed at home, some with enemy damage.

This had been three Berlins in a row for Geoff Ward:

> 'Trip went uneventfully except some difficulty in getting height; crossed Dutch coast in at 15,000 ft. On return to base after getting pancake did one overshoot due to the u/carriage not coming down (according to lights). On making a turn to port for second approach into funnel at indicated height of 500 ft aircraft did a gentle shallow dive to starboard. Did not respond to controls but crashed. Crew unhurt.'

They were due some leave anyway. Newton and W4964 had a week off as well. Berlin, for the moment, could be forgotten.

It was around this time, with J-Jig on thirty-two trips, that the idea of a special identity for the aircraft was translated into reality by the station artist, A-flight ground crewman Corporal Pattison. W4964 became J-Johnny Walker, 'still going strong', with a large picture of the top-hatted and monocled whisky gent striding along beside those three and a bit rows of bombs on the nose.

With the new month, the battle began again, on 2 December. Newton went to Berlin in W4964. Phil Plowright – one who would come to know J-Johnny well – and Wing Commander Porter were among the twelve who went from Bardney. It was not a good night, in any way.

Plowright's rear gunner was Norman Wells:

> 'When we went into the briefing room and saw we'd got Berlin for our first, we thought Christ Almighty and yet, at the same time, it was something good. We were going to Berlin. That was the heart of the war. But when we got there, God, it was horrendous. We all thought, we can't get through this. It was a mass of searchlights, and with the flak and the photoflashes going off and the bombs

The skies over Berlin, 2 December 1943, where J was on her thirty-third op.

exploding, it was as bright as day. Nothing hit us but we could see plenty of other aircraft going down, plenty. I wasn't expecting fighters over the target, not with so much flak, so I could rotate my turret and I could look kind of forward, past the wingtip. Of course, I didn't do that for long, and soon we were on our way out of all the light and mayhem and we crossed some sort of invisible line and there we were, instantly, in black darkness, where we knew the fighters were waiting for us, and I realised that in all the light over the target I'd lost my night vision. Pretty scary, that first one. When we got back and walked down those steps and stood on the ground, we felt elated. We felt, thank God for that. Then we said, wouldn't have missed that one for the world. Well, we could say that, couldn't we? We were home.'

The bombers had been given a direct route in that briefing, straight to the target, and there were no diversionary raids. The weather forecast was incorrect, the pathfinders couldn't compensate, the bombing and the bomber stream were scattered and the boars, both wild and tame, scored heavily. Of the 440 heavies setting off, thirty-nine Lancasters and two Halifaxes were lost to enemy action – 9.3 per cent.

Trying to get in at Gamston, Nottinghamshire, was Pilot Officer Ken Warwick, also experienced but only aged 20 and badly shot up by a fighter. His mid-upper gunner was Sergeant Richard Emerys Jones, 22, a married man. Jones had flown with Reg Knight in W4964 to Milan, back in August, well before the Berlin winter set in. He and most of the rest would fly no more.

The squadron was struggling to make its full contribution despite the losses, some crews being transferred to pathfinders and aircraft temporarily out of action. Whatever the reasons, only seven could be sent to Leipzig the next night, among them Denis Froud and crew on their first op, and Phil Plowright and co on their second, in J-Johnny.

There was a Mosquito diversion on Berlin and that was where the main force appeared to be heading, so when they turned off for Leipzig they found less opposition than usual. Losses on the way home rather made up for that, when a large part of the stream missed the Frankfurt bypass and flew over the city instead, but nothing was as bad as Berlin.

One of No. 9's Lancs was attacked by fighters but got away with serious damage and a wounded mid-upper gunner, but Froud, Plowright and the others avoided trouble and thought the raid good. It was, too, with the Junkers factories in the old World's Fair buildings battered and much further destruction making this the most successful hit on Leipzig of the war.

The December moon and poor weather gave all the heavy bomber squadrons a break, which ended on the 16th with Berlin again. This turned out to be the worst night of all – the most aircraft going and the most falling, a night remembered as Black Thursday. Newton was in J-Johnny, Plowright was there and Bill Reid and nine more as the squadron's share of the record 483 Lancasters set off. Their share of the fifty-four lost was two.

The fighters got in among the bombers on the way there, over the target and especially on the way home, and twenty-four went down over occupied Europe by this means or another, but the explanation for Black Thursday lay not entirely with the human enemy and his machines.

German radio said of this operation: 'The enemy by their air raids will never destroy the will to win of the Berlin population. Factories in Germany are working full blast to produce the weapons of retaliation which will come … attempts to divert the German defences by a mock attack against another target (five Mosquitos dropping decoy flares south of Berlin), false orders transmitted from British short-wave stations to the German night-fighters, and the projection of special luminous rays, were not successful.'

The Times of 18 December: 'An exceptional number of flares were dropped by fighters. RAF crews reported "lanes" of light along the last 10 miles of the route leading to the capital.' The Air Ministry stated: 'More than 1,500 tons of high-explosive and incendiary bombs were dropped. Thirty of our bombers are missing.'

For once, British official sources were being economical with the truth. Twenty-four were missing in the ordinary way – such as failed to return, nothing heard from this aircraft, no signals received – but an astonishing thirty had been either abandoned by their crews because they couldn't land at home or, mostly and fatally, had crashed because they tried to do so. So, the majority of those were not missing. The Ministry knew where they were, spread out as scrap on the moors or the fens of their homeland.

As the bombers approached the shore, they found the entire eastern part of England covered in thick fog. There was nowhere to get down. Some couldn't wait and, short of fuel, bailed out. Others took a chance on finding a friendly spot beneath the blanket of mist. No. 7 Squadron had already lost four in Germany. Now 100 Squadron lost four in England, 101 Squadron lost two away and two at home, and a pathfinder squadron, No. 97, lost two aircraft to abandonments, another five in homeland crashes with most of the crews killed, and they'd already lost one over Berlin.

The Big City had suffered but not to an extent that could be equated with losses of eleven per cent, regardless of the causes. By now, a quarter of Berlin's housing could not be lived in, the railways could hardly function, and many factories, offices and public buildings were laid flat – but the battle was not won.

Attention was switched to Frankfurt on 20 December. It was J-Johnny's thirty-sixth and Denis Froud had to bring her home early when the electrics failed about an hour into the trip. Ward got there, and Plowright. The fighters were very busy – 9 Squadron lost one that had to ditch off Great Yarmouth – and the great majority of the victims were Halifaxes. Three went down from 76 Squadron; 78 Squadron lost five. Out of 257 of this type setting off, twenty-seven were lost – 10.5 per cent, while 390 Lancasters were reduced by fourteen, 3.6 per cent.

The Bomber Command Air Marshals could not have known that, on this raid, the German defenders had been able to follow the bomber stream all the way, pretty well, had been able to forecast the target in advance, and were not unduly concerned by the much smaller diversionary raid on Mannheim. In such circumstances, when the fighters were primed, up and ready, and could attack at will, the Halifaxes made the easier targets and so took the most punishment.

The Times reported:

'Although night-fighters were hurried from all over Germany to stop them, hundreds of RAF heavy bombers on Monday night fought their way through lanes of flares 100 miles long to gain yet another success over the enemy defences and further disrupt Germany's war industries.

... a great number of Lancasters and Halifaxes converged on Frankfurt, one of Germany's 21 major industrial cities and a centre of the chemical industry where, in little over half an hour, they dropped more than 2,000 tons of high explosives and incendiaries.

At the height of the attack, bombs were falling at the rate of 70 tons a minute, many 8,000lb and 4,000lb "block-busters" among them. The raiders left a great oval of fires, stretching from east to west across the city, and pillars of smoke billowing up to a height of 14,000 feet. There was one vivid explosion.'

Plowright thought that 'fires were scattered but developed into one main concentration with a smaller one to the west.' Ward reported that pathfinder flares 'were a bit haphazard and very sparse in number. The attack seemed thin and scattered.'

So it was, with 2,500 houses wrecked, 117 bombs listed in the German report as having hit industrial premises – a considerable part of the bombing falling on Mainz, seventeen miles to the west of the target – but such results were not worth forty-one aircraft.

The thirteen for Berlin from 9 Squadron, two nights before Christmas, included Wing Commander Porter: 'Little sign of concentration ... fires not impressive'; Geoff Ward: 'Did not impress as a very successful operation.'; Denis Froud: 'Fires appeared to be scattered over a very wide area'; and Charles Newton in J-Johnny, who had a hairy time of it: 'Caught by large cone of searchlights. Evaded but caught again five seconds later. Accurate flak. After straightening up found aircraft had overshot flares by approximately one mile. Released bombs immediately.'

The Germans did not latch on to this raid so quickly and that, with the bad weather, meant fewer fighters and lighter casualties – sixteen Lancs lost to fighters and flak, and three more to a crash and a collision – an 'acceptable' 5.2 per cent. Damage to Berlin was minimal, and mostly in the suburbs where the bombers destroyed less than one house each.

A familiar face looked around the door of the sergeants' mess at Bardney. At least, it would have been familiar to some of the WAAFs who worked there, if not to many of aircrew engaged in the Battle of Berlin.

Duncan could have known members of thirty-four crews, flying at the same time as he did his twelve ops in the Spring of the year. Some were old hands then, nearing the end of their tours, some were new boys and some were part the way through. Sixteen of those crews had been lost; seventeen including his own. A few of the others had completed. The rest had volunteered for pathfinders or been transferred to other squadrons – and some of them would be lost too.

John Douglas Duncan had an extra crown on his uniform to denote the rank of Flight Sergeant but otherwise he was the same chap, returned from his *vacances en France*. He would take his new crew to Brunswick on 14 January 1944. On that raid would be two crews he might just have had time to meet in his previous life, in those days under Sergeant W. W. W. 'Tex' Turnbull, the quiet American now a Pilot Officer, and Sergeant Charles Newton, now a Flight Lieutenant and a long server with W4964. Otherwise, there was nobody to ask him where he'd been all this time.

The Times reported that there would be oranges after Christmas:

> 'Oranges have not been available for a long time, the few which have got through being reserved for children up to the age of five years, with occasionally some as well for children up to 16. Now substantial purchases have been made in Spain and Palestine and sufficient will be arriving to permit of 1lb a ration book to everyone.'

With Christmas over it was back to business and Berlin on 29 December when twenty were lost out of 709, with diversions and bad weather again confusing the ground controllers. Sergeant Froud was in J-Johnny on her thirty-eighth.

All ready for the Christmas party, sergeants' mess, Bardney, 1943.

German radio:

> 'The Reich capital was, in the late hours of to-day, again the target
> of a terror attack carried out by strong British bomber formations.
> The sky was covered with a thick layer of clouds and the British
> machines dropped explosives and incendiary bombs on thickly
> populated residential quarters.'

True, they did, but not exactly on purpose, with the average being one
unimportant building destroyed between two aircraft, although 10,000 people
were rendered temporarily homeless.

The report in *The Times* was also accurate, as far as it went:

> 'At well below the average percentage cost in casualties – 20 of
> our aircraft are missing – an extremely powerful force of RAF
> Lancasters and Halifaxes got through to Berlin on Wednesday
> night to make the second attack of more than 2,000 tons on the
> German capital. As the bombers crossed Germany, they flew
> through almost unbroken cloud, but it hindered the enemy night-
> fighters and searchlights more than it did the attackers.
>
> Most of the flyers who had been to Berlin regarded this as their
> most uneventful trip. It was in striking contrast to the last attack
> when the sky was full of fighters and lit by flares.'

In 1943 No. 9 Squadron had lost fifty-five Lancasters on ops and four
more in accidents. Bomber Command had lost 1,117 Lancs, 883 Halifaxes,
418 Stirlings, 327 Wellingtons, 67 Mosquitos, 20 Whitleys and 54 of other
types on ops, 2,886 aircraft altogether plus another 231 in accidents, plus
another 764, mostly Wellingtons, Halifaxes and Stirlings, in training.

The New Year began with two consecutive Berlins, both failures. The first
of the pair was scheduled for 1 January but postponements eventually saw
most of the force taking off after midnight. The fighters found them on
the way in, the marking was very poor in ten-tenths cloud, and many of the
bombs fell in the woods of the Grunewald. The tally of bomber aircrew
killed was 177, which was more than twice the number of Berliners killed on
the ground – seventy-nine.

J-Johnny with Denis Froud and the seven other crews of 9 Squadron who
completed the journey, were back around eight in the morning. Manning
and another had returned early, but the one not coming back at all was
A-Apple, Geoff Ward's kite for the night.

That first Hamburg raid was over five months before, when Ward had
gone on his first op, with the same crew, and Tom Gill had been on a second
Dicky, and Charles Newton in J, Gilbert Hall, Gordon Graham. Since then,
Ward had been on six Berlins, thirteen other ops including three in W4964,
one DNCO, and now a final Berlin, with the same crew throughout except

Date	Aircraft Type & Number	Crew	Duty	Time Up	Time Down	Details of Sortie or Flight	References
1/1.	LANCASTER, JA. 711.	P/O. C. WARD. SGT. J. SUTTON. SGT. E. KEENE B/SGT. G.L. JAMES. SGT. G.F.K. BEDWELL. P/SGT. N.F. DIXON. P/SGT. W.L. IDRAN.	Bombing - BERLIN.	2358.		Aircraft missing. No signals received.	
	LANCASTER. LM. 360.	P/O. A.E. MANNING. SGT. BURKITT, WF. P/O. J.W. HEARN. SGT. P. WARWODA. P/SGT. G.T.W. CAINES. SGT. ZARMITT. JJ. SGT. THOMAS. E.A.	Bombing - BERLIN.	0008.	0242.	No target attacked. Sortie abandoned owing to escape hatch cover over rest bed and on account of M.U. Gunner being unwell. 1538 of	
	LANCASTER W. 4964.	SGT. D.P. PROUD. SGT. F. HARMAN. SGT. D. GARLICK. SGT. L.T. FAIRCLOUGH. SGT. W.H. SHIRLEY. SGT. S.L. JONES. SGT. R.L. BIERS.	Bombing - BERLIN.	0013.	0820.	Primary attacked. 0310 hrs. 22,500 ft. Identified by Wanganui flares. The centre of three of them was in sights. Raid appeared to be scattered, but difficult to form an opinion due to 10/10 cloud.	
	LANCASTER W.5010.	P/O. A.J. JUBB. P/O. S.J. NANCEKIVELL. SGT. J.N. CARTER. P/O. R.G. COLLINS. P/SGT. A.C. JOHNS. SGT. R. WEALLEY. SGT. F. BOLTON.	Bombing - BERLIN.	0011.	0808.	Primary attacked. 0310½ hrs. 21,000 ft. Identified by R/P. flares. M.P.I. of 3 R/P flares in sights. Glow of fires seen reflected on cloud.	

Three I-Johnny crews happen to be all on the same ORB sheet. They would all end up the same way, too.

for one trip, the most recent Berlin, when veteran Flight Lieutenant Gilbert 'Dinger' Bell DFC, squadron Bombing Leader, had stood in for George James.

Twenty ops would have been two-thirds of the way to the end, but they were shot down 100 miles short of the target, near a place called Weyhausen, a few miles from Eschede. The youngest was the mid-upper, Norman Dixon, a nineteen-year-old Nottinghamshire boy. The wireless operator, George Bedwell, was a married man of twenty-four, from Suffolk. With a Canadian in the rear turret and a Yorkie in the pilot's seat, they were the usual sort of mix made into a team.

In their photograph, taken early in their career, possibly on posting to squadron, they look mesmerisingly young and innocent. Geoff Ward's moustache completely fails to make him look any more senior and authoritative. There can be no criteria for what we might expect a rear gunner to look like, but the smart, contemplative young fellow who is Willard Doran surely doesn't fit our preconceptions.

A new kind of statistic was appearing in the British press: bombs dropped per aircraft lost. In the four December attacks, they said, seventy tons of bombs fell on Berlin for every bomber failing to return. On those four raids, 138 aircraft were lost, giving a supposed 9,660 tons of bombs dropped. The bomb load for a Lancaster for such a faraway target was well below the maximum of 14,000lb (6.25 tons) – about 10,800lb was typical (4.8 tons). Just

From the left, back row: Geoffrey Ward, pilot; George James, bomb aimer; George Bedwell, wireless operator; Eric Keene, navigator; front row: Willard Doran, rear gunner; Norman Dixon, mid-upper; Jack Sutton, flight engineer.

short of 2,000 sorties were made to Berlin in December 1943, so that press figure assumes that all of them got there and all dropped their bombs, which obviously didn't happen.

If (in round numbers) 10,000 tons should have fallen, but we take away the bombs of those aircraft shot down before they arrived, those that returned early, and the sorties flown by pathfinders carrying no bombs at all – an unknown but considerable total – we can begin to see the truth in Benjamin Disraeli's alleged statement that there are three kinds of lies: lies, damn lies and statistics.

We know the number of aircrew killed in those four raids was 709. If we make the generous assumption that seven-tenths of the bombs leaving England actually fell on Berlin, that makes a figure for the press of 50 tons per aircraft lost, and 10 tons per man killed – or, again in round numbers, two trips-worth per airman-life.

The statistic always given is the loss rate of aircraft, in this case, for the four Berlins, 6.5 Lancs/Halifaxes/Mosquitos lost per 100 sorties. Another angle on it is thirty-five airmen killed per 100 sorties.

After twenty-eight Lancs failed to return out of the 421 that set off on the first raid of 1944, the next proved to be even worse. With the airspeed indicator iced up and starboard inner overheating, F/O Pearce came back early on J-Johnny's fortieth, which was perhaps just as well for them. Results gained by the German defences were twenty-six Lancasters down out of 362, plus one crashed soon after take-off killing all the crew, an aircraft loss rate of 7.5 per cent. The pathfinder squadron No. 156 lost five Lancs on this night, to add to the four they'd lost the night before, and only one of those nine had any survivors.

Said *The Times*:

> 'The German defences were thoroughly prepared on Sunday night. The bombers made a late start in order to avoid the early moon and a violent, fluctuating wind which rose at times to a 90 miles an hour gale, so that there was no time to follow a roundabout route and their target was obvious long before they reached Berlin. The result was that more German fighters were seen than have been encountered for some time, and during the last stages of their flight the bombers were constantly subjected to attacks by swarms of fighters which had been summoned from a wide area.
>
> These battles (all nine Berlin raids starting 18 November) have cost the RAF 273 aircraft (actually 282) . . . so that more than 51 tons of bombs have been dropped for each aircraft lost.'

There was no explanation for this sudden revision of the bombs-dropped figure. The total number of heavy-bomber sorties so far in the nine attacks was 4,789, giving a figure of well over 20,000 tons of bombs potentially to be dropped, yet the press, quoting the Ministry obviously, is giving a much more realistic picture.

Not so realistic was the description of the results:

> 'The pathfinders arrived exactly to the minute, and by the aid of their flares the main bomber force was able to make a rapid attack which, at its peak, developed to a rate of 70 tons of bombs a minute. Even the very thick clouds did not hide the many fires, which reflected red on the cloud-base and caused a fiery glow visible 100 miles away.'

Bill Read reported: 'Glow below cloud perhaps glow of fires.' Wingco Porter saw some flares and 'bombed the farthest one'. Others reported: 'Scattered markers, no results seen.'

Results recorded by the Berlin authorities were eighty-two houses destroyed, thirty-six people killed, industrial damage insignificant and no large fires. Bomber Command could not know this at the time, nor could they know for certain that 151 of their airmen had been killed, but they had a pretty good idea on both subjects. If they'd had the correct figures, they could have quoted 4.2 aircrew dead for every fatality on the ground.

There was some news so exciting that it was in all the papers and on the BBC. A small cargo of lemons from Sicily would be going to Cumberland, Westmorland, and North Lancashire, including Blackpool and Preston, and more were expected for distribution all over Britain at the rate of one-third of a pound per person. Spanish onions too were going up north, one pound a head, and ration books would not be marked for either.

Compared to Berlin, Stettin was a spectacular success on 5 January. J-Johnny was taken there by F/O Albert Manning and crew, and back again, which was fortunate for them and the press photographer who took pictures of them before and after.

At Stettin, over 500 buildings were destroyed and 1,200 damaged – mostly houses – and eight of the ships moored in the harbour were sunk. Whether this was worth the loss of fourteen Lancs and two Halifaxes, and eighty-seven airmen dead, could not be calculated.

Charles Newton, now a Flight Lieutenant, was back in J-Johnny for Brunswick on 14 January and John Duncan flew his first op since returning to Bardney. It was a big effort from 9 Squadron, sixteen going, and a good hand of J-Johnny alumni – five, with Reid, Plowright and Pearce – but the one lost had not had that experience. The captain, twenty-year-old Flying Officer Edward Argent, and three of his crew were only just back on duty after a December attack by two fighters killed their rear gunner and so damaged their aircraft that they were forced to ditch, spending four hours in the dinghy off Happisburgh, north Norfolk. The skipper and two of his fellow sailors did not survive this time, but the very fact that they were there, and Duncan was there after turning down the chance to go home,

Flying Officer Manning and crew draw their kit before setting off for Stettin, 5 January 1944. Mid-upper gunner Sergeant John Zammit holds his heated suit and looks excited at the prospect of the temperature at 21,000ft. Manning picks up his parachute watched by navigator Flying Officer James Hearn.

Boarding the top-of-the-range luxury coach to be taken to dispersals, Manning checks the passenger list.

Back from the night's work, Manning tolerates the photographer, pausing in the doorway of J-Johnny.

The whole crew, relieved and happy to be home, light cigarettes and crack a smile. From the left: navigator Hearn, Manning, rear gunner Flight Sergeant 'Pinky' Hayler, mid-upper Zammit, flight engineer Sergeant Bill Burkitt and stand-in wireless operator Flight Lieutenant A. G. Newbound. Just visible over Manning's right shoulder is bomb aimer Flight Sergeant Peter Warywoda. Four of this crew would be with Albert Manning at the last.

epitomises life in Bomber Command in mid-winter when the Luftwaffe night-fighter force was at the peak of its strength and effectiveness.

That strength was amply demonstrated on this raid. They found the bombers less than fifteen minutes after they left the English coast, and stayed with them all the way to the target and most of the way back. Thirty-seven Lancs went down on route and two more crashed at home, 7.9 per cent, for the smallest of returns: ten houses destroyed and fourteen people killed.

Duncan saw two large areas of fires. Newton saw one large and three smaller fires, and an explosion. Plowright aimed at a spot where some flares had gone out. Reid saw a few fires, but they were not in Brunswick. They were miles away to the south, where some villages took unexpected hits.

Denis Froud was back from leave and given J-Johnny on 20 January; target, Berlin. Duncan was there too as well as Manning, Plowright and Pearce, all part of a 9 Squadron contribution of fourteen towards a massive, maximum effort of 769 aircraft. Diversionary raids and diversions in the route did not work and the fighters again were ignoring the icy weather, infiltrating and scoring along most of the way in and out.

The Air Ministry stated: 'Large fires were left burning, with smoke rising to a great height. Thirty-five of our aircraft are missing.'

The report in *The Times* was more colourful:

'Once, when the clouds parted for a moment, crews caught a glimpse of streets outlined in the glare of fires. Thick as the cloud layer was, the red glow of the many fires penetrated it ... few of the bombers encountered any opposition on the outward journey. The clouds reduced the effectiveness of the searchlights, while flak was below the usual Berlin standard.'

All of No. 9's squad reached the target, bombed within ten minutes of each other, thought the target marking was good, saw fires that made the clouds glow, and came home. Inexplicably, there are no official German reports of this raid. Crashes and abandonments in the Berlin area, and bombers known to have been hit by the local flak, show that the raid undoubtedly took place; that the whole thing did not happen over another city as has been suggested, but we shall never know if the damage was worth the thirty-seven bombers lost, plus two more crashed at home, and 157 airmen killed.

The Germans had their losses too. The famous ace Major Prince Sayn-Wittgenstein shot down five bombers, making his total eighty-three, before himself being shot down on this night by the crew of a Mosquito.

Of the British aircraft lost due to enemy action, twenty-four were Halifaxes, more than 9 per cent, and worse was to come the next night, at Magdeburg.

Results, in foul weather but with much improved technology, were becoming as unrewarding as in the early part of the war, when Wellingtons and Whitleys flew singleton missions against a choice of six targets. Air Marshal Harris's great advances of 1942 and '43 were being countered by the German defences to such an extent that, without such superbly organised and resourced systems for replacing men and machines, Bomber Command would have been close to giving up.

Sir Archibald Sinclair, Secretary of State for Air:

'Many gallant lives (have been) lost but not one of them was wasted. By such victorious encounters the British and American Bomber

Commands are weakening the power of the Germans to resist. They are thus saving the lives of allied soldiers on all fronts, and shortening the period of the war.'

Of course, that had to be the official line at the time. Looking back, *The Luftwaffe War Diaries* saw matters differently:

'In January the British losses rose to 6.15 per cent of all sorties against Berlin and to 7.2 per cent during the attacks on Stettin, Brunswick and Magdeburg. But the effectiveness of the German defence was not confined to destruction. Harassed all the way to their distant target with bombs on board, many of the bombers were forced to turn back in a damaged condition. Combat and evasive action scattered the remainder over the sky so that they no longer arrived on target as a coherent force. Much as Berlin and the other cities suffered from the bombing terror of the winter of 1943/44, they were spared the total extinction that had been the enemy's prognosis.'

The figures quoted may not be precise but the point is made nonetheless. Even without early knowledge that Magdeburg was the destination, the fighters joined the bomber stream before they crossed the enemy coast and the Tame Boar tactics with running commentary kept them there. Bombers arrived over the target too soon and bombed on H2S readings, leaving fires which competed for attention with the later pathfinder marking and so, with the additional distraction of German decoy fires, the city did not suffer unduly.

The bombers did. Froud in J-Johnny, Duncan, Manning, Plowright and Reid all came home with the rest of No. 9, and Pearce who had been on a small diversionary raid to Berlin, but sixty-two bombers were lost that night, including two which crashed at base, and 291 airmen lost their lives. The Lancaster losses were twenty-three out of 421, 5.5 per cent but the Halifax score was thirty-nine out of 224, a staggering 17.4 per cent.

The month ended with three more Berlins. J-Johnny only went on one of them; the squadron lost one aircraft. Total heavy-bomber sorties for the three were over 1,700; total losses 112.

The subsequent stand-down from operations could not have been more welcome. For the main force squadrons of Bomber Command it was a fortnight off but, after a cancellation on 13 February, there was more of the same two days later – Berlin, the biggest raid of the lot. J-Johnny didn't go; after forty-five ops it was time for an overhaul and that would take up the whole of February, but the crews who knew J carried on.

Duncan, Manning, Pearce with a second Dicky and future J-man, Russ Gradwell, Plowright, Froud and Newton all went to the Big City as part of 9 Squadron's twenty-one strong contribution to the 561 Lancasters and 314 Halifaxes that set out in the early evening. Yet again the target was mostly covered in cloud but this time the bombers had good, if mixed, results with serious damage done to central and industrial districts. Civilian casualties were relatively low; many of the population had fled the city. Aircraft losses were just short of five per cent for a record 2,642 tons of bombs dropped. The stream had taken a long way around, over Denmark; loads would have been a little lighter than usual, so we can say that 600 of the heavies got there and bombed.

Two of 9 Squadron turned back, both with wireless failures. There were no losses among the rest, while so many others went down – four pathfinder Lancs from 7 Squadron, three Halifaxes of 77 Squadron, forty-three altogether. The fighters even found a few on the Denmark dog-leg, thought to be too far for the Germans to reach.

Intelligence suggested that this had been the best raid so far, and Harris's inclination was to follow up swiftly. Raids were planned for the next three nights but all had to be cancelled due to the weather. Forecasts for the following night were better, but wrong, and the target was different – Leipzig on 19 February.

Leipzig was another bad, bad experience for the bombers. Again, two of No. 9's twenty turned back with technical faults – one was an oxygen failure rendering the rear gunner unconscious – and some got themselves lost in a strong westerly wind that blew them miles off track before navigators realised what was happening.

All the way from the Dutch coast, on track or not, the bombers were harried by large numbers of fighters. The Germans had almost 300 in the air and lost only seventeen. A considerable part of the bomber force managed to get to Leipzig before the pathfinders and, circling above the target waiting for the markers, gave the flak gunners some extra shooting time.

Leipzig had been Denis Froud's first, and it was his last. Now he and his crew, blown by the wind, were flying over Stendal, about a hundred miles NNW of Leipzig. Some fifty Stirlings and Halifaxes had been mine laying in Kiel Bay and a group of fighters had been sent there but, as soon as it was realised that Leipzig was the destination for the main force, these fighters were recalled. The town of Stendal is on a line from Kiel to Leipzig.

Froud and all his men were killed in one of the ten bombers known to have been caught by fighters in that area, and one of the stunning, awful total of seventy-eight four-engined bombers lost on the Leipzig raid.

Denis Froud began with a second Dicky on the first night of the Battle of Berlin. When he came home from that, he heard about two squadron losses – Gordon Graham had failed to return, and so had a novice crew on their second trip.

Froud's crew was not settled at the beginning. On his first as captain he took Sergeant Frank Belben as flight engineer, and Frank remembered it:

'A pilot called Froud was on his first op and his flight engineer wasn't available so I was drafted in. I'd had four trips by then and here I was going back to square one with a sprog crew. Anyway, it turned out all right except that when I was getting out of the aircraft at dispersal I slipped on the top step, which was icy, and landed on the concrete. I was out with an injured spine for nearly a month.'

The original engineer, Fred Harman, was available for all the crew's ops from then on, four of them plus a DNCO in J-Johnny. They were a young lot even for that time – two at nineteen, one twenty, one twenty-one, and the ancient captain at twenty-two.

Oberleutnant (later Major) Paul Zorner was operating in that area on the night of 19/20 February, and was credited with four Lancaster victories. We cannot link him directly with Froud, but this is part of his combat report:

'My only difficulty in shooting down the first bomber was that, as soon as he saw me, he slowed down considerably. I helped myself by putting down my flaps and so managed to keep on the enemy bomber's tail. I closed in from a favourable angle without being shot myself, and repeated this tactic successfully in all four cases.'

Zorner would last right through the war, with fifty-nine victories from 272 sorties.

Froud's career, from 18 November to 19 February, included an astounding nine times to Berlin. There would only be one more major raid on the Big City. The Battle, effectively, was over.

CHAPTER 8

The Over 60s Club

February continued with major raids on Stuttgart, Schweinfurt and Augsburg. Duncan, Manning, Pearce, Gradwell, Newton and Wing Commander Porter all featured, plus a once and future J captain Pilot Officer H. C. Clark. The squadron lost three more crews, all killed – one halfway and more through the tour, one on their second op and one on their first.

Stuttgart was special for Charles Newton. He'd finished his tour. Newton and crew had flown in J-Johnny sixteen times, including six Berlins, and now they were done. The captain was posted to No. 5 Lancaster Finishing School.

Stuttgart was a successful raid for Newton to finish on. Losses were relatively light and they hit their main objective – the Bosch factory.

The ground crew man front-centre is holding the 'official' plaque for 9 Squadron bombers denoted WS/Z, which had been known as 'Zola' rather than 'Zebra' since Wellington days. Quite who Zola was we have been unable to discover, but obviously she was a popular girl.

Schweinfurt, centre of ball-bearing manufacture, was less so, despite the new two-wave tactic whereby the force was split in half, taking off and bombing two hours apart. Losses were back up to the 'acceptable' level and damage done was insignificant, although Porter, Duncan, Manning and Clark all thought otherwise.

Date	Aircraft Type & Number	Crew	Duty	Time Up	Time Down	Details of Sortie or Flight	References
24/2/44. (Cont'd)	LANCASTER. LM. 445.	W/C. R.L. PORTER. P/O. W. FOSSEK. P/O. W.A. GALL. P/O. J.A. PRIOR. F/SGT. J. LEVER. SGT. R.G. LOMAS. P/SGT. G.R. BOLT.	Bombing – SCHWEINFURT.	1840.	0224.	Primary attacked 2316½ hrs. 21,000 ft. M.P.I. of five red T.I's in sights. White flares, green and red T/t's seen on run in. Bombed reds. P.F.F. concentration good, but main effort falling short although there were quite a few incendiaries among the T.I.'s. On leaving, a good column of smoke and a few fires were seen from the Northern end of the concentration. Big explosion seen at 2306 hours.	
	LANCASTER. ME. 579.	P/SGT. J.D. DUNCAN. SGT. J.H. PRESTON. P/O. M.E. ANDERTON. SGT. D.C. RICHARDS. SGT. A.T. WEBB. W/O. R. LAWSON. P/O. G.H. WYAND.	Bombing – SCHWEINFURT.	2031	0442.	Primary attacked. 0110 hours. 20,500 ft. M.P.I. of about ten red T.I's and three or four greens in sights. Target covered with one very good fire and several others. Red and greens seen going down. P.F.F. were concentrated but bombing trailed back.	
	LANCASTER. LL. 361.	P/O. A.E. MANNING. SGT. W.P. BURKITT. W/O. J.W. HEARN. SGT. P. WARYWODA. P/SGT. G.T.M. CAINES. SGT. J.J. ZAMITT. P/SGT. T. FINCH.	Bombing – SCHWEINFURT.	1831.	0213.	Primary attacked. 2308 hours. 21,000 ft. M.P.I. of concentration of red T.I's in sights. White flares 22.59 hours followed by greens and then reds. A little ground detail could be made out. A mass of fires seen among T/I's on leaving target with another lot of fires among the woods to the North East. P.F.F. well concentrated.	
	LANCASTER. W. 4235½	P/O. H.C. CLARK. SGT. R.K. GOLDSPINK. P/O. H.P.S. MITCHELL. F/SGT. C.H. REDMOND. P/SGT. A.F.R. HOPGROFT. SGT. M.D. WELTON. SGT. G.R. BRADBURY.	Bombing – SCHWEINFURT.	2035.	0432.	Primary attacked. 0114 hours. 21,300 ft. One T.I. red in centre of cluster. Few green T.I. and many red well concentrated. Woods to the South of the target clearly seen and snow covered ground. Big fires at target all merging and many lines of incendiaries on target. Heavy smoke up to 10,000 ft.	

This was the first time the two-wave tactic was tried. Losses were lighter in the second wave from fighters, as planned, but were heavy enough in the first wave to bring the total to 4.5 per cent.

Augsburg saw another two-wave attack which came to be controversial because the bombing was so accurate. Instead of the usual spread-out to the industrial areas of a compact target like this, the old centre of the city with its many fine civic buildings was totally destroyed. The Germans called it extreme terror bombing.

J-Johnny was back for 1 March, skippered by Phil Plowright wearing his lucky scarf. The officers mess barmaid, WAAF Nancy Bowers, remembered:

> 'Phil Plowright always wore his striped scarf, which was in his college colours, green and orange. That was his good luck charm, and it worked for him.'

Many aircrews had mascots – a teddy bear, a girlfriend's silk stocking – all sorts of things, and a lot them worked at Stuttgart on that cloudy night. The bombing was good and Bosch was hit again, and Daimler-Benz, and only four bombers went down, plus two crashed at home, out of 544 setting off.

Harris was not happy about sending his force to targets like Augsburg and Schweinfurt, small and insignificant as he saw them, when the great goal of Berlin had yet to be realised. He was even less happy about the influences being felt from HQ now that General Eisenhower had been appointed Supreme Commander in Europe, and therefore Harris's new boss.

The invasion of France was still months away and the switch from German attacks to D-Day preparations was not apparent yet, but irritating little diversions were occasionally required. On 9 March Plowright, Clark, Pearce and Porter were part of a small – forty-four Lancasters – and specialised raid on the aerodrome at Marignane (now the Marseille-Provence international airport) and the factories of the Société Nationale de Constructions Aéronautique du Sud-Est, which had been making a new fighter for the French air force àt the start of the war but was now working for the Luftwaffe.

This was a different kind of raid with a select force, and a long-distance one, nine and a half hours return, after some practice on time and distance runs bombing from what was, to Berlin habitués, low level at around 9,000ft. Those on the raid were to meet the new – to them – concept of raid management, which hadn't really been tried since Peenemünde.

Wing Commander Porter went in first and dropped a red spot fire from 6,000ft and got it thirty yards from the aiming point, seeing it clearly in bright moonlight. The rest came in on his instructions, bombed unopposed, and smashed the place to pieces. Returning, after they'd got over the high ground, they flew across France at 200ft all the way, another entirely new experience.

This was the last op for one of our J graduates, gunner Flight Sergeant Pinky Hayler, who had gone with Manning to Stettin and had his picture in the papers. He had joined the squadron in May 1943 and crewed with a second tour pilot, a larger-than-life character, Squadron Leader Dicky

Bunker DFC. A second tour was twenty ops, so Bunker's men still had ten to do when he finished, available for any needy skipper but, as it turned out, taken over by Porter. So Pinky had done his bit and was now Flying Officer Hayler off to 1660 Conversion Unit to show the novices what was what.

Marignane? Morceau de gâteau, they said, but it would be a while before there were any more like that. It was back to Stuttgart, on 15 March, with a force of almost 850 heavies. Duncan, now Pilot Officer, took a second Dicky, a future J pilot – and one bound for more than his fair share of adventure – Flight Sergeant W. R. Horne. Manning was there, Pearce, Clark, Gradwell came home early, and Plowright in J-Johnny on her forty-seventh in a role euphemistically designated as 'supporting aircraft'. This meant you went in first with the pathfinders, not to show the way with your bombing – you had to go around again to do that – but to draw the flak fire away from the boys doing the marking.

It was yet another raid with poor reward. Forty bombers went down on the op, plus three more at home, killing 217 aircrew, while 88 people of Stuttgart died and almost all the bombs fell in open country.

Frankfurt on 18 March was much better with another 800-plus force losing less than 3 per cent and levelling thousands of houses and hundreds of commercial premises. Flight Sergeant Horne was on his debut, in W4964, bombing from 21,000ft with the target indicators in his sights. He got home safely as did all the squadron. They heard four days later that they were going back.

Frankfurt records, quoted in *The Bomber Command War Diaries*, stated:

> 'The three air raids of 18th, 22nd (USAAF) and 24th March were carried out by a combined plan of the British and American air forces and their combined effort was to deal the worst and most fateful blow of the war to Frankfurt, a blow which simply ended the existence of Frankfurt which had been built up since the Middle Ages.'

In fact, the American raid was a diversion from the intended target of Schweinfurt, but the results still combined to make further efforts unnecessary. Plowright was there on the 22nd in 'his' J-Johnny, and others of the J clan, but the squadron lost two, and one of those had the station commander on board, on another of his occasional trips as a passenger.

Group Captain 'Shorty' Pleasance was liable to get in a froth when under pressure but he was a well-regarded, approachable fellow, a First World War veteran with no requirement to go on ops, rather the reverse. Blind eyes were turned to such matters but it was certainly not approved for senior officers to risk themselves unnecessarily. For some, the urge to show willing, to keep in touch with what the boys were facing all the time, was too strong. At first it was thought he'd been taken prisoner; news came through that only the wireless operator, Sergeant Caines, had been so fortunate. Five of the dead were called Manning, Burkitt, Hearn, Warywoda and Zammit.

Albert Manning had not had a settled crew at first, hardly surprising as his mid-upper was killed on their second op and his rear gunner badly wounded. After that he had eight different tail-enders, with Arthur Finch settling into the job at last and flying the final six trips. The captain was on his official sixteenth when he went down, plus three DNCOs, and his second Dicky on the same night as John Syme. Manning had lasted a dozen more ops than Syme, all to Germany except one, with only four Berlins which might have been considered fairly light punishment for this time in the war. He was the tenth J-Johnny skipper to be killed.

The last of the big Berlin raids was on 24 March, when seventy-two heavy bombers were lost out of 793 taking off, 9.1 per cent. That it was not seventy-three was something of a miracle, especially considering the pilot was on his second trip. His only other experience had been in J-Johnny.

SECRET *No. 9 Squadron Combat Report*

Date: 24th March 1944. Time: 00.47. Height: 24,000 ft. Target: Berlin. Lancaster: LL845 WS/L Captain: Flight Sergeant W. R. Horne

On leaving the target the Navigator was using broadcast winds which took the aircraft 60–70 miles off track, which eventually brought our aircraft into the Ruhr. Ten minutes previous to striking the Ruhr the Rear Gunner had gone unconscious due to lack of oxygen, cause unknown. The rear turret was unserviceable also, possibly due to frozen hydraulics.

On entering the Ruhr, a master beam picked us up and the aircraft was immediately coned by approx 30 searchlights and fired on by very accurate heavy flak for 40 minutes, which holed the starboard mainplane, bomb aimer's position, pilot's windscreen, port mainplane, bomb doors and port fin. During all this period the Pilot was wounded and blind, the Bomb Aimer had flak in his leg and the Rear Gunner was unconscious on the rest bed. Through alteration of course and height and diving turns, our aircraft escaped the searchlights and flak.

The Mid Upper Gunner and Engineer were searching and our aircraft was almost at once attacked from the port beam at a range of approx 200 yards by an unidentified enemy aircraft which fired a two or three second burst and broke away starboard quarter down, where we lost him. The burst damaged the MU Perspex. MU Gunner did not see him on account of his searching the starboard beam.

RG Sergeant Parkes fired 0 rounds.
MU Sergeant Morton fired 300 rounds.

This single report more or less sums up the raid. A strong north wind, much stronger than the broadcast estimate and beyond the technology of the time to reassess accurately in flight, scattered the bomber stream. In particular, the stream could not hold together on the journey home, and the flak guns with their radar had a feast, shooting down perhaps fifty of the seventy-two, many of which were flying alone and so more easily picked off, and some of which had strayed into the Ruhr, including Horne's.

Duncan and Plowright and most of the rest of No. 9 somehow got there and back, but W4964 WS/J's fiftieth was an anti-climax, coming home after half an hour with the rear turret u/s. Flight Lieutenant Harry Pooley, second-tour man, was the skipper on his first of many with 9 Squadron.

The Big City was a mess but not a write-off. Many, many aircraft had been lost – over 600 – with 3,000 men killed and 750 taken prisoner. The equivalent would have been if Bomber Command had mounted one major raid from which nobody at all had returned.

Webster and Frankland's official history of the bomber war, *The Strategic Air Offensive against Germany*, states:

> 'Bomber Command was compelled, largely by the German night-fighter force, to draw away from its primary target, Berlin, to disperse its effort and to pursue its operations by apparently less efficient means than hitherto ... The Battle of Berlin was more than a failure. It was a defeat.'

At least it was over, not that the aircrew knew about it, nor could they have guessed at the even more horrendous rate of loss that awaited them six nights hence.

Before that, there was a small, low-level raid on the railway yards at Aulnoye. Pilot Officer Jimmy Ineson and crew had been on squadron one day, and they took W4964. The bombing was accurate and concentrated around the markers, but the markers were in the wrong place and nothing much happened to the railways on this raid, although this was corrected later. There are no precise figures but eighty or more French civilians were killed.

The Germans were now expecting more French raids so another big one on Essen on 26 March caused confusion and the fighters did not get closely involved. Plowright in J, Pooley and Pearce – with surprise second Dicky Ineson, who'd already captained an 'easy' op but apparently needed to see the real thing as passenger over Germany – were among the fifteen of No. 9 and the 683 heavies altogether that did a good deal of damage for small losses, ten due to enemy action and two more crashing at home.

Less than two per cent gone and Essen badly hit – this was a relative triumph. Now came the disaster of Nürnburg.

It was a big force; 786 heavy bombers attacking a city of 430,000 people, which was famous for its arts and crafts, historic buildings and Nazi rallies.

The so-called Nürnburg Laws of 1935 described three sorts of Germans: Aryans, Jews, and mixed race. If the mixed race people didn't have too much Jew in their ancestry, they could marry Aryans and be assimilated.

Defences would be less horrendous than usual on city raids, and the light of the full moon, which would normally have meant no bombing, would be of benefit at the target with clear vision and there would be cloud on the way for the bomber stream to hide in.

A Mosquito weather spy came back from the area with warnings that conditions were likely to be the reverse – clear skies on the way and cloud over the target. Despite this, the raid was not cancelled.

By this time the wild sows were finished. Single-seater fighters and winter nights just did not mix and, in

The young trainee airman Jimmy Ineson, with a long way to go.

any case, the new and much improved Lichtenstein SN2 radar sets were giving the twin-engined tame sows a fresh lease of life.

Extract from *The Luftwaffe War Diaries*:

> 'The high-point was reached on March 30th, 1944, during an attack on Nürnburg, when British Bomber Command suffered the worst losses in its war-time history – exactly two days before Air Marshal Harris claimed that Germany would be forced to capitulate as a result of his own bomber offensive.'

The late evening proved exceptionally clear for the time of year. At fighter bases from northern France to Berlin, crews were in their cockpits, ready and waiting. The moon would rise before midnight. It could not have been better. If the Tommies were foolish enough to fly on such a night, they would pay and pay again.

Yes, the Tommies were coming. A big raid was massing. Those little diversions didn't deceive anyone, partly because the Mosquitos putting on spoof raids didn't carry H2S. No H2S signals to be picked up; no bomber stream, no serious threat.

The first wave was crossing the sea towards the Belgian coast. The fighters scrambled. The question remained – where were they going? By now, Bomber Command were experts at feints and other route trickery. The German commanders ordered their fighters to assemble at radio beacon Ida, near Aachen, and radio beacon Otto, near Frankfurt. Now it was a matter of luck for the Lancasters and Halifaxes. Had the Germans guessed correctly?

The running commentary broadcasts had recently been increased in strength to counter British jamming. The fighter crews listened in:

> 'Couriers flying in on a broad front between the mouth of the Scheldt and Ostend. Many hundreds. Courier spearhead south of Brussels, course 90°, height 16,000 to 22,000 feet.'

Such a course, if continued, would take them close to both radio beacons and, for 150 miles, that's just what they did, without any turns left or right. The wind strength and direction sent back to HQ by the windfinder Lancs were disbelieved, and the wind to fly by, which was broadcast to the main force, was the wind that had been forecast, not the one that was blowing. The result was a scattering of the stream over a breadth, it was said, of fifty miles rather than the recommended five. Safety in numbers no longer applied.

Over eighty bombers were shot down on route, from Belgium to the target. The Me110s with the new Lichtensteins and Schrägemusik had a night to remember.

Those bombers that got there did virtually no damage to Nürnburg. About a hundred bombed Schweinfurt by mistake. Here's Flying Officer John Duncan's report::

'It is thought that position C was undershot due to considerable fighter activity along the route south of the Ruhr and to consequent defensive manoeuvres. It was considered that target had been reached early and no TIs or RP flares were seen and the area was orbited and bombs seen to be dropped by 40/50 aircraft. After orbiting another attack was seen in progress in the distance and it was thought that as no flares or TIs had been seen the correct target had not been identified. Time did not permit the latter to be attacked during the period during which PFF were operating and so bombs were dropped on the area orbited subsequently considered to be Schweinfurt. 01.22 hrs, 22,500 ft.'

Duncan was attacked by a FW190 and then again by a Me110 (considerable fighter activity) but corkscrewed his way out of it (consequent defensive manoeuvres). He flew around and around above a well-defended city. In common with virtually all of his captain colleagues, a combination of unfavourable circumstances, confusion and devotion to duty took him into a fine old mess. Many of the other 9 Squadron skippers also met trouble; two combats resulted in a wounded and a dead gunner, and a third had the ultimate consequence. Plowright, back in J-Johnny, did see flares and TIs, no results of his bombing could be observed, but he had his own near miss. Norman Wells was his rear gunner:

'I don't know what made a brilliant pilot. We thought Phil Plowright was brilliant. Possibly they all were, or most of them, but most of them weren't lucky. One time we were hit and came home on three, then we went on leave and that aircraft went down with another crew. We went to Marseille, got a shell in the tail, came home, and she bought it two weeks later with a very experienced pilot (Manning) and the Group Captain on board, and we were there on the same op in J-Johnny, in among it just like them.

We were nominated PFF Supporter for Stuttgart, which is muggins who flies in front of the pathfinders to draw the fire so they can drop their TIs undisturbed. After doing that, you have to go around and come in again to bomb. We were in J, never got a mark on that one, yet Backwell-Smith, a squadron leader, top man, FTR. Nürnburg, that dreadful, dreadful night, we never got shot at but we damned nearly got rammed by another Lanc heading for the same cloud as we were. He was so close we could hear his engines as well as our own. I went to Berlin seven times,

Frankfurt three times. Goodness knows how many went down on those trips.'

It was 316, Norman.

By the time the bombers turned for home on that dreadful, dreadful night, scattered by the wind and so vulnerable, most of the fighters had used up their fuel and gone back to base. Losses were not as bad as they might have been otherwise.

German reports say that sixty-nine people were killed in the raid, in the town and villages around Nürnburg, and two more at Schweinfurt where the bombs fell in open country. Ninety-nine bombers were lost as the result of enemy action, much the greater proportion to fighters. Six more crashed at home, giving a total for the night of 13.4 per cent of the force setting off.

Dead on the night were 488 airmen. Adding those who died later from their wounds, Bill Chorley gives a figure of 537.

We cannot know how many of the bombers had eight crew, with an extra man to operate the H2S or the new ABC sets, but if we assume fifteen per cent, we have a total of approximately 5,600 heavy-bomber aircrew on that operation, and almost one in ten of them were killed. By way of recompense, the Germans lost five fighters.

(ABC – Airborne Cigar – aircraft carried a special wireless set and an extra, German-speaking operator who ranged the VHF band listening for transmissions by the German night-fighter control system and sent out jamming signals on the frequencies being used.)

It had been a black few months but times were changing, especially for 9 Squadron and its bomber 'family', 5 Group. The invasion by the Allies of mainland Europe was a certainty. Over the next few weeks, southern England would become one great army camp, and the job of the air force was to prepare the ground for the armada to land safely and, first of all, not be driven back into the sea and, secondly, be capable of breaking out of the German defensive ring, all to be done without giving away the location of the invasion point.

The Germans would begin reinforcing as soon as they realised invasion was imminent, so the primary task was to wreck the railway system from the Rhine to the French coast. The commanders made a list of seventy-nine railway targets in France, Belgium and Germany, and split it between the British and Americans, with Bomber Command taking the larger share.

Germany could not be left to feel suddenly secure; men and weapons had to be kept there, on duty and away from the Second Front, and there was still damage to be done to armaments manufacture. Bomber crews would be flying on moonless nights to German targets and on moonlit nights to French ones – and it did feel sometimes as if it was every night.

French targets were not far away. Short trips meant more trips. In the previous year, 1943, Bomber Command had dropped almost twice as much in bomb tonnage as in the whole of the war before that. Now the pace of new aircraft, new crews and new missions increased again, so that 1944 would see twice as many heavy bombers as in 1943, doing three times the work.

A thought occurred to the brass hats at HQ. These raids over France would be much less dangerous than flying over Germany. The first definition of a tour had been 200 operational flying hours in Hampdens, Whitleys and Wellingtons, then it was thirty operations, mostly over Germany. Now we're talking thirty French charabanc outings. So, in future, a French op would count only as one third of a German one. This stricture would last only until 3 May, when a disastrous foul-up at Mailly-le-Camp, depot of 21 Panzer Division, would force a U-turn.

An early example of these one-third raids was 5 April, to an aircraft repair factory at Toulouse. Pooley, Gradwell, Ineson, Clark and six more went as part of a 5 Group-only attack of 150 aircraft. Wing Commander Leonard Cheshire, leader of 617 Squadron Dambusters, one of the great flyers of the war, marked the target. He was in a Mosquito and ten miles from the target he dropped a white marker and the force circled this while Cheshire went in very low to mark the target visually, flying twice over the factory first, giving the workers time to flee, before coming round a third time to drop his flares. Two Lancs of 617 came after, dropping more markers. Cheshire judged that it was good and, acting as master bomber, called the rest in.

Conditions were so clear that the individual skippers of 9 Squadron could identify the boiler house from the assembly shop, and say that one green TI was on the button whereas the other was 200 yards overshot. Of course, a major concern was French civilians, but the force succeeded in destroying the factory without much of what we should now call collateral damage, although there were deaths and injuries when some bombs fell on houses near the plant.

Despite the HQ idea that these shows were mere picnics, the defences had been strong – heavy machine guns and light flak – to which Cheshire's ultra-low flying made him especially vulnerable although his high speed kept the gunners missing on this occasion. Even so, it was clear that another development was needed. It was decided that a pair of Lancasters would go in first, before Cheshire or whoever was in the Mossie, and drop containers of 24-ounce anti-personnel mines to silence the machine guns. Partly because of their excellent and experienced navigators, Russ Gradwell and Phil Plowright of 9 Squadron were the pilots selected out of 5 Group for this little extra job, after which they would have to go round again to bomb with the rest.

No-one told them how they should accomplish their new duty so the crews sat down in the Jolly Sailor at Bardney and talked it through among themselves. Russ and Phil were on very good terms with the owners of the pub and had been ever since Gradwell's first night on squadron, when he went to the pub and asked for a slice off the ham hanging behind the bar instead of his change. He remembered what happened later:

We decided that whoever was in front, me or Phil, when we reached the target we would act as marker and put our nav lights on, so the other could follow and concentrate only on dropping the mines accurately. As the Germans could see just as well, it was expected that the second Lanc wouldn't take too long about it before he took his turn as lit-up decoy for his pal.

After one particularly successful application of this technique, 9 Squadron were debriefing when Cheshire came over on the scrambler telephone to thank the boys for completely silencing the guns and making his job of dropping the markers so much easier. Gradwell:

'Phil Plowright replied that it should be the bombers thanking the Wing Commander, who was so accurate with his marking that it made their ops worthwhile. I said that I didn't believe the Wingco dropped his markers at all, but simply leaned over the side and placed them on the ground. Cheshire was highly amused but pointed out, in that rather posh sort of haw-haw voice of his, that if Flying Officer Gradwell had ever flown a Mosquito he would know that the wings got in the way of such a procedure.'

Within hours of the Toulouse attack, Sir Arthur Harris sent a message to Air Vice Marshal The Honourable Sir Ralph Cochrane, Air Officer Commanding 5 Group, informing him that their method of marking and directing operations was confirmed as officially approved, and that 5 Group could now operate as an independent force. There would be fifteen Lancaster squadrons, including 9 and 617 and two of pathfinders, and a Mosquito squadron.

Railway yards at Tours were attacked by 5 Group Lancasters on the night of 10 April; 180 in the force, seventeen of them from 9 Squadron as was the only loss, shot down by flak. The chief difficulty with the low-level marking technique, apart from it having to be done visually and therefore only in clear weather, was that the master bomber, of necessity, kept his force hanging around until he was quite sure the markers were on the target and not on French housing estates. The bombers, who would go in low themselves anyway, thus gave the flak gunners more opportunities and – as would be seen on later ops – more time for the fighters to turn out.

Cheshire and 617 weren't at Tours (they were attacking a signals station at St-Cyr); Wing Commander Porter in J-Johnny led the op, marking the target with red spotfires which soon disappeared in the smoke produced by accurate bombing. Some crews bombed visually, which produced more smoke, and some went around twice to be sure. The yards were wrecked, so Porter ordered himself and the last few home without bombing, to avoid civilian casualties.

Next night, Ineson was in J-Johnny for Aachen, a medieval town full of churches (Aix-la-Chapelle to the French and the Belgians) but also with important railway junctions and aerodrome. This was not a precision raid on the railways, however. It was an old-style hammering of a German town, and 341 Lancs went to do serious damage. Losses were light and Duncan, Pooley, Clark, Gradwell and the rest got a full point on the trip meters, not a third of one.

Juvisy-sur-Orge on 18 April, was a return to the lines of reinforcement and a 5 Group special attack, with Cheshire and three more 617 Squadron Mosquitos marking. Squadron strength was building at No. 9; they provided sixteen, with Plowright in J-Johnny, the first of twelve in a row for this team of crew and aircraft, many of them in their new role as low-level machine-gun silencer.

Juvisy, a town of 14,000 people or so, had a Paris-sized railway station with connections to most of the major cities in France. The captains reported concentrated bombing, hits on the marshalling yards and generally a good demolition job, but the town suffered badly too, and much of it was destroyed. Once again the only loss of the raid was a 9 Squadron crew.

Something similar happened at La Chapelle, a major railway junction in Saint-Denis, northern Paris, when seventeen of No. 9 went, including Plowright in J-Johnny. There were no losses this time although six went down from other squadrons. The target was smashed but 640 locals were killed.

Eighteen of No. 9, the most so far, were warming up and lining up ready for take-off to Brunswick, which was to be the first trial of the 5 Group, low-level Mosquito marking technique on a German city. It all happened, not especially well, but without most of No. 9. Only three got away before the fourth swung off the runway and burst into flames, blocking the rest. Two came home. The crew lost were on their second op. One of the homecomers was Flight Lieutenant D. H. Pearce, tour complete, who had not quite made it to Berlin in J-Johnny way back in January, with a double J graduate Stanley Jones as his mid-upper, who was killed with Froud. Pearce was away to No. 5 LFS, and the rest who flew in J with him also survived the war.

Much better results for the new method were obtained at Munich on 24 April. The squadron could only send thirteen but all the captains commented on the accuracy and efficiency of the marking. Phil Plowright in J on her fifty-eighth:

> '8 red spot fires in sights. Yellow TIs seen at Datum point followed by flares over the target and red spot fires and green TIs. The latter were well concentrated and illuminated the built-up area. A good conflagration had started and a large explosion was observed when leaving the target.'

Almost 2,500 buildings were destroyed or badly damaged in the centre of Munich. The railway station and various public buildings were levelled.

It was a successful raid, with ten Lancs lost out of 234, the local flak scoring at least as well as the fighters.

Harry Pooley was hit by flak on the Schweinfurt failure on 26 April, and had to come home on three engines, while twenty-one other Lancaster crews were not so fortunate, out of 206. The captains of 9 Squadron reported good concentrations of fires around the markers but the markers were in the wrong place. For ten per cent losses, the return for the bombers was two people killed in Schweinfurt and many holes in the countryside.

For the next three weeks there were no German targets for No. 9, but the French ones would prove to be just as dangerous. First up was the explosives factory at Saint-Médard-en-Jalles, between Bordeaux and the coast, using information provided by the local Resistance. The Lancasters of 5 Group, sixty-eight of them, went to see to it. There was haze over the target, compounded by smoke from errant marker flares setting fire to the woods nearby. The crews waited for the master bomber's orders, and waited, and waited, orbiting the target for almost an hour.

Plowright in J was windfinder, an extra job to assess the strength and direction of the wind over the target so that adjustments could be made to the Mark 14 bombsight. He returned to his aerial post from doing that at 02.28. He received the order to go home at 03.24 and landed with his full bomb load still on board.

It all had to be done again the next night, 29 April, and up ahead again was windfinder Plowright in J-Johnny, on her sixtieth op, with rear gunner Sergeant Norman Wells:

'We flew up and down, up and down at about 6,000 feet, being shot at, until Lucas (navigator) was happy that he'd got the wind just right, then he passed that to Harry Hannah (wireless operator), who sent it back to base, who worked out the numbers and transmitted those to all the 5 Group aircraft so they would know what to feed into their bombsights, which calculated accordingly. We did that, then we flew up and down some more, and we flew up and down for sixty one minutes until the rest arrived.'

Within fifteen minutes of the rest arriving, the factory was no more. Plowright and Gradwell bombed from 4,000ft while Horne, at a slightly safer height from which to bomb a gunpowder factory, saw flames up to 4,000ft, and Ineson saw an explosion sending debris up to 5,000ft.

There were no losses here and none either at Toulouse on 1 May, where the main target was the aircraft factory. Ineson was there; Wing Commander Porter, Clark, Plowright in J, Gradwell, Horne and Pooley with no problems in conditions clear enough to see exactly what they were doing. The brief for 3 May must have sounded much the same – Mailly-Le-Camp, a German army base, admittedly, depot of 21 Panzer Division and a big centre for tank training, but another piece of French cake otherwise.

It was a big force – 346 Lancs and sixteen Mosquitos led by the four Mossies of 617, with Cheshire as Marker Leader. Some of what went wrong is known about; some remains conjecture. Cheshire the perfectionist may have taken too long over his marking but the markers were spot on. He transmitted this information to the master bomber, Group Captain Laurence Deane DSO, DFC, who couldn't hear it because he was being unintentionally jammed by American Forces radio. Also, Dean's W/T was set to the wrong frequency so he could not have relayed instructions if he'd got them, and he couldn't inform his deputies of his predicament.

The attackers milled about, awaiting orders, which gave sufficient time for more night-fighters to arrive. Eventually, the raid got under way when the deputy controller, Squadron Leader Sparks of 83 Squadron, took over.

Well before that, the bombers had flown through incessant fighter attacks on the way in, and when they got through, they found more fighters at the target.

'It was a shooting gallery'. 'Bombers all around were going down in flames.' 'There were fires burning all over the place and not from bombs, from our aircraft.'

Norman Wells, with Plowright:

> 'The markers had to be put down at two minutes past midnight, because the soldiers in the barracks would all be in bed by then. The time came and went and we saw no markers. Nobody knows quite what happened. There were stories about Cheshire arriving too soon, flying over and coming back late, and more about radios not working. Whatever it was, it was a disaster for us. We smashed up the barracks all right and left the town unharmed even though it was right there next door. I heard that the only French civilians killed were by a Lanc which crashed into their house.'

The first target indicator was seen by another crew at 0.01. Phil Plowright:

> 'First marking not much good, but some aircraft bombed this although no orders were given. Orders to bomb received at 0.24.'

It is true that no bombs fell outside the target. Despite all the confusion, the bombing was very accurate indeed and did enormous damage as well as killing and injuring hundreds of German soldiers and destroying many tanks and other vehicles, but also killing about eighty French POWs and forced labourers. The bombers, circling above, waiting for their instructions, and later attacking with meticulous care after dummy runs to be sure, did their job as near perfectly as could be, but they were being shot down at a tremendous rate, and five fallen Lancs smashed into houses killing twelve civilians. Sixteen more were killed at the near-by village of Poivres, where four Lancasters crashed and twenty-eight airmen were buried in the local churchyard.

Of the 346 Lancs taking off for Mailly, forty-two were shot down on route both ways, and over the target, and another crashed at home. Only a few were from flak; the fighters got the rest. Some of the more experienced skippers ignored briefing orders and hung around some distance from the camp. Others stayed above Mailly, among them Jimmy Ineson and crew. Five weeks on squadron was perhaps insufficient to give Ineson the confidence to move away from the worst danger. In any case, their Lanc was among those waiting for orders that were shot down before receiving them, crashing at Normee, a few miles north-east of Mailly.

The bomb aimer, kiwi Flying Officer Les Porteous, parachuted out and was taken prisoner. Mid-upper Sergeant Henry Chappell also jumped and got back to England with the help of the Maquis. The other five died.

The heavy losses at Mailly forced a rethink. French ops would now count one on a tour, not a third of one.

Pilot Officer James Ineson receives his pilot's wings.

Sgt Henry Chappell, centre, with Maquis members and the wreckage of his Lancaster.

Extract from *The Luftwaffe War Diaries*:

> 'Slowly the fighter crept up behind its prey – a Lancaster. Unsuspecting, the latter went on flying straight and level. Drewes (Major Martin Drewes, fifty-two victories) adjusted his speed to that of the enemy and began to climb again. They were now only fifty yards off, and the small projection representing the air-to-ground radar installation (H2S) was clearly visible. There were no other modifications. The Lancaster was still without a ventral gun position, and was thus from below still blind and vulnerable. Were the British really unaware that the majority of their losses were due to attack from that quarter?'

The Lancaster was originally designed and armed with a ventral or belly turret, but no crew member was designated to fire it and nobody could have got in it. The two machine guns, .303 inch, had to be fired by a man standing inside the fuselage, who could only see directly a very small area below the aircraft and who otherwise had to look around with a periscope. Squadrons that had the first Lancs tended to remove the belly turret as neither use nor ornament and it was soon dropped altogether.

When the true menace of Schrägemusik became clear, some squadrons were instructed to combat it by fitting a single .5 inch gun, manned inside the aircraft as before, but firing through a hole in the floor. One of the aircraft selected for the experiment was W4964 WS/J, and she flew with it to the aerodrome and seaplane base at Lanveoc-Poulmic, near Brest on 8 May, captained by Phil Plowright getting very near the end of his tour.

Lanveoc was rear-gunner Norman Wells's twenty-sixth op, his thirteenth in J-Johnny, and the aircraft's sixty-third:

> 'Mick Maguire came with us, the armaments officer. He'd rigged up an extra gun in the belly of the aircraft, where the under-turret had been in the original design. We had a second Dicky with us as well so we were quite a party.'

The new boy was Sergeant George Langford, having his only time in J, who would be shot down at St Leu d'Esserant and taken prisoner.

Mick Maguire was indeed there, and remembered it well:

> 'The idea (of the under-gun) was a bit late in arriving and there didn't seem to be any special urgency or impetus behind it. Some squadrons never bothered with it at all, and ammunition was in short supply. We fitted it to three aircraft, including J-Johnny Walker. I flew with Phil Plowright to test it a few times. The notion suffered with the usual problem of a point five gun at that time, which was that the breech mechanism left it with one up the spout after it had been fired, and the hot barrel meant that it would pop this round off at any moment. It was disconcerting at first but you got used to it and remembered to keep the thing pointing the right way.'

Group Captain McMullen, the Bardney station commander, checked on progress. Was the new gun ready to go on ops? Maguire said it was, and he'd like to go with it, in J-Johnny. McMullen said: 'What? You want to go on the operation? Are you sure you have the time?'

At the briefing, they were told they were going to an airfield south of Brest, on one of the promontories of the Cap Finistère. It was going to be an all-5 Group show, with fifty-eight Lancs and six Mosquitos to mark the target. Maguire:

> 'Our load was eighteen 500s and a 4,000 pound cookie. Off we went, and we got some flak over the Channel Islands. The wireless operator, Harry Hannah, was not at all keen on having a big hole in the floor of J-Johnny and when he went to the Elsan he clung to the fuselage like a rock climber. Approaching the target there was a lot of light flak then suddenly we were caught by searchlights. I'd got a smoked Perspex screen over my goggles so I wasn't dazzled even

though the inside of J-Johnny looked like it had been whitewashed. Phil was on his run and the bombs went (at 6,250 feet), more or less as I fired the point five at the searchlights. He and the mid-upper, Sergeant Corr who was right above me, both said 'Christ, what the hell was that?" and the searchlights went out. Now, I don't think I shot them out although everybody said I did. I think the aircraft behind us had hit them or the generator with his bombs.'

Regardless of Maguire's modesty, a painting of a searchlight was added to the battle honours on J's nose.

At the debrief – called the interrogation – Maguire went to the armaments table where the gunners went to report on any problems they might have had. Instead of the usual one man to take the reports, there was a gang of armourers, including Maguire's right-hand man, Flight Sergeant Harrison, the armaments 'Chiefy'. Maguire:

'"What are you doing here?" I said. "Why aren't you in bed?" And Chiefy looked at me, with a tear in his eye, and said "I thought, if you'd got killed, I'd have your toolbox".'

Later, the Group Captain sent for Maguire and showed him a signal from HQ 5 Group: 'Technical officers will not fly on Operations under any circumstances'.

It had become apparent that, at the heights necessary for German ops, the hole in the floor transformed the Lancaster from a fridge into a freezer, but it was kept on for a while yet.

Plowright was on twenty-seven, J-Johnny was on sixty-four, and the target was the marshalling yards and locomotive repair sheds at Lille-Fives. The marking was perfect and so was the early bombing, so the markers disappeared in the smoke. Plowright and many others had to orbit the target while it was remarked.

Eighty-five Lancs were on the job, of which twelve were lost, all to the fighters it is believed, with many exploding in mid-air as was often the way with Schrägemusik. Only one man survived from those twelve crews. No. 9 Squadron lost two aircraft, all men killed; one crew were on their first, having been on station a week.

One night, when a spare bod was needed in the bomb aiming compartment, the squadron's bombing leader Dinger Bell stepped forward. He'd done a similar thing with Newton in J-Johnny. Maguire:

'In the Jolly Sailor that evening he left a pint of beer on the mantlepiece and said he'd be back for it. The Jolly Sailor had that pint of beer on the mantlepiece for a long, long time. He was very popular, Dinger.'

Flight Lieutenant Gilbert Bell DFC, 9 Squadron bombing leader, is shown here, third from the left, in a scratch crew with Wing Commander Burnett, fourth from left, in November 1943. The Lanc is ED700 WS/O – fifty ops.

They were shot down by a fighter over the rail yards at Lille with all crew killed.

That was 10 May. Next night they were off to the German military establishment at Bourg-Léopold in the Flemish Belgian province of Limbourg. It had been a Belgian army camp of 40,000 men between the wars, properly known as Camp Beverlo, named after the near-by village. Plowright in W4964:

> 'No target attacked as on second approach to target order to cease bombing was received at 00.21 hours followed at 00.33 hours by an order on W/T to return to base.'

Half the force of 190 Lancs had the same experience. With the marking made uncertain by low lying mist, the risk to civilians was too great, as the bombers had already proved unknowingly, hitting the Zuidstraat in Beverlo, killing seventy-seven of the populace.

It was only a three-and-a-half-hour trip, and they didn't bomb, but it still counted for Phil Plowright and his men. Twenty-eight down, two to go, and it was more railway yards on 19 May, at Tours again, only this time it was the yards in the middle of town, not the ones on the outskirts. Marking and bombing had to be very precise, and there to watch it with Plowright in

J-Johnny was a second Dicky, Flying Officer Douglas Melrose, at the start of an association with W4964 that would prove to be the longest of them all. There were five second Dickies that night; two would make it through.

Despite all the careful planning and orchestration of the raid – most 9 Squadron crews made two or three bombing runs before dropping, and they were uninterrupted by fighters – some 700 houses were destroyed around the railway station, which itself was severely damaged, and another 700 houses were hit. No figures are available for the number of civilians killed but it was in the hundreds.

The Plowright crew now had sixteen J trips and twenty-nine all told. They would know of crews shot down and killed on their thirtieth. It happened. Thirty was a magic number for bomber crew but it made no difference to the enemy.

Aircrew morale was a matter of importance to squadron and station commanding officers, although perhaps not quite as important as technical problems such as aircraft maintenance and readiness, weaponry supply, raid planning, training and practice and everything else that went into successful bombing. If the crews were physically fit enough to fly, what was there to worry about? The over-riding attitude then – 'do your duty, get on with it, here we go again, we're all in this together to win the war' – meant that individual concerns about life on a fragile tightrope were usually kept private.

There was no sin so great as damaging the team spirit and this in men who had to deny or submerge their most basic human instinct – to keep themselves alive – every time they went to work.

Just out of training, with no real idea of what they were in for, spirits would be high. You can see it in the photographs of those young men in their smart uniforms, smiling for the team shot. Then came the first few ops, staggering experiences to every man without exception, occupying every faculty. Flying against the enemy in a heavy bomber was such a complex thing to do that it consumed every man's abilities and completely filled his mind. Flying into mortal danger in the dark, for gunner, wireless operator, navigator, engineer, bomb aimer, pilot, it was more full-time than any job on the ground. At the start of it all, there was no time or space to feel fear.

Of course it was exciting, in more ways than one, but until they acquired some professional experience, until they learned to expect all the little and big events of a flight, rather than find everything a surprise, there was no room for contemplation.

When a crew reached five or six ops, spirits might droop. Other crews, maybe experienced crews, had been lost in the meantime, and the sheer weight of the task had become obvious.

On the other hand, as one skipper put it: 'We reckoned if you got through six you'd probably got the hang of things and the crew would be operating and co-operating well, and you might even think you'd get to the end of it.'

It didn't take long for the novelty to wear off. Those who survived the first few had, by their very survival, become battle-scarred veterans and had recognised the price of life. For one crew to get through, it seemed clear that half a dozen other crews had to fail.

At some point along the way, an individual might start to believe, with some justification, that his luck was about to run out. Such Jonah-ism, or depression, could not be shared, or shown. Perhaps a reaction might be to swing to the opposite pole, to adopt a carefree attitude: 'The fighters and the flak haven't killed me yet, and they're not going to, not after all I've been through.'

These sorts of reactions we modern folk can imagine. We cannot imagine quite what it was like to be in a bomber over Berlin, but we can try. Maybe the most difficult emotional phenomenon to understand is the addiction some came to have. The adrenaline-fuelled craziness of the wildest sports at least leaves a certain amount of control in the hands of participants. To become addicted to the Russian roulette of flying bombers was something else again, and it did happen.

And so to the end. 'Will the gods of fortune, the gods of aviators, or any other gods for that matter, be inclined to let me through, or are they going to let me think I'm there, only to have the last laugh as I spiral down, burned at the stake of a Lancaster?'

CHAPTER 9

Anatomy of an Operation

It would be Plowright's finale and the first for Melrose and three more. For those four novice crews today, there was an entirely new kind of tension. Here it was at last. For the pilots it was the culmination of almost three years of training, some of it in South Africa, Canada or even the USA. The British pilots had to go there to train in peace. All the crew had trained long and hard, to satisfy their instructors that they could do their various jobs, but there was no exam they could pass to prove they could cope with other men trying to kill them – no exam, that was, apart from the reality.

Plowright and his men had passed that exam many times over, but they had expected their last one to be another French target. Norman Wells:

> 'When we saw it was back to Germany, we couldn't help but feel a few butterflies. There were no easy ops but after all those Berlin trips and Stuttgart and Essen and whatnot, you'd pick France if you had a choice, which we hadn't, of course. There was no choice. Duisburg it had to be.'

The novitiates did know something about it. They'd flown three or four miles up, in the cold night. They had felt the loneliness of droning along in a tin tube with wings, with nothing to reassure them except the vibration of the machine and the occasional few words in their headphones. The navigator had his little orange-coloured light, in his tiny office behind a curtain, while those in the front seats had the subdued green glow of their instruments, but the general view was of blank emptiness in cloud, or that other emptiness of stars and part moon, that reminded everyone of how insignificant they were.

That much they knew, from their training. What they had no real idea about, and Plowright and his boys couldn't tell them, was the hours in enemy territory when no moment was out of danger, the shocking white blindness of searchlights, the fiery hosepipes of the light flak, the silent explosions of the heavy flak at a distance or the banging, juddering, hammer blows when it was near.

They'd had those curiously-named exercises called fighter affiliation, when friendly foes tried to catch them out, but the German fighters were keen on a different sort of close relationship. Those new boys didn't know what it was like to see another bomber exploding, or getting the worst of an exchange of tracer bullets and plunging down and down to finish, silently again, as a flash of flame, Macbeth's brief candle gone out.

The technical details of the op were taken down and studied as the various trade leaders told them what to do and what to expect. As always, Wing Commander Porter told them what a terrific chance this was to strike at the very guts of enemy war production, a message that may have been noted by the new boys but passed over the heads of the old men, whose minds were already elsewhere.

Like Norman Wells, the other old men had become used to the smaller, more precise type of French raids that 5 Group had been doing, but this was back to main force, 500-plus Lancasters on a mass attack against massed defences.

One crew on their last, four on their first and fourteen at various stages between, ate the traditional pre-flight, haute cuisine meal of bacon and egg.

Bob Woolf was Melrose's Australian wireless operator:

'When the Battle Order was posted up on the notice board, all those listed for the trip felt the tension, and this would continue to build up right through the briefing, the preparation for the flight and the pre-flight meal. Sometimes the reaction would be instant. Suddenly some fellows would need to go to the toilet in great haste. Others would try to show a forced kind of levity, cracking jokes and laughing too easily. Others would become quiet and withdrawn. Nobody wanted to reveal the fear they felt inside but it was deep in our souls and I know that I always gave a thought to whether this trip would be the one from which there would be no return.'

Some men had great difficulty hiding their fear, while some could hide it even from themselves, most of the time. Some wrote a letter to mum, sweetheart, sister, whoever, and left it to be posted, if.

Duisburg. Well, the flak, the searchlights and the night-fighters would all be there, waiting. It was a major city, like Sheffield say, population 430,000, growing up where the Rhine met the Ruhr to become a great industrial and railway centre, and an inland port. It was the first big raid there for a year. The briefing didn't mention that forty-seven Lancasters had been lost there in the past. The previous WS/J had gone down at Duisburg, Plowright might have been interested to know, and the J before that had been hit by flak there. On the other hand, if you were seeking lucky omens, this J had been there on her third and come back. That had been with George Saxton.

That more than several Lancasters would go down tonight was certain. The force would be 510, so twenty-five would be acceptable, a little under five per cent.

The first stage of the journey was a trip in the back of a truck, driven by a WAAF, smiling and cheerful but never, ever saying anything like 'Good luck, you fellows'. Just being nice and warm made them the polar opposite of an op over Germany, and that was enough to make the crews feel a little better about it all.

With passengers disembarked, the WAAF drove back, to wait for their return. She'd be picking some of them up again in about six hours' time. Maybe she and her colleagues would be picking all of them up, all of them aged by rather more than six hours, boyfriends perhaps, some of them. Bob Woolf:

> 'By the time we were taken out to dispersals the tension had reached a high peak and in the buses there was quite an amount of heavy humour and repartee between crews. Those young WAAFs who drove us out to our aircraft were so considerate and friendly, and they did much to soften the emotional stress of the occasion. So, we clambered aboard and set about checking our equipment once more, leaving nothing to chance. This busy activity was good for our nerves and the familiarity of it was reassuring as we waited for the word "Go".'

There would be still an hour to that word 'Go', lots of time put aside in case a fault was discovered that could be attended to before take-off. Usually, everything checked out so there was more waiting, more chatter, more silence, and another couple of cigarettes. Bob Woolf:

> 'As it happened, on our first op we needed some of our spare hour. I was doing my tests and found that one of the two generators wasn't working. That didn't matter in theory. We only needed one generator and had the second as back-up. Still, it wasn't the best thing to happen on your first operation. The skipper spoke to the control tower and the Chiefy of the electrical section came out. He checked the instruments and concluded that, yes, it was indeed the case that we only had one generator. The point was, should we go? Dougie asked me what I thought. We both asked the Chiefy what he thought. He assured us that a second generator failure was most unlikely. It was decided. We would go. We would carry our four thousand pound cookie and our load of incendiaries to Duisburg. Doug signed Form 700, to certify that the aircraft had passed into his command in a serviceable condition and Chiefy went his way.'

Came the sound of seventy-six Rolls Royce Merlins starting up, and the op was surely on. Even at this last moment there could be scrub, with yellow flares fired from a Very pistol by someone in the control tower, but no signal came and the nineteen messengers of destruction began rolling around the perimeter track towards the head of the runway, steered by brakes and outer engines. Four Merlins produced about 6,000 horsepower. Four times nineteen produced a sound that could hardly be described.

At the front of the queue was DV396 WS/G, skippered by Flight Sergeant Ernie Redfern, who'd recently done his first to Bourg-Léopold and would – months hence – take J-Johnny on one of her last. The pilot controlled the engines at this stage, revving up towards take-off power, keeping the brakes hard on until he saw the light of an Aldis lamp change from red to green, a lamp in a Perspex dome in a little hut painted in black and white squares, a hut that had once been a caravan.

Redfern was away at 22.36 Double British Summer Time. Releasing the brakes of the best flying machine of its kind in the world, he set off along a mile or so of tarmac road, a road that led to the sky, at fifty miles an hour, sixty, stick forward to get the tail up and rudder under tension. The flight engineer took over the throttles as Redfern asked for full power. Seventy miles an hour, eighty, ninety, stick back, a hundred ... airborne. Away.

There was quite a gap of eight minutes before the Aldis lamp flashed again, then it was Clark at 22.44, Gradwell at 22.46, more at one- and two-minute intervals, Plowright eighth away at 22.51, then Melrose at 22.53, and another, and another, until the last great ship, DV395 WS/T, a veteran of over thirty ops captained by Flight Sergeant Ray Cornelius, veteran of half a dozen.

There was nobody issuing instructions over a radio, or any kind of instruction at all apart from the Aldis lamp. That was all it took to send a Lancaster to Germany. Bob Woolf:

> 'We'd found out during training that our skipper had a very bad habit. No sooner were we off the ground and climbing than he would fall asleep for about half a minute, but we rather hoped he wouldn't do it on ops. Luckily, Ted (Selfe, flight engineer) was on the ball and kept us going upwards while our captain took his nap, and was always ready for it after that. Doug would never believe he did this until one day Sammy (Morris, bomb aimer) broke all the rules and took a camera with us and got a photo of Doug in the land of nod while at the controls of the King's Lancaster WS/J.'

Blackout was resumed at the Bardney aerodrome and the night fell silent. While the squadron climbed to assembly height and made for the rendezvous point, those left behind could do no more. The watchers in Germany would soon be aware, taking bearings from those in the bomber stream carrying H2S radar, plotting the likely target, or guessing.

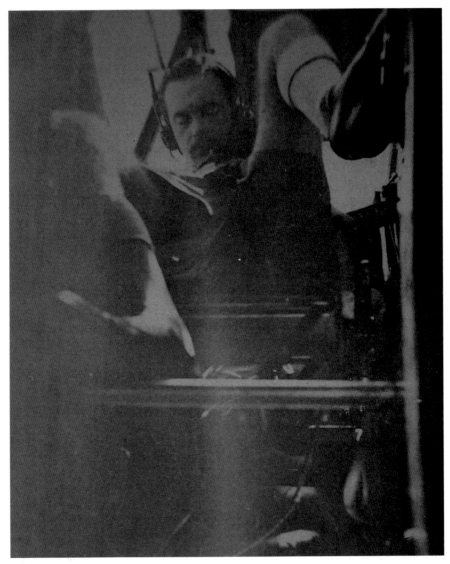

Dougie Melrose takes his customary thirty winks after the rigours of take-off.

None of the Lancasters of No. 9 had turned back. Mechanical faults often didn't show themselves until the bomber was up and away, despite air and ground tests. Illnesses too could occur in flight, real or imagined, but tonight all achieved straight and level flight at the height and on the course ordered, and crews settled in to their routines. Bob Woolf:

'We functioned well on our first trip. We did our various jobs by the book as the skipper liked but, with ten tenths cloud over the

Ted Selfe, Melrose's flight engineer, had been groundcrew on a Spitfire squadron before retraining as aircrew. He and wireless operator Bob Woolf were fine singers, harmonising over the intercom when circumstances allowed.

target, there was not much to see in the way of results. I somehow managed to fulfil all my wireless-operating tasks while keeping half my attention on the remaining generator ammeter and the other half on Monica.'

Monica was another airborne radar, the bombers' equivalent of the Lichtenstein apparatus, but not as good. The earlier (1942) versions were

Jimmy Moore, Melrose's navigator, another Australian, at thirty-some was quite elderly for aircrew but his mature, unflappable nature was much appreciated.

sound only; an aerial on the bomber's tail sent out a pulse and if there was an aircraft behind, the device emitted pips, and the closer together the pips, the nearer was the aircraft. This was often fed into the intercom so all the crew could hear it, but Monica could not tell friend from foe. In the bomber stream, the pips could be almost continuous, getting on everyone's already stretched nerves. The Mark III that Woolf had gave a visual indication but still only of the vaguest, with no directional information. Even worse,

Bardney from the air, showing Lancasters parked at dispersals around the perimeter.

the Germans had captured a set soon after Monica was introduced and developed an instrument called 'Flensburg', which was fitted to fighters, picked up Monica's signals and used them to home in on the transmitting aircraft from as much as forty miles away.

Nobody realised this until a German fighter pilot got lost and landed in England by mistake. Engineers soon worked out what his Flensburg was for and Monica was withdrawn in September 1944, probably having killed many more bomber crews than she'd saved.

In J-Johnny, Flying Officer Pearson – standing in as bomb aimer for the regular man, Sergeant Allen – had already fed into his Mark 14 bombsight the target's height above sea level, the local barometric pressure and the terminal velocity of the bombs. The height of the aircraft and the airspeed were recorded automatically by the box of tricks inside the bombsight, actually a small, valve-driven computer. The navigator, Flying Officer Lucas, would provide his best opinion on the wind speed and direction.

To an experienced man like Pearson, aiming at flares through ten-tenths cloud, as he was now doing, might have made all that information and computing seem a bit excessive. To novices like Flying Officer Morris and the other three new bombardiers, whether they had a stickler skipper like Melrose or not, the job had to be done as near perfectly as possible. The problem was that Morris couldn't see any markers. There was no aiming to be done, so they dropped their bombs on Estimated Time of Arrival.

The incendiaries in their SBCs (Small Bomb Container) would be scattered far and wide as the SBC opened above the ground, before impact. The 4,000lb cookie, the blast bomb, basically just a dustbin full of high explosive, went off on impact and could flatten a street. Standard bombs, which could pierce as well as blast, might have delays built in, to disrupt the work of the German emergency services.

Looking down as the bombs fell silently and invisibly, Melrose and his men could see only a patchy red glow. The job was done for the first time. The photograph would be meaningless but had to be taken. So, let's go home.

Back at Bardney, in the control room, in the watch office, the usual tensions began to be felt as the time for returning approached. The senior officers drifted in trying to conceal the anxiety that everyone felt. Two WAAFs sat in front of candlestick microphones, waiting for voices to call in to their heavy black headsets. Messages exchanged during the mission would have been picked up at 51 Base ops room Waddington, but Bardney would have heard nothing yet.

Aircraft VHF radios were much better than they had been. Those old sets, the TR9s, had had a very short range. The WAAFs then got their first inklings when the bombers were only three or four minutes flying time away, that is, if they could hear what the pilot was saying through the interference. The modern sets were more powerful and, normally, there was hardly any crackle or buzz.

As the clock ticked past 02.30, the squadron's crews were flying over their last few miles of sea, expecting on a clear night to see the tall tower of St Botolph's church at Boston, the 'Stump' as it was known, and then the River Witham to guide them to the less elegant stump of the Bardney sugar beet factory.

The code word for 9 Squadron's wireless identification was 'Rosen'. Thus the duty WAAF would expect to hear, for example, 'Hello Bardney, this is Rosen Apple,' and then a few words to indicate the state of play – everything was as it should be, or they had a wounded man on board, or they were on three engines, or whatever. If all was fine, WS/A-Apple would be instructed accordingly: 'Hello Apple, pancake,' meant to land immediately; 'Hello Apple, aerodrome, one thousand,' meant to get into the circuit over the airfield at 1,000ft and await further instructions. If, say, Rosen Charlie called in at the same time, he might be told 'aerodrome twelve fifty'.

Pip Beck, R/T WAAF at Bardney, spoke those words many times, and many times hoped to hear words that never came:

> 'You had to be cool and calm. You couldn't start flapping about, and if your boyfriend didn't come back, well, you had to carry on. If you were heartbroken, you had to leave it til afterwards. You couldn't burst into tears and go all hysterical on duty. And nobody did. It was very hard sometimes but you had to get used to it and quick.
>
> The routine was always the same. Stack them up, bring them in. You might have a complication if the runway became blocked or there were some other special instructions to make you depart from the script. If a crew was very late, we might get a phone call from another aerodrome to say they were down there. We might get a stray from another squadron, with wounded or dead maybe, or a shot-up aircraft, and he would make a Darkie call.'

Lost, damaged, whatever serious trouble the ship might be in, once he knew he was in home territory the pilot didn't say 'Mayday'. He said 'Darkie, Darkie' and left his set on transmit, long enough for ground stations to get his bearing and tell him where he was. Or, he might need rather more help than a course for home, and the WAAFs had to sort him out.

There were no Darkie calls this night, but the first thing the WAAFs heard was not quite what they were used to. Norman Wells:

> 'We were determined to be first back and when it was time to call base, Phil dispensed with the usual routine. Instead of the Rosen Johnny over business, he just said "Johnny Walker, still going strong. Get some in!"'

They were first down, at 03.09. They beat Redfern by a minute.

They taxied to dispersal and climbed out of J-Johnny for the last time to ride in the usual comfort back to the scruffy collection of buildings they had called home since last November, all those Berlins ago. Still, it wasn't quite over yet. There was the interrogation, with tea and free cigarettes. Norman Wells:

> 'After that, we had a few drinks, and later on our flight commander signed my log book, that was Flight Lieutenant Mathers, and the CO, Wingco Porter, he signed it and wrote "First operational tour completed: twenty nine and a third sorties". A third? I don't know which one they were counting as a third. Our flight engineer Sticky Lewis had missed a few in April and so had to stay on to finish.'

Sergeant William Charles Lewis would indeed stay on, to the very last.

9 SQUADRON.

20 25 .35

Date	Hour	Aircraft Type and No.	Pilot	Duty	Remarks (including results of bombing, gu		Flying Time Night
		LANCASTER			(29)		
19.5.44	22.20	J-W4964	P/O Plowright	Gunner.	OPS — TOURS　RAILWAY YARDS		5.20
21.5.44	22.50	J-W4964	P/O Plowright	Gunner	OPS — (30) DUISBURG		4.15
					TOTAL FLYING TIME FOR MAY	3.55	36.45

SIGNED .... *Richmathers* F/Lt
o/c 'A' Flight

TOUR COMPLETED.

TOTAL FLYING TIMES FOR 9 SQUADRON
DAY　21.45
NIGHT.　211.20
First operational tour completed + 29⅓ sorties.
SIGNED .... *...................*
C.O.
9. SQUADRON

TOTAL TIME ... 116.20 | 261.70

Hip, hip, hurray! The last page of Norman Wells's log book, and a rarity. Tour complete, twenty-nine and one third ops, otherwise known as thirty.

It was late. Crews with nothing more to celebrate than getting home mostly went for their fried egg and then bed. Some didn't bother with the egg. Pip Beck:

'The aircrews went to bed, they knew what the chances were and the war had to go on. It was no good waiting up and biting your nails. You'd never cope if you did that.'

It hadn't seemed a particularly successful trip, they said in the interrogation. The marking had been hard to pick or not there at all, and no results were observed. In fact it had been a good raid with a lot of damage done, but they hadn't seen that. One had been attacked three times by a fighter which made him overshoot the target; one hadn't found the target at all so bombed Mönchengladbach instead; one had flown around and around above the clouds but couldn't find anything so just came home, jettisoning his cookie in the sea.

Flight Lieutenant Mathers was down at 03.44 in the new C-Charlie, followed by an eternity of eight minutes when the also-new O-Orange turned up at 03.52.

LANCASTER W4964 WS-J IX SQDN BARDNEY 1943

CREW L TO R
P.E. PLOWRIGHT. R.P. ALLEN. F. CORR. N.H. B. LUCAS. N.F. WELLS.
FRONT
W.C. LEWIS. H. HANNAH

Phil Plowright and crew pose with J-Johnny, seemingly in early March 1944 although the caption reads 1943. WS/J has done over forty ops and Plowright's men are about a third of the way through their tour. At the end of May 1944, Plowright was posted to 17 OTU and Lucas to 1654 CU, and the rest to other peaceful billets, apart from Sticky Lewis.

There were two not yet back: fresher Melrose and slightly more of an old boy Cornelius. Plowright had been first back on his last and, almost an hour later, Melrose was, at last, back on his first.

Next day, the word was that Cornelius was definitely missing. No messages had been received. He hadn't landed anywhere else. He'd gone for a Burton, he and his very young, all-sergeant crew, unless they'd parachuted out and been taken prisoner – but they hadn't been so taken. They were lost without trace. Eventually, their names would be carved on the stone of Runnymede, to commemorate six trips there and back, and one more that ended in death.

Melrose and the others heard the news and, for the first time, knew the standard aircrew feeling. Bad luck. Could have been me, but glad it wasn't.

CHAPTER 10

The Start of Something Big

Melrose had come on to operations at what would prove to be one of the busiest times of the war for Bomber Command – in preparation for D-Day and after that in support of the invading armies – but tonight, they were going back to Germany. The squadron had lost one yesterday. What would happen today?

There were nineteen again, for Brunswick, with some debutants, some very experienced captains and crews, some who had done a few, some who had done one. Melrose was in J-Johnny, the sixty-eighth op for this venerable old bird. His exact contemporary, Pilot Officer Leslie Baker, aged twenty-two, was in a much newer machine, fifteen ops, but they were both equally serviceable and there was no difference anyone could measure between captains and crews.

Crossing the Dutch coast and heading south-east across Germany, a fighter picked up Baker's Lancaster and shot it down near Lingen, on the River Ems. The navigator got out but the rest died, including a man whose wife had had a baby three days before, the wireless op, Paddy McKee. Much the same thing happened to twelve other Lancasters, all with seven men inside, most of them killed, but Melrose and the rest of 9 Squadron flew home to tell the intelligence officers that the attack had been scattered, no great shakes at all, the marking confused and communications faulty with the master bomber. It had been cloudy when the forecast had been for clear skies. It had been a poor show, and another crew lost.

Later reconnaissance showed that Brunswick had suffered very little. The German report notes the raid but records few bombs and no casualties.

The next outing for J was a poor show too, with the experienced Pilot Officer Clark taking her on a small, specialist raid to the Philips HQ at Eindhoven, which was recalled. The master bomber would not risk bombing the Netherlands unless it could be seen clearly, and ten-tenths cloud prevented that.

At least they could say no losses. May so far had not been a merry month on No. 9. After Ineson had gone on the 3rd, there had been two more FTR on

Date	Aircraft Type & Number	Crew	Duty	Time Up	Time Down	Details of Sortie or Flight	References
22/5/44. (Contd).	LANCASTER. W.4954.	P/O. J.D. MELROSE. SGT. E. SELFE. P/O. J.W. MOORE (AUS). F/O. S.A. MORRIS. F/O. R.G. WOOLF (AUS). SGT. E. HOYLE. SGT. E.E. STALLEY.	Bombing – BRUNSWICK.	2242.	0520.	Primary attacked. 0125 hrs. 20,250 ft. Centre of concentration of fires under recce. flares in sights. Flares seen on approach, with many sticks of incendiaries beneath. One green T.I. also seen. Just after bombing a red Wanganui flare was dropped, also a green T.I. Bombing covered area of 3 or 4 miles.	
	LANCASTER. LL.845.	P/O. H.C. CLARK. SGT. R.K. GOLDSPINK. F/O. H.F.S. MITCHELL. W/O. C.H. REDMOND (CAN). SGT. A.F.R. HORSECROFT. P/O. S.C. MATTHEWS. SGT. G.R. BRADBURY.	Bombing – BRUNSWICK.	2240.	0423.	Primary attacked. 0131 hours. 19,750 ft. Green Wanganui flare in sights. Target was obscured by a patch of cloud which prevented visual identification. Controller ordered a Wanganui attack about 0128 hours and this appeared to develop reasonably well, although there was a good deal of scattered bombing beforehand.	
	LANCASTER. LM.519.	P/O. L.J. BAKER. SGT. E.J. BRITTAIN. SGT. J.M. STEPHENSON. F/O. J. McKEE. SGT. R.W. ENGLAND. SGT. G. GOW (CAN). SGT. N.R. PIKE.	Bombing – BRUNSWICK.	2242.		Aircraft missing.	
	LANCASTER. ME.757.	P/O. L. YOUNG (NZ). SGT. V. PLANT. F/SGT. A.R. BARRINGER. P/O. J.F.J. GREIG. F/SGT. L.H. HEASON. SGT. D.M. WILFONT. SGT. P.F. HILL.	Bombing – BRUNSWICK.	2234.	0508.	Primary attacked. 0128 hours. 20,000 ft. M.P.I. of R.S.F's in sights; the glow of which was plain through cloud. A few scattered undershoots seen but in the main bombing was concentrated around P.S.F. Numerous fires none outstandingly large.	

Melrose and Baker began together last night. Tonight, one crew came home and one was met by a German fighter.

the 10th, another on the 11th, and more on the 21st and 22nd. That was six in three weeks. If things went on like this, none of the new crews starting in May would be operating past midsummer's day. To cap it all, Air Chief Marshal Harris chose this moment to send a letter to all squadrons:

'I have always considered that the strain imposed by sustained Bomber Operations requires that aircrew personnel should enjoy the maximum amount of freedom from restraint and should be relieved, as far as can be done without loss of efficiency, of routine Station duties. This policy, and I can see no reason for changing it, places on Station, Squadron and Flight Commanders the responsibility for ensuring that such privileges are not abused.

Unfortunately, my attention is continually drawn to the lack of discipline prevalent amongst operational aircrew, and to causes of complaint such as irregularities of dress, lack of smartness in bearing and appearance, slackness in saluting and a degree of untidiness in some of their living quarters which practically amounts to squalor. Apart from the bad impression created both inside and outside the Service, such symptoms cannot help but have an adverse effect on the behaviour in the air of the personnel concerned, as conditions of modern warfare, and in particular the gruelling task of Bomber crews, demand instantaneous and unhesitating obedience to orders, combined with a degree of physical and moral stamina which can only result from a high standard of self-discipline.

It has become apparent that an attitude, or perhaps I should call it an affectation, which rates the normal obligations of Officers and NCOs in matters of smartness and cleanliness as of negligible importance, or even slightly contemptible, is more or less general amongst aircrew personnel. It is clearly essential that such an attitude, to which most of aircrew shortcomings are attributable, should be eradicated. The junior aircrew members of today are the Flight and Squadron Commanders of tomorrow, and the Station and Base Commanders of the future, and unless they grow with an understanding of and a sincere regard for, the right ideals and best traditions of the Service, our efficiency and our prestige will inevitably decline. The conduct of our aircrews on operations has won, and continues to win, the admiration of the world. It is particularly undesirable, therefore, that their conduct on the ground should fall short of this magnificent standard, and should excite unfavourable comment by the other members of the Royal Air Force, by other Services, or by the general public.

The last thing which I would wish to do would be to impose on aircrew personnel an irksome regime of inspections, parades and "spit and polish". I want their special privileges in the way of leave, petrol, extra rations and freedom from routine Station duties to continue and everything possible be done to relieve the strain of operations and to increase their fitness for their primary role. Station, Squadron and Flight Commanders, and even Captains of Aircraft themselves must, however, ensure by leadership, encouragement, education and personal example, that those measures are re-inforced by that strength of mind and body which derives from right thinking and right living.

Constant steps must be taken to see that aircrew personnel take sufficient physical exercise to keep them fit, particularly during lulls in operations. They must be educated in matters of general, as well as Service, knowledge. They must be made aware of the achievements, both past and present, of the Royal Air Force, and thus gain pride in their membership of our Service. Finally, they must be reminded that, as aircrews of Bomber Command, they form the spearhead of the national offensive, and as such lay claims to be called a "crack Corps", but that every "crack Corps" which has ever existed in any arm of the services in any country, has been distinguished for its all-round efficiency, smartness and esprit-de-corps, just as much as for its valour and fighting skill. Let us see to it that Bomber Command aircrews do not forfeit in the eyes of the world, through ignorance fostered by poor leadership, their full claim to that title.'

Whatever the 9 Squadron boys thought of the rest of it, they could certainly agree with that bit about the juniors of today being the commanders of tomorrow. At the rate they were dropping, dead men's shoes were going to be continuously vacant.

D-Day minus eight, 27 May – fairly typically for this period, over a thousand bombers went on seventeen separate ops, to Bourg-Léopold (army camp), Aachen (railways mainly), Rennes (airfield), five different coastal gun batteries, Le Havre (mine laying), and various other places including Nantes, which was where 9 Squadron were sent. There were a hundred Lancs – seventeen from No. 9 – and four Mosquitos marking. Melrose was in J-Johnny and in the van, as it were, among those who got there first and bombed, so accurately that half the force was told to orbit and wait for the dust to settle, and then to go home because the railways and workshops were wrecked. That was J's seventieth. Melrose's men would have to give way to two different crews for seventy-one and seventy-two.

At Ferme-D'Urville, near Cherbourg, was the most important German radar/listening station on the Normandy coast. Halifax squadrons had failed to damage it in poor visibility on 1 June, so the Lancs of 5 Group were sent there two nights later. The Mosquitos put their markers down on the very spot, the weather was clear and the defences inconsequential. Russ Gradwell in J-Johnny saw two red TIs 150 yards apart and a green TI between them, and thought the bombing well concentrated. He was right too. The target had disappeared from the earth.

Tomorrow was D-Day, the start of Operation Overlord. The railway system in France was severely disabled and would soon be almost no use to the Germans for bringing up reinforcements. The task for the moment was to neuter the coastal defences while not giving away the secret landing grounds, so for every mission against the Normandy guns there were two elsewhere.

Squadron 218 in Halifaxes and 617 in Lancs dropped huge amounts of Window, zigzagging slowly across the Channel many miles to the east and west of the invasion point, giving enemy radar the impression of invasion fleets approaching. In the early hours of the morning of 5 June, the rest of Bomber Command mounted, at the last possible moment, a raid on the Normandy guns featuring 963 four-engined heavies and forty-nine Mosquitos, dropping 5,000 tons of bombs, the most so far in the war, and another 110 aircraft flew the fighter routes jamming enemy signals.

Seventeen went from Bardney to Pointe-du-Hoc, near the small town of St Pierre-du-Mont, where gun batteries overlooked Omaha Beach. Others attacked the guns at Fontenay, Houlgate, La Pernelle, Longues, Maisey, Merville, Mont Fleury, Ouisterham and St Martin-de-Varevilles. Only one of the batteries escaped with little damage and only six bombers were shot down. Flying Officer Peter Blackham was on his second op, in J-Johnny, having been on squadron for six days, no time for a second Dicky. Like the others, he thought the bombing accurate.

Tomorrow, the US Rangers would be wading ashore and fighting their way up Omaha Beach, their job made feasible, at any rate, by the lack of action from the heavy guns.

The night of 6/7 June had No. 9 attacking German army positions at Evel, near Argentan, a small town in the department of Orne, Normandy. This was another thousand-bomber night, frustrating German attempts to come up to the beach-head and, ultimately, helping to clear the way for the Allies' push into France, but there was a more difficult balance to strike now between the urgent matter of the invasion and the likelihood of French civilian casualties. Several towns suffered badly; Argentan lost its railway station and many other buildings while Melrose in J-Johnny and nineteen others bombed their markers through the smoke, and Argentan was by no means the worst hit.

So it went on for WS/J and Melrose – Rennes, Orleans, Poitiers, Aunay sur Odon, Châtelleraut, railways, fuel dumps, roads, troop positions, six raids in nine days, experience rapidly gained for the newer men, like Blackham and the future J flyers Ben Taylor, Ernie Redfern and Charles Scott, and for the old men like Gradwell and Clark.

Poitiers was the first for Taylor and Scott, in skies that were clear of cloud but not of confusion. Melrose: 'Instructions received to bomb red, then cease bombing, then bomb red again, and finally to bomb green. Explosion at

01.54, otherwise no results observed. Gradwell: 'After instructions to cease bombing, orders were given to bomb red TIs and this was done. Two minutes after bombs were gone, orders were given to bomb green Tis.'

Even so, Poitiers had the best results out of six similar raids, with little hurt done to the town.

Châtelleraut produced a new threat for Melrose and J – fire from their own coastal defences as they flew home. The gunners could see W4964 on their radar screens but the blip should have shown as a friendly one, made so by the aircraft's IFF machine (Identification Friend or Foe). It wasn't, and the colours of the day, frantically fired off by the wireless operator, were not visible through the cloud. Oh well, no serious hurt was done, so it was just another something to bear in mind.

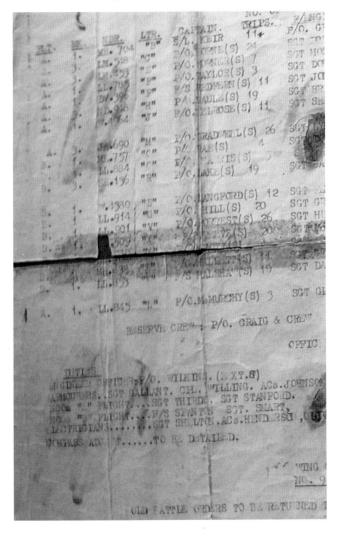

This is part of the battle order for 17 June – an op that never was. The ORB only says 'Operations were put on but cancelled later', which is true if light on detail. These captains and their crews saw their names on the mess wall and had to assume they were going, and prepared themselves accordingly. There would be another cancellation next day, then the Watten recall, and then Gelsenkirchen, when the last man on this list, Pilot Office McMurchy, would FTR, skipper and two crew were killed and four POW.

Allied ground forces were moving and their latest positions were not always known to the bombers. With so many bombing raids on targets so close together, by so many aircraft, perhaps organised chaos was the best description of this short period of the war. A new addition to the list of priorities was the V-weapon sites, and J's seventy-ninth was for such a target near Watten, twenty miles or so inland from Calais and Dunkirk. Better known today as the Éperleques blockhaus, it was a massive concrete structure designed for fuelling and launching V2 rockets, hidden in the woods and meant to be bomb-proof. The Allies only knew it was important, and to do with secret weapons. It was attacked again and again by the RAF and the USAAF, so never did fulfil its purpose. On this occasion, nothing happened to it because the mission was recalled after an hour in the air. Bob Woolf:

> 'We were after flying bombs and expecting a hot reception. Whether for this or another reason they gave us an extra gunner to operate the point five undergun. Only three kites had these guns, which we didn't think a great deal of and which usually went unmanned. They caused a lot of humorous remarks in the Mess. We'd heard about Mick Maguire, the armaments officer, actually getting airborne to test out this idea in anger, and we'd heard all the jokes and witticisms that generated.'

Three J graduate crews were on the next trip, another switch in priorities connected with the invasion, the synthetic oil refineries that were keeping the Wehrmacht motorised and the Luftwaffe flying. There were two targets on the night of 21/22 June, visited many times before but never seriously inconvenienced, Scholven-Buer and Wesseling, near Gelsenkirchen. Bob Woolf:

> 'The flak was very evident, very heavy, very solid, and we all had a few holes here and there. There was no warning before a sudden burst in fiery red and the rattling sound of shrapnel against the sides of the aircraft. Over a well-defended target there was no let-up of the continual flashes in the bomber stream, producing the inevitable bright cascade of colours when an aircraft was fatally hit and blossomed into a huge ball of flame, gradually falling earthward like some giant firework.'

Horne, Melrose, Gradwell and sixteen more of 9 Squadron were among the 123 Lancs heading for Scholven-Buer. At the other target, Wesseling, 44 Squadron lost six Lancasters, 49 Squadron also six, 57 Squadron lost five, 619 Squadron six, and 630 five. Altogether, thirty-eight Lancasters went down on the Wesseling raid out of 133, which was 29 per cent.

As the bomber flew, Wesseling was a few miles further along the route and, for no accountable reason, the Scholven-Buer force got off relatively lightly, losing only eight plus one crashed at home. Bob Woolf:

> 'The flak was very close and tossed us around but we were lucky and damage was not so severe. The night-fighters were having a go as well. We lost one over the target and another which was hit by flak and dived thousands of feet upside down. The pilot ordered the bomb aimer and second Dicky out but couldn't go himself as some of his crew were wounded. He got home on two.'

That was Horne, who had taken J-Johnny to Frankfurt on his first op (J's forty-eighth) three months before. After that other time on his third, when he was coned, hit by flak, attacked by a fighter and carried on while blinded with an unconscious rear gunner, he might have thought he'd had his share.

At 01.30 hours they were hit by flak and/or cannon fire. As both gunners were wounded, cannon fire from a fighter would be the best guess, but that hardly mattered as the aircraft fell almost vertically with the starboard inner engine and rear turret in flames. There was a second Dicky on board – what a baptism for him – and the bomb aimer was filling in for the regular man Sergeant Johnson, otherwise they were all the same men who had gone to Frankfurt in J.

Somehow, in a power dive, Horne managed to give the order to bail out. The two 'foreigners' did get out through the front hatch (the bomb aimer was killed) but the rest couldn't move. Skipper Horne, engineer Powell, navigator Shirley, wireless operator McReery, wounded gunners Morton and Parkes, had begun this dangerous life together and now would surely end it together. Their aircraft, hurtling ever faster to the ground, still carried the full bomb load.

They had been hit at 17,750ft. In Horne's own words: 'Captain finally managed to pull aircraft out of dive at 2,000 feet and flew back to England, landing at Wittering 04.05.' The ORB monthly summary was even more succinct: 'The Captain succeeded in bringing his aircraft back to base.'

Flight Sergeant Robert Hugh McFerran, later Pilot Officer, had already had his gong, his DFM, for the earlier incident. Pilot Officer William Robert Horne would get his DFC for this one.

In June 1944, Dougie Melrose and his crew flew ten ops, two air tests, two cross countries returning from diverted landings, one bombing practice and the recalled op to Watten, all in WS/J-Johnny. That made a total of fifteen for Melrose, fourteen for the crew, and eighty-four for the aircraft. The last four of the month were all French:

- Limoges – railways and the Gnome and Rhône factories where aero-engines were made for the Germans, also the war-film star, the Wehrmacht motorcycle with sidecar.

Here we see part of the Gnome and Rhône site before and after the bombing raid of 23 June. 'Bombs seen to hit markers, and large explosion seen', reported Peter Blackham. Melrose in J reported 'Marking and timing were good and bombing was well concentrated around the markers'. They were right.

- Prouville – V1 site near the coast, fiercely defended, where fifteen Lancs went down, mostly to night-fighters, including three from No. 9.
- Vitry-le-François – railway yards, described as 'uneventful trip'.
- Beauvoir – V1 site, 9 Squadron's first daylight raid since the early part of the war. No marking was seen, nothing was heard of the Controller, there were no fighters about, so they bombed anyway and came home in time for tea.

By 15 June, the Germans had fifty-five launching sites in France operational for the flying bomb, the V1, the buzz bomb, the doodlebug, and by noon of the 16th, they had fired almost 250 of them. They were unreliable at first, as likely to blow up on launch as to hit any precise target, but by midnight London had taken over seventy hits. The general effect of these unpredictable and somehow ghostly missiles was greater than the damage they did, on the people and on the military. Hitler's secret weapons became a top priority.

Clark flew his last and was through. He and his crew would last the war apart from his mid upper, Flying Officer Sid Matthews who, as Flight Lieutenant DFC, on his second tour, would lose his life in a most extraordinary episode (see Epilogue).

John Duncan proved he couldn't get enough of it by joining 83 Squadron pathfinders. Five of 9 Squadron's crews had failed to return in the month of June, three of them not on squadron long enough to get to know anyone, and there was a new CO, Wing Commander Jimmy Bazin, replacing Porter who would soon be back flying, as a raid manager with pathfinders but without Duncan's luck.

July began with cancelled ops on the 1st and 3rd, and a cancelled cricket match against RAF Woodhall Spa (617 and 627 Squadrons) on the 2nd, but J-Johnny was soon flying to more transport targets and V-bomb sites, starting with Creil. These secret-weapon ops were regarded with some misgivings; the bombers were attacking Hitler's last hope and crews expected tough resistance.

There was an extra dimension on this one for Melrose and J, because they were selected as one of the five aircraft of the first wave to stay over the target to examine results.

Creil itself, a small town with some industry and a railway junction sixty-five miles from the coast in the department of Oise, north of Paris, was not the important point. Nearby was a warren of rock caves and natural tunnels spread underground over thousands of yards which the villagers of St Leu d'Esserant had for years been using to grow mushrooms. The Germans saw ready-made, bomb-proof bunkers, decided that these were more important than the mushrooms of the local paysans, added some more facilities by way of railways and flak guns, and shipped in partly assembled doodlebugs and all the supplies that went with them.

Allied intelligence had identified St Leu as a flying bomb store in March, but it wasn't until June, when Enigma-decoded messages proved the intelligence, that priority was assigned.

The first to have a go was the USAAF on 27 June, doing some damage but nowhere near enough. More decodes gave Bletchley Park a clear understanding of how much material was being shipped in; matching these numbers with the latest V1 launches showed that St Leu must be the main depot. Local spies were seeing train-loads of equipment being moved into the caves and convoys of lorries leaving at night with their loads covered up.

There was no hope of collapsing the caves so the objective had to be to block the entrances and moonscape the surrounding area so that the caves were useless. Carrying the new Barnes Wallis super bomb, the 12,000lb Tallboy, 617 Squadron watched Cheshire drop his markers from 800ft and bombed between 01.31 and 01.44, 5 July. The rest of the force saw that too and attacked immediately, having already suffered several losses from night-fighters. Other large raids on railway targets in the same region had spread the fighters around but those attacks were finished now and St Leu was still going on. It was a clear, moonlit night; combats and combatants were visible all about the sky and the fighters did not have it all their own way.

On the night, the Lancaster gunners and intruder Mosquito crews claimed fifteen definites and two probables, but the bombers lost more, twenty-eight altogether, thirteen of them on the St Leu raid, with one from No. 9. Many went down on the way back and many more were attacked. Bob Woolf:

> 'One fighter had a crack at us, a Me410 but Ernie (Stalley, rear gunner) gave him a good squirt while we corkscrewed like hell and he broke off and we lost him. Guess we were lucky. We saw quite a few kites shot down.'

That 9 Squadron Lanc lost at St Leu had had a second Dicky on board; all eight men were killed. The practice of giving new pilots such risky trials by combat was about to end, but Russ Gradwell had had one with him, Flight Sergeant Tweddle, another future J man, and Gradwell would be taking the last 9 Squadron second Dicky with him the next time to St Leu, night of 7/8 July.

The caves had to be put right out of action. Buzz bombs were falling on London a hundred times a day. The raids so far had been good, but aerial reconnaissance showed great efforts at repair so, clearly, the job was not finished.

Gradwell had been on station since 10 February and he'd been pretty well everywhere, but not getting his turn in J until June. Counting those early French trips as ones rather than thirds, the second St Leu was Gradwell's 33rd op, the crew's 32nd. Officially, the skipper would be tour expired after this one, with his crew one short but they would go on another to finish together.

After all that, they had never been attacked by a fighter. Going to St Leu there were dogfights everywhere they looked, and bombers going down. Gradwell:

> 'There was nothing we could do except plough on and, about half-way between the coast and the target, it came to our turn. We were flying south east, into the moon. Anyone behind us would have seen the unmistakeable shape of a four-engined bomber against the circle of light.'

Les Sutton, rear gunner, had been a gamekeeper in civilian life. He had exceptional night vision, even for aircrew. His sudden imperative, shouted over the intercom, brought the instant, life-saving reaction that the best pilots had. 'Corkscrew port, go!' he almost screamed as he fired a burst from his guns.

They believed they'd avoided the worst of the fighter's fire. They knew they'd been hit, but not – yet – fatally. The fighter was still there, they had to assume, preparing a second charge and, as Gradwell put the Lanc through the rivet-straining torture of the corkscrew, another sound penetrated the thick atmosphere of anxiety inside the craft as the crew, invisibly, drew together in that moment all aircrew feared.

Somebody was laughing. It was Bill Best, the Canadian mid-upper. The fighter's cannon had ruptured the hydraulics in the turret and Best was slowly revolving, with nothing to do about it except see the funny side.

'Level out,' shouted Les Sutton in the rear turret. 'Level out, skip.'

This was not an orthodox order from a rear gunner, who in effect had command of the ship when being attacked from behind, but Gradwell did as he was told and watched as the fighter flew underneath the Lancaster, with the pilot seemingly dead in his seat. With the controls loose, the aircraft had gone into default mode and would fly straight and level until the petrol ran out.

The Lanc was flying in fully serviceable fashion and nobody was hurt, so Gradwell decided to carry on. They would rather be in the bomber stream with a u/s mid-upper turret than flying home alone with same. They reached the target, saw the markers, and the pilot took his last look about him before eyes-down on his instruments and flying to the instructions of his bomb aimer, Atch Atkinson.

Gradwell saw a flame in the port wing. It was only a little flame. They would bomb, turn for home, and put the fire out.

It was indeed a moonlit night and, with ex CO Wing Commander Porter as master bomber of a force of over 200 Lancs, the damage done in such clear conditions was sufficient to render the place unserviceable for some weeks. The cost, though, was high. Thirty-one Lancasters were shot down, plus one

DATE	AIRCRAFT TYPE & NUMBER	CREW	DUTY	TIME Up	TIME Down	DETAILS OF SORTIE OR FLIGHT	REFERENCES
7/1 (Contd)	LANCASTER W.4964	F/O. J.D. McLROSE	Bombing ST. LEU D'ESSERENT	2240	0215	Primary attacked. 0121 hrs. 11,750 ft. Bombing in area 1,000 yards long, 500 yards wide along left side of river., with much black smoke.	
		SGT. E. SELFE					
		P/O. J.W. MOORE (AUS)					
		F/O. S.A. MORRIS					
		F/O. RG. WOOLFE (AUS)					
		SGT. E. HOYLE					
		SGT. B.E. STALLEY					
	LANCASTER JA.690	P/O. R.S. GRADWELL	Bombing ST. LEU D'ESSERENT	2245		Aircraft missing.	
		F/L. J.W. OLMORE					
		SGT. T. LYNCH					
		P/O. P.E. ARNOLD					
		P/O. R.B. ATKINSON (CAN)					
		SGT. J.T. PRICE					
		SGT. W.F. BEST (CAN)					
		SGT. L. SUTTON.					
	LANCASTER DV.161	P/O. L.E. MARSH	Bombing ST. LEU D'ESSERENT	2245	0210	Primary attacked. 0120 hours. 14,800 ft. Bombing well concentrated.	
		SGT. C.L. HARRISON					
		P/SGT. A. BROWN (CAN)					
		F/O. J.A. CARR (CAN)					
		F/SGT. C.I.G. DAVIES					
		SGT. S.J. MARSHALL					
		SGT. F.R. RICHES.					
	LANCASTER JA.957	P/O. P.D. BLACKHAM	Bombing ST. LEU D'ESSERENT	2245		Aircraft missing.	
		SGT. J.D. MURRIE					
		P/O. J. WENGER (CAN)					
		P/O. J.D. ELPHICK (CAN)					
		P/O. G.A. WHITE (CAN)					
		SGT. V.C.A. STOKES					
		SGT. J.M. HICKEY (CAN)					

The 'easy' short trips over France didn't have the searchlights and efficient, well-practised flak batteries of the German ops, but the fighters, in large numbers and with no distance to travel to find the bombers, were more than making up for that.

crashed at home. Losing five were 207 and 106 Squadrons; losing three were 57, 50, 49, 44, and 9.

Peter Blackham and crew had been on squadron a day or two over five weeks. They took J-Johnny on their second op, J's seventy-second, to the D-Day guns, and to the flying bombs at Prouville. They'd also been to Ferme d'Urville, Argentan, Rennes, Orleans, Poitiers, Limoges, Vitry, Beauvoir, St Leu and again St Leu. It was the same crew throughout, with the engineer Sergeant J. D. Murrie the only one to escape death (evaded and got home). Crashing near the small commune of Ecquevilly, west of Paris, we can assume it was a night-fighter that caught them. They were quite an elderly crew – three in their mid-twenties, one married and over thirty, and four of them Canadians.

Gradwell's little fire was inside the wing. The fighter must have shot a hole in a tank and a spark from an engine had set it alight. Engineer Pete Lynch feathered both port engines and switched all the fuel off on that side, but no improvement came. While Gradwell fought to keep the Lancaster straight on the starboard engines, that flame burned brighter, and it was moving, very slowly to be sure, but moving, across the wing.

Lynch said: 'I think we've had it, skip'. He had been an apprentice at A. V. Roe, the firm that designed the Lanc. He could see in his mind's eye what was happening inside the wing. When the flame reached the main spar it might give up, or it might cut through. Gradwell:

> 'A Lanc with one wing was no good to anybody so I gave the order to bail out. Pete Lynch dished out parachutes to me and the second Dicky, Oldacre, and we put them on. Atch jumped, followed by Oldacre, Pete and Tommy (Arnold, navigator). Bill Best was still going round and round in his turret although not laughing so much by this time.'

Best had quite a bit to do before he could jump. There was a leather stirrup the gunners used to get a leg-up into the turret. He stuffed that into the machinery, stopped the rotation, and let himself drop down onto the fuselage floor, missing by a fraction the hole they hadn't realised they'd acquired, which was easily big enough to allow a man without a parachute to pass through. Jim Price, the wireless operator, met the gunners at the rear door, all with parachutes now, and called the captain to say goodbye.

Price made the mistake of picking up his chute by the release handle, which opened the package inside the aircraft. There was no spare, so he had to try and hope.

To keep the Lanc flying, the pilot needed to force the rudder full over to the right with his foot, while pulling the joystick similarly right over with both hands. He would have known about the twenty-year-old Pilot Office Leslie Manser of 50 Squadron who had been awarded the posthumous Victoria Cross for keeping a Manchester going, in a similar situation, after the Thousand Plan Cologne raid. The crew had all jumped but Manser could not.

Gradwell's Lanc was, as yet, not in such a bad way as Manser's Manchester had been, but the problem was the same. As soon as the pilot let go, the aircraft would power-dive to port and go into a spin, sticking him immovably inside a giant centrifuge.

Very gingerly, Gradwell got out of his seat and stood on one leg on the cockpit floor, his other foot stretched out to the rudder bar and his hands on the stick. All right so far. He could see the bomb aimer's hatch open, below and in front of him. It was simple, really. All he had to do was let go of the controls and simultaneously scramble the few feet to the hatch and leap out. Biggles would have done it. James Bond hadn't been invented yet but his was the sort of talent Gradwell felt he was lacking, not to mention parachute practice. The only instruction bomber crew received in this matter was in how to put one on and which handle to pull. Oh well.

One. Two. Three. Go.

> 'Next thing I knew, I was swinging from my parachute, descending in the moonlight towards a forest. I had no real idea how I came to be there, in the French July air. I landed in a heap on the ground, stowed away my chute and mae west, realised I was in enemy territory on my own and began imagining a German soldier behind every tree.'

Second Dicky Oldacre, a few miles away and, in varying circumstances, the rest of Gradwell's crew, were doing much the same except for Sergeant James Thomas Price, wireless operator, aged 21. He was lying dead in the same forest. His body would not be found until February 1945 and so, as far as 9 Squadron knew, all the company were lost without trace.

Gradwell knew he was somewhere north of Paris (in fact, near Beauvais in Oise, about fifteen miles back from the target), so fifty or sixty miles from the coast and an unknown distance from the Allied lines. He headed north west, stumbling about in the dark woodland, coming out on a lane that seemed to be going in the right direction. Jumping into a ditch as a truck went by, he saw it was full of German troops, obviously out looking for the crew of the fallen bomber.

The lane led to a village, where he heard shots. It would make sense, he thought, to lie low for a while, so he hid in a cornfield and went to sleep. The sun was up when he woke to the sound of a reaping machine. He could run for it; he could stay where he was until discovered; or he could step out and say 'Bonjour' to the reapers, whom he hoped were not of the grim variety. Gradwell:

> 'I knew French, a rare thing among aircrew, but I'd never tested it in a French cornfield before. "Hey, Messieurs. Je suis Royal Air

Force" was the best I could manage, and it didn't seem to be good enough. The two French farm workers looked blank. I pointed to the wings on my uniform and the letters RAF. "Ah!" they cried. "Vous êtes Royal Air Force." '

A conversation between the two reapers and a young couple who had turned up, contained bits that Gradwell could understand, including some mention of hiding:

'I was taken to a farm, a very big farm, and word had gone ahead of me because formed up outside the farmhouse were a dozen or more people, all anxious to shake hands and kiss both cheeks with the brave English flyer. As I worked my way down the line, I really did wonder at it all. If the Germans had arrived they'd have shot the lot of them. Anyway, with formalities complete and protocol satisfied, everyone went back to their work except for Madame Carron, the farmer's wife. Inside the house, she wanted to know if I was hungry. RAF procedure on an escape was to accept food only if you were desperate, because the French were themselves desperately short. So I said "Non, non merci, je suis bien".

Madame Carron gave me a nod and a smile and went down the cellar steps. She came back with the biggest steak I had ever seen, which she began to fry in about half a pound of farm butter on top of the wood-burning stove. While that was doing, she produced a gorgeous white loaf, more butter and a bottle of red wine. I hadn't seen white bread since the war broke out and I had a year's ration of butter in front of me.'

Purely out of politeness he got through this ordeal, including the steak which would have caused a riot outside the butcher's at home. As he sat back with a satisfied smile, Madame Carron placed a large bowl of strawberries on the table with a jug of fresh cream. Cream was illegal in Britain.

Gradwell had to be inspected and examined, to make sure he was not a German plant. The first inspector was a small boy who looked him up and down but didn't speak a word, followed by an elderly and rather up-market lady who spoke good English and could test her interviewee on Welsh geography (Gradwell came from Llandudno). At last she said 'I am sure you are an officer in the Royal Air Force. I will fetch assistance.'

Two men arrived, introduced themselves as M. Maigret and M. Thibou, and asked for the names of the rest of Gradwell's crew. Good. They had been found. Only one was missing. M. Maigret took out a camera. The Germans had revamped the French ID card so the RAF-issue photos carried in escape kits were u/s. Maigret and Thibou had their ID-card blanks straight from the printer, with official stamps supplied by a cleaning lady at German HQ.

Gradwell became Roger l'Anglais, which the Frenchmen thought highly amusing for a Welshman. Once again, Gradwell could only wonder at the spirits of these people. The Germans would not have hesitated for a moment in shooting them dead. It also crossed his mind that, although they might hesitate, the Germans would probably shoot him dead too.

There was still a war on at Bardney, whatever losses might be suffered, and Wingco Bazin was living up to his reputation as a slave driver. There was bombing practice every day. Ops were planned and cancelled, so more practice, until the show went live, 12 July, Culmont-Chalindrey, a railway target in the Haute-Marne.

A dozen squadrons were there and the pilots of 9 Squadron, all of whom followed the Controller's orders, complained about some of the others. Horne: 'Other crews were bombing without instructions from the Master Bomber and their photo flashes greatly impeded those who were trying to make a correct attack.' Melrose in J-Johnny: 'Controller's instructions not adhered to by many crews.'

Well, somebody certainly did good work. A local report stated that the depot was completely thrown down and everything was annihilated – rails, points, sidings, buildings turned into craters 25m deep, forty-two engines destroyed, and the near-by viaduct at Torcenay badly damaged. This witness estimated 1,500 bombs had fallen, killing only four civilians and two railway workers.

Bad weather diverted Melrose to an American base at Balderton, near Newark. Bob Woolf:

> 'It was always a delight to be diverted to American aerodromes because the breakfast we received was so much richer and more selective than anything the RAF could provide. Imagine, as many eggs as we could wish for, and a variety of food that otherwise we could only dream about. This was all served up with a warm welcome from the American personnel who always showed a great interest in us fellows and our Lancaster. When we landed and Doug opened the bomb doors, one Yank looked up in awe and shouted "Goddam, it's a flying bomb bay!"'

The invading Allies had met strong resistance at Caen, and a great deal of bombing and artillery fire had already reduced the city to rubble. Most of the civilian population had left, but not before a thousand and more had been killed. By this time, 18 July, there were really only Germans left around the place, refusing to give in to Montgomery's troops. A force of almost 1,000 bombers was sent to hit five fortified villages to the south of Caen, in a dawn raid. Melrose and his crew were on leave so J-Johnny was put in charge of a new pilot, Flying Officer Morrison. No fighters were seen and the flak was largely ineffective, so losses were few. When the Canadian 3rd Division moved up into the area, they found wrecked tanks everywhere,

Melrose and co after an American breakfast: from the left, Selfe, Hoyle, Melrose, Woolf, Morris, Stalley, Moore.

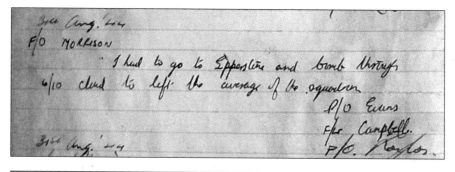

Wainfleet and Epperstone were practice bombing ranges.

many German dead, and many more wandering about, shell-shocked from the bombing and unable to fight.

This op was the first for No. 9 featuring novice pilots officially denied a second Dicky, although Morrison was not the first to go unofficially without one.

Aileen Walker was an eighteen-year-old WAAF serving in the 9 Squadron officers mess:

> 'The telephone rang and it was the CO. "Wing Commander Bazin here. Can you get Morrison for me?" I looked about and couldn't see him. Where's Eddie Morrison, I said. Somebody piped up "He's in the windsock". That's how naive I was and they knew it. Sorry, sir, I said. Flying Officer Morrison isn't here but you'll find him in the windsock.'

Of the fifteen pilots and crews arriving at 9 Squadron in the month of May, eight had been lost by mid-July and the other seven had been so busy that they were roughly halfway through their tours. Other, newer boys had not reached that far and some never would, including a crew on their third with a twenty-year-old skipper at Courtrai, or Kortrijk, Belgium. This was another railway target linking Germany and occupied Netherlands with northern France. The railway station, sidings and yards were flattened on the night of 20/21 July but so were many city buildings, the station being in the centre of town. Freshman Tweddle, or Tweedle as the WAAF typist styled him, was in J-Johnny and already on his fourth trip at the end of his first week, which was J's eighty-ninth.

The first raid on Kiel for well over a year, and the first big raid on a German city for two months, featured Melrose on J-Johnny's ninetieth and over 600 Lancs and Halifaxes, 23 July. The general opinion, given the cloud cover, was that the bombs hit the markers and so it was. The port facilities, U-boat yards and many other important areas of the city were severely damaged. Surprise, deception and radar-jamming were so effective in combination that the confused defences could only shoot down four Lancasters, but almost made it five. Bob Woolf:

> 'We'd dropped our bombs when suddenly we flipped upside down, and J-Johnny fell in a long spiral, and we remembered something similar happening to Horne at Scholven-Buer. We all thought we were goners, of course, except we had Doug and Ted, and they likewise managed to pull us out of it somehow and we levelled out flying low over Germany. Just where in Germany we didn't know, and the boys to tell us were somewhat hampered by an accident to a tin can, what you might call a jerry can, that we used to save us from venturing all the way to the Elsan at the back of the aircraft. The fluid in the can had spilled during our rapid descent and

saturated our Gee box and radio, so they were no help. The front half of J-Johnny was filled with Window flying about, and Jimmy Moore had lost his navigation chart.'

Aircrew were not permitted to take any private documents on an op, but navigator Moore had 'forgotten' to take a letter from home out of his pocket. It was three pages, written on one side only, so he pinned this useful paper to his little table and drew on it a map of the region, with latitudes and longitudes. After some calculation and inspiration, he gave Melrose a course for home. Once over the coast of England, navigation to base was no problem to the intrepid Australian. Woolf:

'At Bardney, in interrogation, the Intelligence Officer said "Where's your chart, Moore?". It was very hard not to laugh as Jim sheepishly presented him with a three page letter from Australia with Schleswig-Holstein drawn on the back.'

Flying Officer Melrose became Flight Lieutenant Melrose, leading A Flight of 9 Squadron on 25 July. In two of the busiest months of the war, if you survived, you could go from new boy to commander of half a squadron, in this case heading for Saint Cyr-l'École, a short step from Versailles. The historic airfield, scene of much aviation pioneering, and the Napoleonic military academy had become a German signals centre.

It was a daylight, up around 17.00, bomb from 10,000ft two hours later, back at around 21.45, which left behind a devastated target but also 300 civilian dead and very few houses left standing in the town, which was nine-tenths levelled.

Two bombs almost hit J-Johnny from above, something the crew would never have known about on a normal night op, and a flak shell came through the fuselage between the two Aussies, navigator and wireless op. When the ground crew patched up J, they recognised their colonial cousins by adding a kangaroo to the aircraft's already extensive nosepaint.

Next night they were on for the railways at Givors, a round trip of about nine hours to this town near Lyon. Most of them got there and did the job, but it was the weather that stayed in the memory. Bob Woolf:

'We were in electrical storms continually and the whole aircraft was alive with St Elmo's Fire. There were static sparks everywhere and the exterior of J-Johnny was covered with blue flames. Aerials, guns and wings were brilliantly alight. The props were just four circles of flame. Visibility was almost zero though enough for us to see three aircraft hit by flak and go down very close to us. There were hailstones. Rain poured into the aircraft making the floor awash with water. In such foul weather there would be no fighters about so the Master Bomber gave the order to turn on navigation lights. Immediately the surrounding sky was filled with red, green and white lights showing just how close and heavily populated the bomber stream was. Terrifying.'

Glaswegian Charles Scott took charge of J for her ninety-third, Stuttgart on 28 July, and they were the only 9 Squadron crew attacked by a fighter. They managed to shake it off, unlike the forty Lancasters that were shot down in the moonlight, mostly on the way in to the target when the fighters got among the bomber stream. This was the last raid in a series of three over five nights, aiming to stop the war output of Daimler-Benz, VKF and Bosch and eliminate the city as a centre of any kind of major activity, which they did.

What the Luftwaffe and all the flak gunners of Germany and Occupied Europe could not achieve, one of 9 Squadron's own almost succeeded in doing. A daylight op to Cahagnes, Normandy, in support of the advancing American army, was recalled two hours into the flight, when they were over the cloud-obscured target, with the signal 'Apple pie'. Quite a queue of J-Johnny alumni, past and future, landed back at Bardney with all their bombs still aboard – Horne, Taylor, Redfern, Scott, Tweddle/Tweedle, Pooley – but Flying Officer Macintosh, on his third trip, ordered his bombs to be jettisoned at far too low a height. The shrapnel from the explosion riddled the aircraft and put her out of action for almost a fortnight.

During the month of July, 9 Squadron lost eight Lancasters and crews, while ten new aircraft were delivered. LM221 went down first time out, at Culmont-Chalindrey, likewise JB116 at St Leu d'Esserant. LM220 arrived on the same day and lasted sixty-five ops.

CHAPTER 11

Ton-up Kids

Bois de Cassan V1 storage depot on 2 August, and Redfern reported: 'Leaders did not keep leading.' Horne said: 'Leaders split up before the target' but that was his last report. He was through. Flying Officer Horne DFC and Bar, shot up and wounded over Berlin in March, defying death in a power dive after being attacked at Scholven-Buer in June, captain of J's forty-eighth, had flown his last one. He had three of his original crew with him – engineer Powell, navigator Shipley, wireless operator McReery, and they had finished too. It would be too late for them to be called back for a second tour, and too early for them to be offered a tour continuation, as would happen later in the year to those who completed. For Horne and his three merry men, the war was over.

The date of 4 August would prove to be significant for 9 Squadron and, eventually, for Melrose and J-Johnny. For the first time, No. 9 flew with 617 Squadron only, twenty-seven of them together. The target was a difficult one, a railway bridge at Étaples, on the Canche estuary, so obviously it had to be a daylight raid. The Tallboy deep-penetration bomb was 617's weapon of choice but supplies had not arrived, so both squadrons went with the usual 1,000lb bombs to try to cut this German reinforcement supply line.

Flight Lieutenant Camsell, a future J man, thought his bombs had hit it. Ben Taylor hit it with three bombs, Charles Scott with four. Melrose saw bombs falling on either side of the bridge. Redfern saw bursts on the bridge, Pooley wasn't sure, Tweddle believed it was a successful attack, and Macintosh said that on leaving, the bridge was seen to have been destroyed. When the smoke cleared, it was still there. Bob Woolf:

'We had one touchy moment when a piece of flak hit our aircraft's left windscreen, shattering it and spraying particles over Doug and Ted Selfe. Ted had a few cuts and fragments in his eyes. I happened to have given Doug a good pair of sunglasses and he was wearing these in the bright sunlight and they probably saved him from worse injury. Of course, if the flak had been two inches to the left it would have taken his head off.'

Next day, 617 were beginning their Tallboy assault on the U-boat bases, starting at Brest, so 9 Squadron went back again to the bridge, fourteen of them on their own. Captains' reports were less optimistic than before, but when the smoke cleared this time, the job was seen to have been done. Bob Woolf:

'Much to our pleasure we had successful results with our attack. Having flown with No. 617 Squadron, the Dambusters, who missed the target, we are feeling rather full of ourselves at present. There wasn't much opposition, peculiarly enough, and only our squadron on it. Up to today, this squadron has operated on fifteen days out of

The railway bridge at Étaples, on the Canche estuary, during and after the second raid. This time when the smoke cleared, extensive damage could be seen, at both ends and in the middle. The craters on either side are from the previous day.

seventeen. Some of the chaps, armourers and so on, haven't been to bed for three days. Groundcrew never receive the recognition they deserve.'

Keeping a diary was not just frowned upon; it was strictly forbidden. Careless aircrew might take their diaries with them to the pub and have them stolen by secret agents. Or, worse, they might take them on ops, get shot down, and have to hand over their diaries to the Germans. Even so, quite a few aircrew did keep a diary, including Flying Officer Robert Woolf, Australian wireless operator:

> 'August 8th, Tuesday. Had the same kind of panic today as is usually found with these daylight tactical targets. Panic this morning, then we were on and off all day, and finally it was all scrubbed just as we were about to go out in the buses. It's a bad show. We get so hot and perspiring with all the rush and bother and then it's freezing cold when we get up high. The build-up of tension and then the deflation is hard to take.'

August 9th, Wednesday. Arose at 01.00. Take off scrubbed, back to bed. Up again, mad rush to take off at 07.00. Target was La Pallice on west coast of France. Trip went OK, not too much flak, over six hours in the air. Signals were a shambles due to badly planned briefing but no damage done. This was another joint Op with 617 who attacked the U-boat pens with Tallboys while 9 Squadron hit the oil storage with conventional bombs.

August 10th, Thursday. Our crew not on the battle order. Sammy (Morris, bomb aimer) went as spare bod with Squadron Leader Pooley (to Bordeaux oil depot). Our a/c J-Johnny became serviceable today and we went up for an air test. J has been repaired after some clot took her on ops and nearly blew her out of the sky. He jettisoned his bombs from a ridiculously low height and the shrapnel nearly wrecked our beloved plane coming very close to 100 trips.'

This is a 9 Squadron crew's view of La Pallice during the raid of 9 August.

It was the ninety-fifth, to Brest on 13 August. General Patton had issued his famous order 'Take Brest' on 1 August because the port could accommodate big ships direct from the USA and thus supply the invasion but, like all the U-boat bases, Brest had been classified as 'Festung' (fortress, to be held at all costs). Although the German forces were hemmed in on the peninsula, they were fighting with great resolve to prevent the harbour falling. As it turned out, the American army would not take Brest until 18 September, by which time the place was a wreck from bombs and shelling.

Meanwhile, the small target for J-Johnny and No. 9 was an old ship, a tanker that intelligence reports suggested was going to be sunk in an awkward place to block the harbour. While 9 Squadron saw to that, 617 Squadron were to attack an old battle cruiser, the *Gueydon*. Ben Taylor saw 'Bombing very concentrated around tanker and no scatter whatsoever.' Doug Melrose in J saw bombs 'Hit the stern of the ship which was burning well.'

The bomb-aimer's post-drop camera shot from J-Johnny shows bomb bursts on and around the target ships and nothing hitting the town.

They had to go back next day, with a much larger force. Once again 617 was after the *Gueydon*, still there obviously, and 9 Squadron was given another old warship to destroy for the same reason, the *Clémenceau*. Bob Woolf:

> 'Bombing was not as accurate as yesterday's. Don't know how 617 got on. I think Group is pitting 617 against 9 to see who is best. Flak was worse today and just as precise. We all had holes in our aircraft. It was a very scary effort.'

Woolf was almost right about 617 and 9, but it was not so much a competition to see which was better, as training in co-operation over precision targets, with one very special target in mind.

The tides of war seemed to have turned decisively in favour of the Allies. The armies had landed in southern France and were breaking out of Normandy. It was time to reopen the bombing offensive against Germany and a massive operation was mounted, over 1,000 bombers, against nine

The same raid a little later shows hits on the harbour wall and U-boat pens.

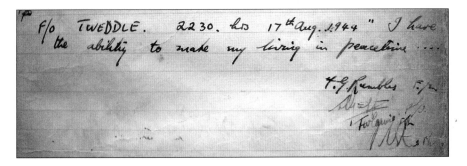

night-fighter bases in Belgium and the Netherlands as a preparation for that. As part of a force of 100 Lancs, 9 Squadron was assigned to the base at Gilze Rijen; Ben Taylor and crew were in J-Johnny. A Dutch eye-witness reported seeing the Lancs coming in at 3,000ft, and almost no bombs

At the front, three unnamed (and unsung) groundcrew. At the back, from left to right, bomb aimer 'Lucky' Holmes, wireless operator Ken Burns, rear gunner George 'Moose' Young, engineer Dennis Doherty, mid upper George Freeman, pilot Ben Taylor and navigator Jock Cunningham.

Gilze Rijen under attack. Redfern: 'Airfield well plastered with bombs.' Macintosh: 'Airfield appeared obliterated.' Taylor in J: 'Smoke to 8,000 ft.'

dropping outside of the aerodrome. He was right about the bombs but 9 Squadron pilots dropped from around 16,000ft and the photograph from a 9 Squadron crew backs up that rather more reliable impression.

The U-boat pens at La Pallice had been considered impregnable by the Germans, but that illusion had been destroyed by 617 Squadron's Tallboy bombs which had made big holes in the massively thick concrete roofs. The next attack on 16 August, did not add to the damage as the aiming point could not be seen though cloud. The Melrose crew were on their thirtieth. Bob Woolf:

> 'We were Controllers, with Dougie giving directions over the R/T and me confirming with my Morse key. They painted our tailfins white for the occasion, so that the Germans knew who was in charge. There was a fair amount of flak but not as accurate as our last two trips to Brest. J-Johnny's ninety-sixth – what a great plane we had.'

Skipper Melrose in his favourite seat, probably taken after La Pallice second time.

Actually, it was the ninety-eighth. Two ops had gone missing from the count, probably the Watten recall and one of the Berlin DNCOs so long ago.

Wing Commander Porter fell at last to the Germans, on 17 August while directing some mine-laying in the Baltic Sea at Stettin Bay, part of a diversionary operation in support of the main force attacking Stettin itself. Stories later circulated that he would not bail out, preferring death to capture, which was speculation based on his known, deep hatred of the enemy. In fact, his aircraft went down in flames and he and all his much decorated men – two DFMs and two more DFCs besides Porter's DFC, and a second bomb aimer, were killed.

Pathfinders of 97 and 83 Squadrons had dropped markers for the mine-layers, flying very low to get the fine accuracy required, in the face of an intense flak barrage. Porter, almost through his second tour, was master bomber. He was coned and hit, and radioed to the effect that the aircraft was being abandoned. Such a low altitude made it unlikely that anyone could have survived. The bodies of three of the crew were never found.

Canadian Flight Lieutenant Camsell took J-Johnny next, the thirtieth skipper so to do, at La Pallice again on 18 August, with 617 taking Tallboys for the pens, 9 Squadron taking a normal load for the oil storage. Everybody thought it a successful raid, with more Tallboy holes in the roofs and the oil depot a mass of smoke, according to Camsell.

La Pallice during the raid of 18 August, with hits showing on the pens below the U-boat dock.

The raid on the E-boat pens at Ijmuiden, 24 August, J-Johnny's 100th.

The same stratagem was deployed on 24 August, against the E-boat pens at Ijmuiden, also with excellent results. Camsell was in J-Johnny, on her hundredth trip although not so counted at the time. No. 9's bombs scored direct hits and Camsell, Morrison and Tweddle all saw Tallboys hit the pens. They would have had a special interest in this because, on the previous evening, an extensive programme of practice bombing had taken place. It was the squadron's first practice with the Tallboy.

Apart from another attack on a ship in Brest harbour, with Aussie Flying Officer Arndell taking J on his second and her one hundred and first, there were no more ops for No. 9 for a while. It was practice, practice, practice, with no inkling given of what it might be for. From their record, on operations and in the monthly inter-squadron bombing competitions on the ranges, No. 9 had been selected to join 617 as a Tallboy squadron, and they were the only two units in the RAF to carry this bomb in wartime.

'Upkeep', the bouncing bomb used against the dams, had not been judged useful against other kinds of target. A more orthodox Barnes Wallis design, the 12,000lb 'Tallboy' was a bomb like other bombs, using the same

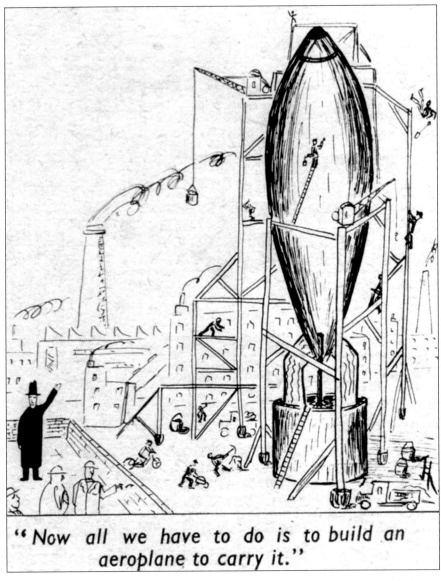

"Now all we have to do is to build an aeroplane to carry it."

The readers of Aeronautics *magazine in 1944 possibly thought this was science fiction.*

technology, except that it was the biggest thing that could possibly fit in a Lancaster's (modified) bomb bay and, it was believed, the heaviest thing the aircraft could possibly carry for any great distance. Its highly finished, streamlined body in special steel allowed it to penetrate deep into the ground so that, assuming it didn't actually hit a difficult target, such as a railway viaduct, it would explode beneath, bringing the structure down with earthquake strength tremors.

6th Sept. '44.

After practice bombing with A.V.M. Cochrane A.O.C 5 Group. F/O. Tweddle said " The A.O.C. said that I was one of the finest pilots he had ever flown with & had been instructing a long time before"

B. Taylor. F/C
Atkinson F/o

4th Sept. 1944   F/o Taylor

I went on a "discip" course at Brighton ("A" course naturally) + I did so much P.T. that it cost me over £50 to get unfit again.

Atkinson F/o
Aitken F/o.

The bomber chiefs saw it differently; as a means of battering the allegedly indestructible secret-weapon blockhouses and the naval bases hiding U-boats and E-boats beneath reinforced concrete twenty feet thick and more. Its first use, by 617 Squadron on a railway tunnel at Saumur in early June, had proved that point.

As well as practice in dropping dummy Tallboys, experiments were conducted to maximise fuel economy, with Lancs flying up and down for hours on end, trying out different combinations of propellor pitch and throttle settings. Wherever they were going to drop this bomb, it was obviously going to be somewhere far, far away.

CHAPTER 12

Adventures in France and Russia

In France the Resistance had reunited Atch Atkinson, bomb aimer, with Russ Gradwell, pilot, and relocated them to the tiny village of Villiers St Barthélemy, near Auneuil, where Marcel and Germaine Dubois had a three roomed cottage. Marcel, who did farm work, was an escaped POW so was himself always in danger. His wife, who had been a high-class Paris hat-maker, earned a few francs with her sewing skills. They shared their poor lot with the airmen, who did what jobs they could to help, including their own variation on the dawn raid, searching the woods for snails and mushrooms.

After six weeks of this, the airmen's identity was still a secret, as was that of the rest of the crew, minus Oldacre and Price, whom Maigret and Thibou had moved into another house in the village, where they all met up on Sundays.

One fine morning, Russ, Atch and Marcel, very local-looking locals, returned from their mushrooming and found a convoy of German trucks parked on the road. The soldiers, like soldiers everywhere and always, were concentrating on the matter in hand, which was breakfast. They had no business with three peasants wandering about, but a shock was in store over the peasants' own breakfast (mushrooms) when a stream of Germans marched past the window and set themselves up in next door's barn.

Two days later, with no alarms so far, Russ Gradwell was busy with the housework:

'I turned to find a large German soldier in the doorway with a couple of eggs in each hand. He wanted me to make an omelette for him. I waved at him to say, stay where you are, and went into the kitchen, and persuaded Germaine to cook the eggs, on her

164

condition that the soldier ate them outside. I called the man over and passed the eggs to Germaine. We stood there, enemies divided by a cottage doorway, although only one of us knew the whole of it, and conversed as best we could. My French was a lot better than his. He was a typical conscript squaddie. He didn't want a war. He didn't want to kill anybody or be killed for the fatherland. All he wanted was to get back to Dresden, to his wife, his family and his rose garden.'

Next day the Germans decamped and all of a sudden there were British troops in the street, a reconnaissance unit. The airmen were told to stay there until the infantry came through but, before that could happen, Maigret and Thibou picked up the six and took them to a château, where resided Madame Ravel, the upmarket lady who had checked Gradwell's geography. Gradwell:

'The table was set for a magnificent luncheon with different wines in their own glasses to accompany each course. At the end came brandy, real Cognac which we hadn't seen for years, and real coffee. Real coffee, made from coffee beans. We couldn't have been more impressed if she'd ordered up a Lanc to take us home.

In fact, our real journey home took us through parts where fighting had been fierce. In some places, the German bodies had been bulldozed to one side to open the road. In others, they still aimed their guns from their foxholes but could not see anything to shoot and never would. Once back in Blighty we found that, of course, we had been listed as missing and immediately sent off telegrams to our relatives, who had assumed – because there had been no news on the BBC of capture for all this time – that we had been killed.'

The two Canadians, Atkinson and Best, were repatriated and the other four were given the glad tidings that, although they were one and a half trips short, they were counted as tour expired and could transfer to non-operational jobs, which they did.

The battleship *Tirpitz*, sister ship to the *Bismarck*, had eight 15-inch guns, twelve 6-inch, sixteen 4-inch, eight quad torpedo tubes, a mass of anti-aircraft guns and 2,400 crew. Top speed was over 30 knots; range 9,000 miles at 19 knots.

That was why she was an ever-present threat. Surveillance of this titanic weapon was constant, as had been attempts to remove her from the war. Over thirty such attempts by 700 British, Russian and American aircraft and midget submarines had failed, partly because of her armoury, partly because of her armour, which was the main problem for an aerial attack.

From six-and-a-half feet below the waterline to the gun battery deck above, there was armour plating over a foot thick. Above that it was 6 inches thick. The plating protecting against bombs was less so, but the *Tirpitz* had been built to withstand anything an aeroplane could throw at her. But then, so had the *Bismarck*.

After the *Bismarck* went down, the *Tirpitz* hardly ventured to sea, staying otherwise in Norwegian fjords, now in Kaafjord, protected additionally by anti-submarine booms and nets, shore batteries of anti-aircraft guns, smokescreen gear and nearby squadrons of fighters. In Kaafjord, she was also beyond the reach of heavy bombers flying from the UK.

Arthur Harris later told the short story of how the job of sinking the *Tirpitz* was passed to him.

> 'Churchill rang me and said "I want you to sink the *Tirpitz*". I said "Why bother, Prime Minister? She's not doing any harm where she is". Churchill replied "I want you to sink the *Tirpitz*". So I sent the boys out and they sank the *Tirpitz*.'

The boys to fill the bill were those of Nos 9 and 617 Squadrons, and sending them out was not so simple. There was time pressure for as the war swung more in the Allies' favour, the likelihood increased of *Tirpitz* being sent into battle, so she needed to be tackled before the long Norwegian winter's darkness postponed the attack to 1945.

Tallboy was the only weapon that could defeat the ship's armour, but with one of those on board and full standard and extra tanks, even with the mid-upper turret removed, the total weight of a Lancaster would be 70,000lbs, which was 5,000lbs over the designed maximum.

In any case, two squadrons of Lancs flying to Norway would be spotted. The *Tirpitz*, and the fighter protection, would be waiting, ready. A high-level approach, needed to keep the bombers away from the ship's armament, would make hitting the target even more difficult.

Kaafjord was about 600 miles from Archangel, in the land of the Russian ally. Stalin had been keen on sinking this battleship that overlooked his supply convoys. He would surely be equally keen on a plan in which he could be involved.

Alas, Plan A was a bit crazy. The bombers would fly to Scotland, top up on fuel, fly through the night, attack the *Tirpitz* at dawn, fly on to an airfield near Archangel and, after 2,000 miles, land, recuperate, and fly home.

This plan was briefed to the two squadrons on 8 September. Most of the Lancs would take the Tallboy; some the untried 'Johnny Walker' mine (no relation), a self-powered, roaming mine that – allegedly – rose and fell in the water, 'walking' here and there if it didn't hit anything. It would have been better named the Heath Robinson mine, and aircrew noted that its power unit was a bottle of compressed hydrogen, and that they were to jettison these new devices if they came under attack. So which order came first, 'corkscrew' or 'jettison'? Mick Maguire:

'If by some remote chance one of them had hit the *Tirpitz*, the armour plating would have shrugged it off. It had a very small

These low level photographs of the Tirpitz *were not what the bombers would see. To them, the mighty ship would be no bigger than a matchstick, firing on all guns, with a smoke screen.*

charge. I thought they were a bloody waste of time and it would have been far better to have all the Lancs carrying Tallboys.'

The weather forecast rendered Plan A inoperable. September tended to be cloudy in those far northern parts, and it would be disheartening to fly all that way to find the target invisible. Plan B was to miss Scotland, fly directly to Archangel, and stay there until a clear day occurred. The bomber crews heard about this around midday on 11 September, along with orders to pack some kit for a few days in Russia. Takeoff would be at 5pm. They would reach an island called Yagodnik, in the river Dvina, which had a grass airfield, at dawn. If it was a fine afternoon, they would attack the *Tirpitz*.

The task force was twelve Tallboy Lancasters from No. 9, fourteen from 617, six from each with a dozen of the mines, and two unarmed B24 Liberators of 511 Squadron, Transport Command, carrying the groundcrews and HQ officers, all in the charge of the Bardney station commander, Group Captain McMullen. An extra Lancaster of 463 Squadron had cameras and a film crew, and a Mosquito of 540 Squadron was for reconnaissance and additional photographic duties. Just short of 300 RAF men were off to the Arctic Circle, to sink the *Tirpitz*.

The Liberators would need to add fuel at Lossiemouth so they set off first from Bardney, followed by 9 Squadron led by Wing Commander Bazin, plus the camera Lanc. Wing Commander Tait led 617 from Woodhall Spa.

First disaster: one of No. 9's Tallboys worked itself loose and had to be jettisoned, and the aircraft came home. Apart from that, on the longest fully loaded flight ever attempted by Bomber Command in this war, hardly anything happened until they got there, the exception being one 9 Squadron Lanc with an engine bursting into flames about seventy-five miles from the Norwegian coast. The engineer extinguished the fire, feathered the prop, and on they went on three.

Armaments officer at 9 Squadron, Flying Officer Mick Maguire, presides over a raid's worth of Tallboys at Bardney.

All the crews were expecting visibility six miles at Archangel. The Russians had forecast ten-tenths cloud there, down to a few hundred feet, with heavy squalls, but that information never found the bombers, likewise the radio navigational signals, because frequencies did not match. Navigators had been issued with army maps from the First World War, which didn't help much while flying over infinite stretches of pine forest and marshland largely hidden in cloud.

Bob Woolf, flying with Melrose in J-Johnny, believed to be on her century mark:

> 'We encountered extremely bad weather on route and for the last hour of the flight cloud was down to 300 feet combined with rain. None of the promised radio aids were available and the navigating was done by means of dead reckoning and map reading. Jimmy (Moore, navigator) and Sammy (Morris, bomb aimer) did a wonderful job and Doug flew so well considering the poor weather. We ultimately landed at Yagodnik after 10.25 hours in the air. A very exhausting time in a tin tube.'

No navaids, the filthy weather and empty fuel tanks led thirteen Lancaster crews astray. They had been told only about one airfield, so when they saw another they thought it was the right one. Some got down all right, some didn't. By a miracle, nineteen Lancasters landed safely where they were supposed to, at Yagodnik. Eleven landed some miles away at Kegostrov, one of which was permanently u/s. Otherwise the score was: two at Vascova of which one was u/s and one was stuck in a bog. Two at Onega could be made serviceable, but the four at Belomorsk, Chubalo-Novolsk, Molotovsk and Talagi, all rather wild spots even by local standards, could not. Somehow, with the help of Russian search parties, all the crews were assembled at Yagodnik over the following day, 13 September.

Apart from a brass band to play the heroes in, the Russians had supplied very little except for voracious bed bugs in the billets, which included a moored paddle steamer and some subterranean huts. Every aircraft needed work and petrol supplies were quite inadequate. Over two days and nights, groundcrews, augmented by well-meaning Russians, struggled to get as

F/o. Morrison, after a forced landing in a swamp in Russia, states in his report on the incident "I touched down lightly on three points"

S. Taylor. F/o.

many Lancs as possible into an airworthy state, robbing the crashed ones for spares.

The opportunity thus arose for the Russians to provide entertainment for the aircrew. There were films, very long films in Russian, and a dance, also without subtitles, and a mess dinner. The meal was raw fish, borsch and roast meat not identified, and an endless river of toasts in vodka and red wine, to King George, General Secretary Stalin, President Roosevelt, Winston Churchill, the Royal Air Force, the Red Air Force, Bomber Command, 9 Squadron, 617 Squadron, Yagodnik aerodrome, the Avro Lancaster, Barnes Wallis, Uncle Ivan Cobleigh and all.

The first attack on Thursday 14 September turned into a scrub because of the weather. Next day they were on – ten Lancs of 9 Squadron, seventeen of 617 Squadron, twenty of them with Tallboys and the rest with Johnny Walker mines.

Force A, the Tallboy aircraft, began taking off at 09.30 local time, 617 Squadron first. All were up and on their way soon after ten. From the operation report:

> 'Force A was to be disposed in a height band of 14,000–18,000 feet and attack in four waves of five aircraft in line abreast, each wave occupying 1,000 feet in height with a distance between waves of a few hundred yards … (At a) point 140 miles due south of the target … the three 9 Squadron wind finders were to be three minutes ahead … approximately 60 miles from the target Force A was to lose 2,000 feet to gain speed, this distance being considered the limit of surprise.
>
> The operation proceeded as planned until the final run up to the target, when a large alteration of course was necessary as (the Force) was several miles west of track. On the run up a small amount of low cloud drifted over the fjord which, together with the smoke screen, prevented some crews from bombing on their first run. Two 9 Squadron aircraft (C & V) had their bombs hung up and did several runs.'

Most of the Tallboy aircraft attacked from astern of the battleship, about three miles above her, looking at smokescreens, a sky filled with flak and shellfire, occasional visible pieces of ship and flashes from the big naval guns. It was all over in thirteen minutes.

WS/J, Flight Lieutenant Melrose bombed at 10.55 from 14,900 ft. 'Stern of ship seen in sights. Five Tallboys seen to burst between ship and boom.'

WS/U, Flying Officer Tweddle; 10.56, 15,800 ft. 'A large column of brown smoke rising from target.'

WS/L, Squadron Leader Pooley; 10.57, 14,000 ft. 'Three bursts seen; one looked as if it might be a possible hit.'

WS/B, Flying Officer Taylor; 10.57, 12,500 ft. 'Two Tallboys seen to explode, one of which seemed close to the ship.'

WS/P, Flying Officer Jones; 11.00, 12,500 ft. 'Results not seen. One plume of smoke seen at estimated position of ship.'

WS/O, Wing Commander Bazin; 11.04, 15,000 ft. 'Smoke started at 10.55.'

WS/C, Flying Officer Dunne. 'Hung up, Tallboy returned to base'.

WS/V, Flying Officer Scott. 'Target not attacked. Tallboy would not release in spite of making four runs over target. It eventually fell off through bomb doors.'

The other two 9 Squadron aircraft had Johnny Walker mines.

The record shows that Melrose in W4964 WS/J was first to drop, followed a minute later by Tweddle and five of 617 Squadron, led by Wing Commander Tait. Tait never saw Melrose and Melrose said that, regardless of the official timings, he saw Tait bomb a few seconds before him. None of the 617 pilots reported a hit of his own, only some near misses. In among the smoke and explosions, it was generally thought that there had been one or perhaps two good hits.

Intelligence confirmed it as one hit and three near misses and the 5 Group 'Plot of calculated strike position of Tallboy bombs' showed that, of the first bombers, Tait had fallen short by 700 yards, Oram (617) was 450 yards to port, Stout (617) had overshot by about 350 yards and Pooley (9) was

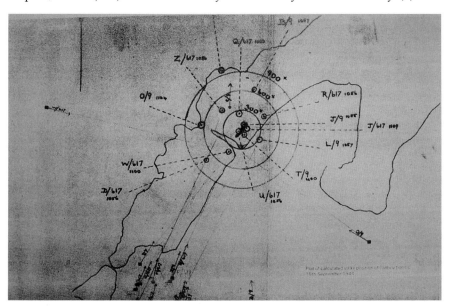

The chart shows WS/T bombing at 11.00 and near-missing, but WS/T was the American pilot Ed Stowell carrying mines. The only 9 Squadron aircraft to bomb at 11.00 was WS/P, Flying Officer Jones, so it has to be assumed that P goes for T as a clerical error on the chart. What happened to the Johnny Walker mines is not recorded in any detail. Some fell in the fjord. Some fell on the land. None hit the target.

300 yards to starboard on dry land. Howard (617) was nearer, less than 300 yards off the port bow.

Pryor (617) and his bomb aimer, Pilot Officer Hoyland, missed by a whisker. Their Tallboy, dropped at 10.56, exploded just off the starboard side, a minute after another of these fantastically terrifying weapons, surely unknown to – and unimagined by – the German sailors, smashed through the foredeck, dropped at 10.55 by Flight Lieutenant Dougie Melrose and bomb aimer Flying Officer Sammy Morris, from W4964 WS/J-Johnny Walker.

Every Lancaster was hit by flak and/or developed mechanical faults, except for J-Johnny and one other. At least there had been no fighters.

Norwegian intelligence and German coded messages gave different accounts of the success of Operation Paravane. In sum, one hit had drilled through the foredeck at an angle and come out of the ship's hull near the

YEAR 1944		AIRCRAFT		PILOT, OR 1ST PILOT	2ND PILOT, PUPIL OR PASSENGER	DUTY (INCLUDING RESULTS AND REMARKS)
MONTH	DATE	Type	No.			
—	—	—	—	—	—	— TOTALS BROUGHT FORWARD
SEPT	9	LANCASTER	J	SELF.	CREW + 1	AIR TEST & BOMBING
	10	LANCASTER	J	SELF.	CREW +	BOMBING (141")
	11	LANCASTER	J	SELF	CREW	To ARCHANGEL (RUSSIA)
	15	LANCASTER	.J	SELF	CREW	OPS Nº 31 "TIRPITZ" ("ALTEN FJORD NORWAY)
						JOHNNIE'S 100ᵗᵗ TRIP + TALLBOY
	17	LANCASTER	J	SELF	CREW + 2	FROM ARCHANGEL (RUSSIA)
	22	LANCASTER	J	SELF	CREW + 15	TO EXETER & RETURN
	23	LANCASTER	J	SELF.	CREW	OPS Nº 32 DORTMUND - EMMS
						CANAL (TALLBOY brought back
	30	LANCASTER	M	SELF.	CREW + M	BOMBING landed swindon +
						* Lyneham 141" @ 20,000' B.S.E50'
				Summary SEPT 1944	1. LANCASTER	
				Unit N⁹ 9 SQDN.	2. _____	
				Date 1/10/44	3. _____	
				Signature J. Melrose ofa.	4. _____	
					T. A. Bazin	W/CMDR O.C. 9 SQDN
				GRAND TOTAL [Cols. (1) to (10)] 6 45 Hrs. 15 Mins. 66650		TOTALS CARRIED FORWARD

Melrose's logbook showing the Tirpitz *op.*

waterline before exploding some distance away. Had it exploded inside the ship it might well have sunk her.

On *Tirpitz*, the heavy gun ranging officer was Lieutenant Willibald Völsing:

'What we had expected happened on the 15th September. Twenty-five 4-engined Lancasters, so-called "Flying Fortresses" (sic) were announced over the PA system by our own observation posts (on the mountains). We opened up with our 38cm guns at 25km. The attack was thus interrupted because they had expected no firing at that range. A direct hit caused the fore part of the ship severe damage. From that time we could only operate 3 nautical miles from the coast, i.e. Tirpitz was no longer any use on the high seas. During this raid, on the spit of land where we lay an un-exploded bomb had dropped* – 9 metres long. When we saw this 6 tonne bomb, it was obvious that a direct hit from a bomb of this size would mean the end of our ship.'

*This was probably ex-J man (Berlin, March) Squadron Leader Pooley's bomb, which seemed to have been the only one to hit dry land near the ship.

The boys hadn't sunk *Tirpitz* and now there was no need to, but only the Germans knew that. They also knew that sailing her down the coast at 10 knots for repairs was not an option, and the repairs would take months anyway. Better to leave her in the fjords, still a great threat so long as the Allies didn't find out she was u/s for war, and therefore still a drain on resources.

There would be two more raids by 9 and 617 before she was sunk at last, but J-Johnny didn't go, being retired by then.

Indeed, J's last five ops were bound to be something of an anti-climax after *Tirpitz* although, being all in Germany, it didn't seem like that at the time, nor was the tale of life and death finished yet.

Harris had been put back in complete charge of Bomber Command, no longer under Einsenhower. Orders would still come from above on special occasions but generally the emphasis was back on German industrial targets. The fighters were no longer the menace they had been but these ops were still very hard going.

First up was an evening raid, takeoff in daylight at seven. Melrose led A flight to aqueducts near Münster on the Dortmund-Ems Canal. It was the last time that all the original crew flew together, and the last time they flew in the beloved plane. Assuming they got back, Melrose would be up to thirty-two ops, including twenty-four in WS/J, and the others all would have thirty or more. After this one, they could wave goodbye.

The Dortmund-Ems was a ship canal, not like the UK narrow-boat meanders, and was hugely important to the Germans. The bombers had breached it and drained it on several occasions and they would do it again tonight, with a force of 136 Lancasters, seventeen with Tallboys from Nos 9

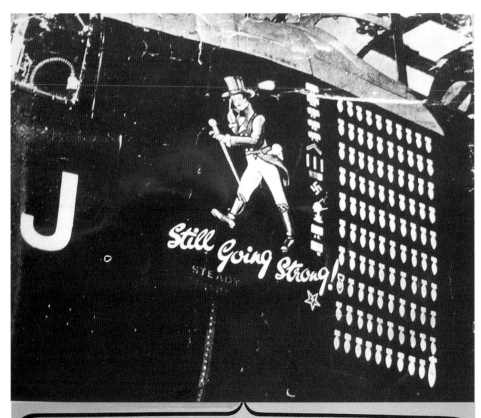

Rolls Royce took some of the credit for J's success in their advertising, and the makers of Johnny Walker whisky wrote a congratulatory letter saying they had taken the liberty of forwarding a case of one dozen bottles of Black Label.

istian names: JAMES DOUGLAS   Surname: MELROSE.

k: FLYING OFFICER(ACTING FLIGHT LIEUTENANT)   Official number: 51126

roup: 5 GROUP, BOMBER COMMAND.   Unit: NO. 9 SQUADRON.

251

Total hours flown on operations:..........171.45

Number of sorties.........................32

Total hours flown on operations since –
receipt of previous award...................N/A

Number of sorties since receipt of
previous award..............................N/A

Appointment held.......................... Pilot. Captain of aircraft.

Recognition for which recommended..........Distinguished Flying Cross.

Particulars of meritorious service for which the recommendation is made:–

    This officer has completed 32 successful sorties as Captain of aircraft. His
sorties have included attacks on heavily defended targets in Germany and on precision targets
in occupied Europe, by day and by night. He also played a prominent part in the recent attack
on the German battleship "Tirpitz".

    On every occasion Flight Lieutenant Melrose has shown courage and
determination of the highest order, together with the greatest keenness to operate as often
as possible. He has several times acted as deputy leader of the Squadron on daylight
operations, and more than once as leader, a task he has fulfilled most successfully. The
Bombing results achieved by his crew have been consistently successful and are proof of
Flight Lieutenant Melrose's high standard of captaincy. He has, in fact, set the very highest
example, both in the air and on the ground, not only to his crew, but to the whole Squadron.

Date: 12th October, 1944.

                     WING COMMANDER, COMMANDING
                     R.A.F. STATION, BARDNEY.

Remarks by Base Commander.

    A consistently successful and determined captain. Strongly recommended.

Date: 19th October, 1944.

                     AIR COMMODORE, COMMANDING
                     53 BASE, R.A.F. WADDINGTON.

Remarks by Air or other Officer Commanding

    Recommended for an award of the Distinguished Flying Cross

Date: 3.11.44

                     AIR VICE-MARSHAL, COMMANDING
                     NO. 5 GROUP, ROYAL AIR FORCE.

Citation for the Distinguished Flying Cross, Dougie Melrose.

and 617. Most went for the canal banks at Ladbergen, while No. 9 went for the aqueducts. Bob Woolf:

> 'There was a panic to get airborne. We didn't have enough Tallboys on the station so we and three other crews went to Woodhall Spa (617 Squadron) to pick up our bombs and go to the briefing, which was a shambles as far as I was concerned with no gen at all for wireless. It was throwing it down as we took off and things got worse over the Channel as we saw two kites go down together. They must have collided. We saw the yellow ball of flame slowly falling, leaving a streak of fire hundreds of feet long, before being scattered in a bright glow along the coastline.'

When they got there, they found ten-tenths cloud. It was pointless dropping Tallboys if you couldn't see the target, so they brought their Tallboys home. For the Melrose boys, that was it. They had achieved where so many had failed, a tour of bomber ops, and had stayed alive for the four months it had taken to do it.

Another ex-J crew on the same op only managed three-and-a-half months. Flight Lieutenant Charles Scott and his crew failed to return from Münster. Their tour ended on the way home, over Gelderland. Scott had twenty-eight ops, the rest had twenty-seven.

From the left: back row, Sergeant Jack Simkin, flight engineer; Flight Sergeant Louis Harding, navigator (father of the entertainer Mike Harding); Flight Sergeant Langley, bomb aimer (survived as POW); Sergeant Les Hambly, rear gunner. Front row, Sergeant Maurice Hayward, wireless operator; Flight Lieutenant Charles Scott, pilot; Sergeant Frank Saunders, mid upper gunner.

Scott had come on squadron with four other skippers; two were still there. Scott and his crew had done the French targets – Poitiers, Aunay-sur-Odon, Limoges, Creil and so on. They'd had their first aerial combat in J-Johnny at Stuttgart. They'd been to the U-boat pens and the Étaples bridge, and Russia. Two more to do, after this one.

A newish bomb aimer on squadron, called Jim Brookbank, had a captain by the same name:

> 'Our skipper was Flying Officer W. Scott. He, and all of us, were posted as killed, printed in the 5 Group news sheet, instead of Flight Lieutenant C. B. Scott's crew. When the Service Police came to clear up our quarters and started taking our stuff, it was a stroke of luck that some of us dead men were there or the telegrams would surely have gone out to the wrong crew's families. A few days after that I was walking down Lincoln High Street and a lad I knew from training in Canada came up to me and asked me what I was doing there, seeing as I was dead.'

It was Karlsruhe on 26 September. For J-Johnny, in the hands of Flying Officer Arndell, it was her 104th. 'Fires were seen covering a large area.'

Kaiserslautern was a much smaller target for the night of the 27th, a town of 70,000 in Bavaria with steelworks and factories. Arndell took J-Johnny again. 'Fires were seen to be numerous and especially well concentrated around the church spire.' More than a third of the town was destroyed in its only mass attack of the war.

On October 5 eighteen of No. 9 went on a daylight to Wilhelmshaven, where the war had begun for the squadron in 1939. In ten-tenths cloud, Redfern, in J-Johnny Walker on her 106th, observed no results.

Bremen on the 6th was the last and best of over thirty raids on this city. On a clear, moonlit night, 250 Lancasters destroyed around 5,000 houses and fifty factories, including some of Focke-Wulf and Siemens, for the loss of five aircraft. It was the last too for J-Johnny, driven there and back on her 107th and final journey by Flying Officer Alf Jeffs: 'Fires were seen covering large area between the river and the marshalling yard.'

It was retirement at last. W4964 WS/J-Johnny Walker was going strong no more, one of over seventy Lancasters delivered to 9 Squadron in 1943. All of those seventy-odd, every one of them, had been lost except for one transferred to other duties, J-Johnny, and her near equal, EE136 WS/R Spirit of Russia with ninety-three ops, that went on to reach 109 with 189 Squadron.

W4964 had flown eleven Berlins, all four Hamburgs, Peenemünde, all the Ruhr targets, *Tirpitz* – outlasting the 1943 intake plus a great many of the 1944 new ones, and she'd outlasted many of the men who had flown in her.

W4964 was allowed to keep her mid-upper turret, her kangaroo patch and her decorations won during her long and gallant flying life. She was

"A" FLIGHT.

MK.	NBR.	LTR.	CAPTAIN.	SQR.	F/ENGINEER.	NAVIGATOR.	A/BOMBER.	W/OPERATOR.	M.U. GUNNER.	REAR GUNNER.
3.	LB. 146.	"A"	F/O. SCOTT(S)	3.	SGT. BAKER.	F/S. HAYDON.	SGT. BROCKBANK.	F/S. MOSSINSON.	SGT. GRAY.	SGT. JONSON.
1.	LM. 289.	"B"	F/O. FOLLETT(S)	2.	SGT. FLANAGAN.	F/O. HOWARTH.	F/O. MITCHELL.	SGT. STEVENSON.	SGT. VOTER.	SGT. LONG.
	LM. 548.	"C"	F/O. BUCKLEY(S)	1.	SGT. DAVES.	S/LD. SHUTLER.	F/O. NOLAN.	F/S. MOODY.	SGT. POUND.	SGT. GANTENWALTER.
	NF. 937.	"E"	F/O. ARUNDELL(S)	4.	SGT. JONES.	F/S. CANTRELL.	F/O. FOSTER.	SGT. MEADS.	SGT. BROWN.	SGT. RICHARDS.
	LB. 213.	"F"	F/O. READ(S)	-	SGT. WHITE.	SGT. FEATHERSTONE.	SGT. WILLIS.	SGT. McARDLE.	SGT. DONNWELL.	SGT. LEWZED.
	LB. 596.	"H"	F/O. REARS(S)	35.	SGT. SCOTT.	SGT. ALTON.	F/S. BATES.	SGT. CURRIGAN.	SGT. BRACE.	SGT. WROTH.
	W. 4964.	"U"	F/O. REDFERN(S)	35.	SGT. WILLIAMS.	SGT. COOPER.	F/O. HULL.	SGT. ROBERTS.	SGT. BOAD.	SGT. TUBB.
	LL. 845.	"J"	F/O. JEFFS(S)	3.	SGT. HIGGINS.	SGT. MOUSLEY.	SGT. FISHER.	SGT. McMILLAN.	SGT. THOMAS.	SGT. SWANN.
	LM. 745.	"M"	F/O. MARSH(S)	12.	SGT. HARRISON.	F/S. BROWN.	F/O. CARR.	S/LD. DAVIES.	S/O. MARSHALL.	SGT. SEELE.

"TABLE."

| | | | P/O. WILLIAMS(S) | 7. | SGT. LEVIS. | SGT. LOCKERBIE. | SGT. GOLD. | SGT. SKINNER. | SGT. THOMSON. | SGT. KELLY. |

"B" FLIGHT.

MK.	NBR.	LTR.	CAPTAIN.	SQR.	F/ENGINEER.	NAVIGATOR.	A/BOMBER.	W/OPERATOR.	M.U. GUNNER.	REAR GUNNER.
	NP. 929.	"P"	F/L. CAUSELL(S)	19.	SGT. ANDREWS.	SGT. ASLIN.	F/O. THOMAS.	F/S. WEBB.	SGT. HERBERT.	F/S. BOW.
1.	LM. 220.	"?"	F/O. AYRTON(S)	3.	SGT. HUDDLESTONE.	SGT. HEWES.	F/S. BARDSLEY.	SGT. SMITH.	SGT. CHALGRAFT.	SGT. DAVIES.
3.	LB. 136.	"R"	F/O. WATERS(S)	1.	SGT. BOOTH.	SGT. MILLS.	SGT. COXON.	F/S. FRENCH.	SGT. JONES.	F/L. GARFIEL.
1.	LB. 736.	"S"	P/O. COSTER(S)	2.	SGT. PINNING.	F/S. BLACK.	F/S. BOAG.	SGT. EAST.	SGT. MORRISON.	SGT. JONES.
3.	LM. 448.	"T"	F/O. REES,(S)	4.	SGT. MAYHEW.	SGT. HAMMOND.	F/S. McINTOSH.	SGT. MORROW.	SGT. KING.	SGT. HERRELL.
1.	LD. 198.	"U"	F/O. HARPER(S)	2.	SGT. WHITWORTH.	F/O. HOME.	F/S. WILLIAMS.	SGT. IRWIN.	SGT. McCANN.	SGT. HERRELL.
	LM. 594.	"D"	F/O. DAVIES(S)	1.	SGT. RICE.	SGT. WARD.	W/S. HARRISON.	F/S. NEWMAN.	SGT. MARR.	SGT. WRIGHT.
	LM. 713.	"Z"	F/O. NEWTON(S)	3.	SGT. GREGORY.	SGT. GRANT.	SGT. MANN.	SGT. KELLY.	SGT. COOPER.	SGT. PHILLIPS.
3.	LM. 715.	"O"	F/O. JAMES(S)	-	SGT. POCOCK.	F/S. WATT.	F/S. CURRIE.	W/S. REDWOOD.	W/O. LEGG.	SGT. READY.

Officer i/c flying........W/C. BAZIN.

(sgd) J.M. Bazin,
WING COMMANDER, COMMANDING
NO. 9 SQUADRON,   R.A.F.

Redfern, into his second tour on thirty-five sorties, skippered J on her penultimate. Jeffs was on three, and would take J on her last. Sticky Levis was still around, in the spare crew.

J's nosepaint after Tirpitz showing 100 ops, four DFMs and three DFCs earned by crew but not yet Melrose's and Morris's, searchlight for Mick Maguire's shooting, various stripes for hurts received, more medal ribbons, a Russian star, two kangaroos, a swastika for a fighter down and a chevron to denote a year's active service – not many Lancasters got that one.

Melrose and all the original crew with J, just before retirement.

pensioned off to a new career, dull but safe, as Ground Instructional Airframe 4922M. Eventually scrapped, a centre section of the fuselage was used for many years as a shed by a farmer. You can still see it, if you go to Newark Air Museum.

Epilogue for the J Men

In round numbers, RAF Bomber Command in World War Two lost 9,000 aircraft of all types while flying 300,000 sorties and dropping one million tons of bombs and mines. The busiest months were August 1944 (20,659 sorties) and March 1945 (21,341). The quietest was November 1939 with nineteen. About ninety per cent of the bombing effort happened after February 1942 and Harris's appointment. Of the seventy German cities attacked, only twenty or so were left with better than half their buildings standing.

Von Rundstedt, commander of the last great German offensive against the invading Allies, said: 'Air power was the first decisive factor in Germany's defeat. Lack of petrol and oil was the second, and the destruction of railways the third. The principal other factor was the smashing of the home industrial areas by bombing.' He might have saved himself a few words. The second, third and other factors were all part of the first.

Number 9 Squadron flew approximately 6,000 sorties. During the 2,500 in Wellingtons, over 100 aircraft were lost. During the 3,500 in Lancasters, approaching 200 aircraft were lost, one every seventeen-and-a-half ops and one of the largest totals of Lancasters lost by a single squadron.

C-in-C Air Chief Marshal Sir Arthur T. Harris:

> 'We are ending this war on the threshold of tremendous scientific developments – radar, jet propulsion, rockets and atomic bombing are all as yet in their infancy. Another war, if it comes, will be vastly different from the one which has just drawn to a close. While, therefore, it is true to say that the heavy bomber did more than any other single weapon to win this War, it will not hold the same place in the next.'

In those few years of World War Two, the arts and sciences of bombing with explosives from petrol powered aircraft had developed from almost useless to almost perfect, to be rendered obsolete soon afterwards. On

18 May 1951, the prototype of the Vickers Valiant, the first of the V-bomber jets, flew in expectation of carrying an atomic bomb at the speed of sound at 50,000ft.

That was all after the war. J was finished, and her story of 107 operations with thirty-three different captains and crews, 240 men altogether. But for some of J's graduates it wasn't over yet. The total of 103 of her men killed in action had not yet been reached.

Doug Melrose, J-Johnny champion with twenty-four ops as skipper plus one as second Dicky, finished the war as Squadron Leader DFC and Bar, he and most of his crew having elected to run straight on to a second tour of fifteen after finishing the first of thirty. Most of the other later J captains and crews also survived – Pooley, Arndell, Morrison, Macintosh, Camsell, Tweddle, Taylor, and their men. Two crews and two individuals did not make it.

Ernie Redfern had elected for the forty-five like Melrose, with a different crew, and his fortieth was 12 January 1945, the Tallboy joint attack with 617 on the U-boat pens at Bergen. It was a daylight, with fighter escorts, a Polish squadron of Mustangs.

The Mustangs had been sighted briefly on the way over. At the target, they dived down on to the flak emplacements and strafed them, while a flock of FW190s arrived high above and attacked the bombers.

Three of 9 Squadron's Lancasters had tremendous battles against three, four or five 190s at a time, and somehow escaped. One was Flight Lieutenant Larry Marsh:

'We were attacked by five FW190s who peeled off in turn and the attacks went on consistently from 13.09 to 13.27. We ended up at 900 feet with 360 mph on the clock after corkscrewing continuously. After seeing the fighter escort at the concentration (assembly point, Scottish coast) we never saw them again except for one which stood off and watched us near the end of the attacks.'

Something very similar happened to Ernie Redfern, witnessed by a bomb aimer called Dennis Nolan:

1Our Lancaster and another were flying on a similar course but the other was about two thousand feet lower, and we had three more aircraft in our view, which were FW190s. They stooged about while we watched them make up their minds. They were choosing. The sods were selecting which bomber to go for, us or him. They chose him. He corkscrewed and appeared to be getting free when one of his engines caught fire, and then another. That Lanc hit the sea in a way which clearly said to us, watching from above, that there would be no survivors but the fighters carried on shooting into the burning wreckage until they had no ammunition left. They couldn't attack any more Lancasters, such as ours for example, so they flew away. I thought that here were three of the best fighter aircraft of the war, operated by three of the worst or least experienced pilots.'

Melrose and crew saw it too. Most of them did, and the same kind of battles featuring 617. The sky was full of aircraft milling about but, seemingly, not including Mustangs. The Lancaster that fell in flames into the sea was NG257 WS/N, Redfern's. He had joined the squadron as a Flight Sergeant in early May, been promoted to Flying Officer in the July and awarded the DFC. He'd flown some routine missions, like everybody and, like everybody, had been sent to some of the worst jobs. Unlike so many, he had lasted a long time. He was one of the most experienced Lancaster pilots flying that day, and he was still only twenty-two years old. His crew, the ones that died with him at Bergen, were the same men who had taken J on the next-to-last, to Wilhelmshaven.

Flight Lieutenant Sidney Matthews DFC, once upon a time Pilot Officer Clark's mid-upper in J-Johnny to Eindhoven, was flying as a gunner in a B17 Fortress III on radar-jamming duties on 17 March 1945, with 214 Squadron, supporting a raid on the Misburg refinery. The aircraft was hit by flak and severely damaged; the captain gave the order to bail out – although he didn't go himself – and managed to bring his charge home to Bassingbourn.

Of the nine parachutists, four were decorated – two DFMs, two DFCs. All were captured; a group of seven were put in the village school cellar at Huchenfeld, near Pforzheim where, a few weeks before, an air-raid had reduced that town to rubble.

The airmen were under guard, of course, but a mob of Hitler Youth and others overwhelmed the guards and marched the men to the cemetery. On the way, three escaped but the other four, including Sidney Matthews, were shot. The next day, the escapers were caught. Two went to POW camp; one was beaten up and shot, also by Hitler Youth.

The new month of April would be the last of the flying war in Europe. It should have been pieces of cake all the way. On 7 April Number 9 Squadron went to Molbis, a town near Leipzig where there was benzol manufacture. An enormous explosion was seen at 23.10 and that was the end of the benzol plant.

There was another explosion later when an experienced crew died in a brand new Lancaster. HK788 WS/E burst into flames as they flew homewards and crashed near Wantage. Alf Jeffs and some of the others were quite elderly for bomber crew, and four of them were married. They'd taken W4964 on her last trip but they were not the last of WS/J's old boys to die.

That unwanted distinction belongs to a flight engineer, one with over forty ops behind him, one who had flown his first on 3 December 1943 with

Last captain, Alf Jeffs, too junior to go on the Tirpitz raid, is seen here with his flight engineer and bomb aimer.

Phil Plowright to Leipzig and who had looked after J-Johnny Walker sixteen times. A new captain was short of an engineer to go with him on his first op on 8 April, to an oil refinery at Lützkendorf.

The Germans had very little oil left. Luftwaffe fighters hadn't had any stocks issued lately. Destruction of this plant would be a near-fatal blow. It was a long way, near Leipzig, eight-and-a-half hours there and back. The winds were stronger than forecast but the bombing was excellent. There would be no more oil coming from Lützkendorf.

Over the target five Lancs out of 258 were shot down by flak, and in one of them was Sticky Lewis – Sergeant William Charles Lewis. He had been promoted to Flight Sergeant several times but was always busted down again for some indiscretion, generally linked with a few pints too many in The Jolly Sailor. He'd done his tour, no need to be there, not officially on a second tour but seemingly unable to give up flying ops. That was something he had in common with the famous men like Cheshire and Gibson, but Sticky Lewis wasn't famous. He was just there when they wanted him, a slight, smallish, often solitary figure with nothing very remarkable about him. The squadron commanders were happy, of course, to have a thoroughly experienced, Berlin hardened flight engineer to call on when they were short and, for the last time, they were short for Lützkendorf.

One Hundred and Seven
The operations of Lancaster
W4964

	Date	Target	Captain
1943			
1.	20 April	Stettin	Warrant Officer Wood
2.	4 May	Dortmund	Sergeant Duncan
3.	12 May	Duisburg	Sergeant Saxton
4.	13 May	Pilsen	Warrant Officer Wood
5.	23 May	Dortmund	Sergeant Gill
6.	25 May	Düsseldorf	Sergeant Gill
7.	27 May	Essen	Sergeant Gill
8.	11 June	Düsseldorf	Sergeant Gill
9.	12 June	Bochum	Sergeant Gill
10.	14 June	Oberhausen	Sergeant Aldersley
11.	24 July	Hamburg	Sergeant Newton
12.	25 July	Essen DNOC	Flight Sergeant Graham
13.	27 July	Hamburg	Flight Sergeant Graham
14.	29 July	Hamburg	Flight Sergeant Ward
15.	2 August	Hamburg	Pilot Officer Newton
16.	10 August	Nürnburg	Pilot Officer Newton
17.	12 August	Milan	Sergeant Knight
18.	15 August	Milan	Flight Sergeant Hall
19.	17 August	Peenemünde	Pilot Officer Newton
20.	1 October	Hagen	Pilot Officer Newton
21.	2 October	Munich	Pilot Officer Newton
22.	4 October	Frankfurt	Pilot Officer Newton

	Date	Target	Captain
23.	7 October	Stuttgart	Pilot Officer Newton
24.	8 October	Hannover	Pilot Officer Ward
25.	18 October	Hannover	Pilot Officer Ward
26.	20 October	Leipzig	Pilot Officer Ward
27.	22 October	Kassel	Flight Sergeant Syme
28.	3 November	Düsseldorf	Pilot Officer Newton
29.	10 November	Modane	Flying Officer Reid
30.	18 November	Berlin	Flying Officer Reid
31.	22 November	Berlin	Pilot Officer Newton
32.	23 November	Berlin	Pilot Officer Newton
33.	2 December	Berlin	Pilot Officer Newton
34.	3 December	Leipzig	Sergeant Plowright
35.	16 December	Berlin	Flying Officer Newton
36.	20 December	Frankfurt DNCO	Sergeant Froud
37.	23 December	Berlin	Flying Officer Newton
38.	29 December	Berlin	Sergeant Froud

1944

	Date	Target	Captain
39.	1 January	Berlin	Sergeant Froud
40.	2 January	Berlin DNCO	Flying Officer Pearce
41.	5 January	Stettin	Flying Officer Manning
42.	14 January	Brunswick	Flight Lieutenant Newton
43.	20 January	Berlin	Sergeant Froud
44.	21 January	Magdeburg	Sergeant Froud
45.	27 January	Berlin	Flight Lieutenant Newton
46.	1 March	Stuttgart	Pilot Officer Plowright
47.	15 March	Stuttgart	Pilot Officer Plowright
48.	18 March	Frankfurt	Flight Sergeant Horne
49.	22 March	Frankfurt	Pilot Officer Plowright
50.	24 March	Berlin DNCO	Flight Lieutenant Pooley
51.	25 March	Aulnoye	Pilot Officer Ineson
52.	26 March	Essen	Pilot Officer Plowright
53.	30 March	Nürnberg	Pilot Officer Plowright
54.	10 April	Tours	Wing Commander Porter
55.	11 April	Aachen	Pilot Officer Ineson
56.	18 April	Juvisy	Pilot Officer Plowright
57.	20 April	La Chappelle	Pilot Officer Plowright
58.	24 April	Munich	Pilot Officer Plowright
59.	28 April	St Médard en Jalles	Pilot Officer Plowright
60.	29 April	St Médard en Jalles	Pilot Officer Plowright
61.	1 May	Toulouse	Pilot Officer Plowright
62.	3 May	Mailly-le-Camp	Pilot Officer Plowright
63.	8 May	Brest/Lanveoc	Pilot Officer Plowright
64.	10 May	Lille	Pilot Officer Plowright
65.	11 May	Bourg Leopold	Pilot Officer Plowright

	Date	Target	Captain
66.	19 May	Tours	Pilot Officer Plowright
67.	21 May	Duisberg	Pilot Officer Plowright
68.	22 May	Brunswick	Flying Officer Melrose
69.	24 May	Eindhoven recall	Pilot Officer Clark
70.	27 May	Nantes	Flying Officer Melrose
71.	3 June	Ferme d'Urville	Pilot Officer Gradwell
72.	5 June	St Pierre du Mont	Flying Officer Blackham
73.	6 June	Argentan	Flying Officer Melrose
74.	8 June	Rennes	Flying Officer Melrose
75.	10 June	Orleans	Flying Officer Melrose
76.	12 June	Poitiers	Flying Officer Melrose
77.	14 June	Aunay sur Odon	Flying Officer Melrose
78.	15 June	Châtellerault	Flying Officer Melrose
79.	19 June	Watten recall	Flying Officer Melrose
80.	21 June	Gelsenkirchen	Flying Officer Melrose
81.	23 June	Limoges	Flying Officer Melrose
82.	24 June	Prouville	Flying Officer Blackham
83.	27 June	Vitry le Francois	Flying Officer Melrose
84.	29 June	Beauvoir	Flying Officer Melrose
85.	4 July	Creil	Flying Officer Melrose
86.	7 July	St Leu d'Esserant	Flying Officer Melrose
87.	12 July	Culmont-Chalandrey	Flying Officer Melrose
88.	17 July	Caen	Flying Officer Morrison
89.	20 July	Courtrai	Flight Sergeant Tweddle
90.	23 July	Kiel	Flying Officer Melrose
91.	25 July	St Cyr	Flying Officer Melrose
92.	26 July	Givors	Flying Officer Melrose
93.	28 July	Stuttgart	Flying Officer Scott
94.	30 July	Cahagnes recall	FlyingOfficer Macintosh
95.	13 August	Brest	Flight Lieutenant Melrose
96.	14 August	Brest	Flight Lieutenant Melrose
97.	15 August	Gilze Rijen	Flying Officer Taylor
98.	16 August	La Pallice	Flight Lieutenant Melrose
99.	18 August	La Pallice	Flight Lieutenant Camsell
100.	24 August	Ijmuiden	Flight Lieutenant Camsell
101.	27 August	Brest	Flying Officer Arndell
102.	15 September	Tirpitz	Flight Lieutenant Melrose
103.	23 September	Münster	Flight Lieutenant Melrose
104.	26 September	Karlsruhe	Flying Officer Arndell
105.	27 September	Kaiserslautern	Flying Officer Arndell
106.	5 October	Wilhelmshaven	Flying Officer Redfern
107.	6 October	Bremen	Flying Officer Jeffs

All J's Men – the crews

Listed in standard order: pilot, flight engineer, navigator, bomb aimer, wireless operator, mid-upper gunner, rear gunner. Rank is given where no initial is known.

1. H. E. Wood, C. Clayton, Sergeant Chipperfield, T. Mellard, G. T. M. Caines, W. R. Barker, H. G. Watson. Also E. L. Cramp, navigator,
2. J. D. Duncan, S. G. Blunden, H. T. Brown, G. Bartley, S. Hughes, L. G. Warner, D. B. McMillan.
3. G. H. Saxton, D. C. Ferris, W. C. Macdonald, R. M. Morris, J. Reddish, J. C. Owen, J. Buntin.
4. T. H. Gill, M. McPherson, R. V. Gough, B. P. Devine, W. A. Morton, K. McDonagh, R. McKee.
5. J. A. Aldersley, P. Hall, P. Webster, H. Poppleston, G. J. Sinclair, H. F. Poynter, D. G. Tremblay.
6. C. P. Newton, J. Turner, P. Hall, E. J. Duck, J. Ryan, R. McFerran, W. J. Wilkinson. Also L. T. Fairclough, bomb aimer (see Froud crew); Flight Sergeant Allen, bomb aimer; H.S. Sandy, second pilot; G. Bell, bomb aimer; G. W. G. Wickham, second navigator; H. C. Clark, second pilot;
7. G. A. Graham, W. Statham, D. MacDonald, R. M. Innes, A. F. Williamson, H. F. Altus, K. Mellor.
8. G. Ward, J. Sutton, E. D. Keene, G. L. James, G. F. K. Bedwell, N. F. Dixon, W. L. Doran.
9. R. A. Knight, T. W. Bradford, G. A. Munro, J. W. Noble, D. G. Connor, R. E. Jones, R. G. Nelson.
10. G. E. Hall, L. J. G. Field, W. D. Evans, E. Colbert, O. J. Overington, R. A. Chorley, H. G. Williams.
11. J. Syme, Sergeant Whiting, E. Hubbert, J. C. Docherty, D. Cattley, Sergeant Sorge, J. Heron.
12. W. M. Reid, S. W. Richards, R. D. H. Parker, D. G. Moir, B. Harthill, C. J. Wilhelm, G. Brown.

13. P. W. Plowright, W. C. Lewis, N. H. B. Lucas, R. P. Allen, H. Hannah, F. Corr, N. F. Wells. Also W. S. Richardson, navigator; S. J. Nancekivell, flight engineer; J. H. Preston, flight engineer; G. A. Langford, second pilot; J. D. Melrose, second pilot (see also Melrose crew); W. E. Pearson, bomb aimer

14. D. P. J. Froud, F. Harman, D. P. Carlick, L. T. Fairclough, W. H. Shirley, S. L. Jones (see also Pearce crew), R. L. Biers. Also R. Johnson, flight engineer; D. S. Nichols, wireless operator; J. Lever, wireless operator.

15. D. H. Pearce, C. W. Howe, J. E. Logan, W. R. Doran, S. L. Jones, E. A. Thomas.

16. A. E. Manning, W. F. Burkitt, J. W. Hearn, P. Warywoda, A. G. Newbound, J. J. Zammitt, R. G. Hayler.

17. W. R. Horne, T. W. Powell, J. J. Shirley, J. T. Johnson, J. H. McReery, R. A. Morton, J. S. Parkes.

18. H. R. Pooley, S. Bloom, C. L. Griffiths, F. Sowerby, A. R. Manthorpe, J. A. Williams, N. Smith.

19. J. F. Ineson, L. C. Margetts, H. F. Mackenzie, T. L. M. Porteous, H. R. Warren, H. S. Chappell, J. Wilkinson.

20. E. L. Porter, C. E. Bowyer, J. Waterhouse, J. McMaster, B. Owen, J. Michael, C. R. Bolt.

21. J. D. Melrose, E. Selfe, J. W. Moore, S. A. Morris, R. G. Woolf, E. Hoyle, E. E. Stalley.

22. H. C. Clark, R. K. Goldspink, H. F. S. Mitchell, C. H. Redmond, A. F. R. Horscroft, S. C. Matthews, G. R. Bradbury.

23. R. S. Gradwell, T. Lynch, P. E. Arnold, R. B. Atkinson, J. T. Price, W. F. Best, L. Sutton.

24. P. D. Blackham, J. D. Murrie, J. Wenger, J. D. Elphick, G. A. White, V. C. A. Stokes, J. M. Hickey.

25. A. M. Morrison, A. Aitkinhead, F. Reid, L. L. Westrope, F. Black, P. Strachan, F. Hooper.

26. W. D. Tweddle, C. G. Heath, E. Shields, J. W. Singer, A. Carson, J. A. Foot, K. Mallinson.

27. C. B. Scott, J. E. Simkins, L. A. Harding, L. W. Langley, E. M. Hayward, F. A. Saunders, L. J. Hambly.

28. D. Macintosh, R. V. Cosser, N. Hawkins, P. J. Ramwell, P. E. Tetlow, J. A. Wood, G. Owen.

29. B. Taylor, D. J. Doherty, A. L. Cunningham, A. M. Holmes, K. A. Burns, G. C. Freeman, G. M. Young.

30. G. C. Camsell, W. Andrews, P. R. Aslin, R. H. Thomas, D. Beevers, W. J. Hebert, A. E. Boon.

31. K. S. Arndell, P. H. Jones, P. E. Campbell, H. W. Porter, R. Meads, J. Brown, L. J. Richards.

32. E. C. Redfern, J. W. Williams, R. W. R. Cooper, O. P. Hull, L. G. Roberts, W. Brand, D. Winch.

33. A. E. Jeffs, C. V. Higgins, K. C. Mousley, H. A. Fisher, C. M. McMillan, W. Thomas, G. J. Symonds, C. Follett.

Roll of Honour

Men who flew in Lancaster W4964 and perished elsewhere. Names marked * are of men who were lost with ex-J captains but did not fly in W4964. Dates given are those of the commencement of the operation. Again, crews listed in standard order: pilot, flight engineer, navigator, bomb aimer, wireless operator, mid-upper gunner, rear gunner.

13 May, Pilsen

ED589 WS/P. Five crew commemorated at Runnymede.

Sergeant George Henry Saxton, 27, son of Mr and Mrs Robert Saxton of Carlisle.

Sergeant Douglas Claude Ferris, 22, son of William and Maude Ferris of Milton, Southsea.

Sergeant Wallace Reginald Macdonald, Canada.

Sergeant Roger Marshall Morris, 22, son of Ernest and Bertha Morris, husband of Isabella, of Cambridge.

Sergeant John Reddish.

Sergeant John Charles Owen, 24, son of Owen and Mabel Owen of Rhos-on-Sea. Wonseradeel Protestant Churchyard.

Sergeant James Buntin. Wonseradeel Protestant Churchyard.

12 June, Bochum

ED558, WS/N. Two crew buried at Bergh (Zeddam) Protestant Cemetery.

Warrant Officer Herbert Edward Wood, 26, pilot, son of John and Marion Wood of Melton High Wood, Barnetby.

Warrant Officer 2 Herbert George Watson, 19, rear gunner, son of Herbert and Aileen Watson of South Lethbridge, Alberta.

16 June, Cologne

ED487 WS/D. Four crew buried at Schoonselhof (Antwerp) Cemetery.

(Sergeant J. A. Aldersley POW)

Sergeant Patrick Hall.

Sergeant Denis Webster, 20, son of Jack and Sybil Webster of Loughton.

(Sergeant H. Popplestone POW)

(Sergeant C J Sinclair POW)

Sergeant Herbert Francis Poynter, 19, son of William and Eliza Poynter of Islington.

Sergeant David Gerald Tremblay, 27, son of David and Katherine Tremblay of Elm Creek, Manitoba.

31 August, Mönchengladbach

ED551 WS/M. Crew commemorated at Runnymede.

Warrant Officer Gilbert Eric Hall, 23, husband of Beatrice Irene, son of Samuel and Ada Hall of Appleton.

Sergeant Leon John George Field, 26, son of Leon and Emily Field of Hildenborough.

Sergeant William David Evans, son of Robert and Margaret Evans of Carmarthen.

Pilot Officer Clarence Howard Anderson, second navigator, 28, husband of Edith, son of John and Myrtle Anderson of Calgary, Alberta.*

Sergeant Edward Colbert, 27, son of Elizabeth Colbert of Atherton.

Sergeant Oliver John Overington.

Sergeant Robert Alexander Chorley, 27, husband of Joan, son of Robert and Elvira Chorley of Catford.

Sergeant Henry Gordon Williams, 31, son of Mr and Mrs J. T. Williams of Eltham.

5 September, Mannheim

R5744 WS/E. Crew buried at Dürnbach War Cemetery.

Sergeant Reginald Arthur Knight, 23, husband of Maisie, son of Arthur and Florence Knight of Carshalton.

Sergeant Thomas William Bradford, 31, husband of Lilian of Waltham Cross, son of Walter and Emily Bradford.

Sergeant George Alexander Munro, 24, son of George and Jean Munro of Calgary, Alberta.

Sergeant John William Noble, 21, son of Samuel and Ada Noble of Mansfield.

Sergeant David Gordon Connor, 20, son of James and Sarah Connor of Workington.

Sergeant Chester Andith Davis*.

Sergeant Robert Gilchrist Nelson, 22, son of Gavin and Elizabeth Nelson of Glasgow.

ED666 WS/G. Crew buried at Dürnbach War Cemetery.

Pilot Officer Thomas Henry Gill, 25, husband of Mollie, son of Thomas and Ellen Gill of Birmingham.

Sergeant Matthew McPherson, 21, son of Matthew and Jean McPherson of Glasgow.

Flight Sergeant Raymond Victor Gough, son of Albert and Eveline Gough of Cheltenham.

Flight Sergeant Bernard Peter Devine, 22, son of James and Florence Devine.

Sergeant William Alexander Morton, husband of Leading Aircraftman M. E. Morton.

Sergeant Kevin McDonagh, 23, son of John and Margaret McDonagh of Limerick.

Sergeant Robert McKee, 23, son of James and Ruth McKee of Bolton.

18 November, Berlin
DV284 WS/G. Crew buried at Berlin War Cemetery.

Pilot Officer Gordon Alan Graham, Canada.

Pilot Officer John Graham McComb*, second pilot, son of Samuel and Elizabeth McComb of Belfast.

Sergeant Walter George Statham.

Flying Officer Duncan MacDonald, 34, husband of Jane, son of Murdo and Julia MacDonald of Glasgow.

Sergeant Ronald McKenzie Innes.

Sergeant Arthur Fenwick Williamson, 20, son of Arthur and Evelyn Williamson of Tynemouth.

Flight Sergeant Hector Ferdinand Altus, 33, son of Maria Altus of Wilkawatt, South Australia.

Sergeant Kenneth Mellor, 21, son of Henry and Ada Mellor of Lower Hopton.

2 December
DV334 WS/C. Gamston after Berlin. Rake Lane Cemetery, Wallasey.

Sergeant Richard Emrys Jones, 22, air gunner, husband of Edith, son of Richard and Violet Jones of Wallasey.

3 December, Leipzig
ED920 LE/D, 630 Squadron. First three named commemorated at Runnymede; others buried at Berlin War Cemetery.

Pilot Officer John Syme, 26, son of James and Amy Syme of Adelaide, South Australia.

Sergeant George Leggott, 22, son of Mr and Mrs G. H. Leggott of Scunthorpe.*
Sergeant Eric Hubbert, 21, son of Frank and Florence Hubbert of Swinton.
Flying Officer John Christopher Doherty, 22, son of Stephen and Mary Doherty of Carshalton Beeches.
(Sergeant D. Cattley, POW.)
Sergeant Kenneth Swinchatt.*
Sergeant James Heron, 22, son of Frances Heron of Gateshead.

2 January, Berlin
JA711 WS/A.

Flying Officer Geoffrey Ward, 23, son of Arthur and Sarah Ward of Dewsbury.

Sergeant Jack Sutton.

Sergeant Eric Douglas Keene.

Flight Sergeant George Lloyd James.

Sergeant George Frederick Kenneth Bedwell, 24, husband of Joan, son of Walter and Mabel Bedwell of Saxmundham.

Flight Sergeant Norman Frederick Dixon, 19, son of Frederick and Ivy Dixon of Old Balderton.

Warrant Officer 2 Willard Lawrence Doran, 21, son of Lawrence and Minnie Doran of Edmonton, Alberta.

19 February, Leipzig
W5010 WS/L. Crew buried at Berlin War Cemetery.

Flight Sergeant Denis Percy John Froud, 22, son of Percy and Florence Froud of Leyton.

Sergeant Fred Harman.

Sergeant David Brynmor Carlick, 21, son of Samuel and Beatrice Carlick of Treharris.

Flight Sergeant Leonard Thomas Fairclough, 20, son of Paul and Alice Fairclough of Adlington.

Sergeant Wilfred Henry Shirley, 19, son of Mrs W H Shirley of Langley.

Sergeant Stanley Lewis Jones.

Flight Sergeant Robert Lloyd Biers, 19, son of Harold and Sadie Biers of Cochrane, Ontario.

22 March, Frankfurt
LM430 WS/B. Seven crew buried at Brussels Town Cemetery.

Flying Officer Albert Edward Manning, 28, husband of Lilian, son of Alfred and Laura Manning of Ipswich.

Sergeant William Frederick Burkitt, 22, son of Frederick and May Burkitt of Hornsey.

Flying Officer James White Hearn, 30, son of Alexander Hearn of Bonnyrigg.

Pilot Officer Peter Warywoda, son of Michael and Annie Warywoda, Canada.

(Flight Sergeant G. T. M. Caines POW*)

Sergeant John Joseph Zammit, son of Emanuel and Celestina Zammit.

Flight Sergeant Arthur Finch.*

Group Captain Norman Charles Pleasance, station CO, passenger.*

3 May, Mailly-le-Camp

LL787 WS/Y. Five crew buried at Normee Churchyard, Marne.

Flying Officer James Frank Ineson, 22, husband of Monica of Leeds, son of William and Sarah Ineson of Batley.

Pilot Officer Leonard Charles Margetts, 29, husband of Frances of Edinburgh, son of William and Lucy Margetts of Moseley.

Pilot Officer Hugh Fraser Mackenzie, 21, son of George and Cecile Mackenzie of Spirit River, Alberta.

(Flying Officer T. L. M. Porteous, New Zealand, POW)

Sergeant Henry Robert Warren, son of F. J. Warren of Deptford.

(Sergeant Henry S. Chappell evaded)

Sergeant James Wilkinson, son of G. Wilkinson of Urmston.

10 May, Lille-Fives

LM520 WS/X.

Flight Lieutenant Gilbert Bell DFC, son of Frank and Mabel Bell of Exeter. Commemorated at Runnymede.

7 July, St Leu d'Esserant

JA957 WS/D. Six crew buried at Ecquevilly Communal Cemetery, Yvelines.

Flying Officer Peter Douglas Blackham.

(Sergeant J. D. Murrie evaded)

Flying Officer John Wenger, 26, son of John and Pauline Wenger of Regina, Saskatchewan.

Flying Officer Douglas Elphick, 25, son of Richard and Mary Elphick of St Catharines, Ontario.

Flying Officer George Albert White, 27, son of John and Jean White of Markham, Ontario.

Sergeant Victor Clement Arthur Stokes, 20, son of Arthur and Dora Stokes of Smethwick.

Pilot Officer James Martin Hickey, 31, husband of Jean, son of James and Anne Hickey of Peterborough, Ontario.

JA690 WS/M.

Sergeant James Thomas Price, 21, wireless operator, son of Osmond and Mabel Price of Hugglescote. Beaumont-les-Nonaines Communal Cemetery, Oise.

17 August, Stettin Bay

NE167, 97 Squadron.

Wing Commander Edward Leach Porter DFC and Bar, pilot, 33. Poznan Old Garrison Cemetery.

23 September, Münster Aqueduct
LL901 WS/V. Six crew buried at Holten General Cemetery.

Flight Lieutenant Charles Berrie Scott, 22, son of John and Helen Scott of Glasgow.

Sergeant Jack Edward Simkin, 23, son of Charles and Mary Simkin of Seaford.

Flight Sergeant Louis Arthur Harding.

(Flight Sergeant L. W. Langley POW)

Sergeant Maurice Edward Hayward, 21, son of Maurice and Edith Hayward of Ludgershall.

Sergeant Frank Alfred Saunders, 30, husband of Ellen of West Kensington, son of Andrew and Mary Saunders.

Sergeant Leslie Joseph Hambly, 19, son of John and Ruth Hambly of Millom.

12 January, Bergen
NG257 WS/N. Crew commemorated at Runnymede.

Flying Officer Ernest Cyril Redfern DFC, 22, husband of Frances of Salford.

Flight Sergeant John Walter Williams, 20, of Trimdon.

Sergeant Ronald William Riverston Cooper, 22, of Welling.

Flying Officer Owen Percy Hull.

Sergeant Lewis George Roberts, 23, husband of Lydia Jean of Ilsington.

Sergeant Walter Brand, 28, of Sheffield.

Sergeant Dennis Winch, 20, of Grantham.

17 March 1945, Huckenfeld
Fortress HB779 BU/L, 214 Squadron.

Flight Lieutenant Sidney Clayden Matthews DFC, 25, husband of Iris of Edgware, son of Alfred and Maud Matthews.

7 April, Wantage after Molbis
HK788 WS/E. Crew buried at Botley Cemetery, Oxford.

Flying Officer Alfred Edward Jeffs, 29, husband of Bessie Margaret of Birmingham.

Sergeant Clarence Victor Higgins, 23, husband of Irene of Birmingham.

Flight Sergeant Kenneth Charles Mousley, 36, husband of Miriam Grace of Streatham.

Warrant Officer 2 Hugh Alexander Fisher, 24, Dauphin, Manitoba.

Flight Sergeant Campbell McIntosh McMillan, 20, husband of Betty of Kettlethorpe.

Flight Sergeant Willy Thomas, 20, of Cleckheaton.

Flight Sergeant Gordon John Symonds, 20, of Wantage.

8 April, Lutzkendorf
NG235 WS/H. Berlin War Cemetery.

Sergeant William Charles Lewis, flight engineer.

Bibliography

Aeronautics magazine, various issues 1939–1945.

Aspects of the Combined British and American Strategic Air Offensive against Germany 1939 to 1945. Michael Varley.

Operations Record Book, Combat Reports and Squadron Archive, No. 9 Squadron.

RAF Bomber Command Losses of the Second World War, vols 1 to 6. W. R. Chorley.

The Bomber Command War Diaries. Martin Middlebrook and Chris Everitt, 1985.

The Luftwaffe War Diaries. Cajus Becker, 1964.

Despatch on War Operations. Sir Arthur T. Harris, 1995.

Evaders' and other records from the Public Record Office and the National Archives.

Commonwealth War Graves Commission.

How the RAF works. A. H. Narracott, 1941.

Pilot's and Flight Engineer's Notes – Lancaster. Air Ministry, 1944.

RAF Operational Diary, Operation Paravane. Squadron Leader E. S. Harman.

9 Squadron. T. Mason, 1965.

T.A.B.S (9 Squadron Association) magazines, 1981 ff.

The Lancaster Story. Peter Jacobs, 2002.

A Hell of a Bomb. Stephen Flower, 2002.

Sledgehammers for Tintacks. Steve Darley, 2002

Die Deutschen Ubootbunker und Bunkerwerften. Sönke Neitzel.

Quand les Alliés bombardaient la France. Eddy Florentin.

The Mare's Nest. David Irvine, 1964.

The Air War in Europe. Ronald H Bailey, 1981.

Avro Lancaster, The Definitive Record. Harry Holmes, 1997

The Lancaster at War, vols 1, 2, 3 & 5. Mike Garbett & Brian Goulding, 1971 ff.

The Air War in Europe. Ronald H. Bailey, 1981.

The War in the Air. Gavin Lyall, 1968.

Various RAF, RCAF, USAAF and WW2 history websites.

ALL OUR PLANES RETURNED SAFELY

A marked tribute to the skill and courage of our pilots and wonderful testimony to the unfailing performance of the modern aero engine and components. Millions of flying hours have been safeguarded by .

TECALEMIT
full flow
OIL FILTERS

AVIATION DEPARTMENT

TECALEMIT LIMITED   GREAT WEST ROAD   Phone: EALing 6661   HYDRAULIC & MECHANICAL
BRENTFORD MIDDX   (16 lines)   DESIGNING & MANUFACTURING ENGINEERS

Small Parts
for Big Jobs

"Our bombers were out over Germany last night . . ." For success the crews depend on the outstanding quality of the aircraft — outstanding in every detail, down to rivets and distance pieces, screws and bolts. That's why we at Linreads take pride in the many thousands of those small parts we are turning out — small parts good enough for the biggest jobs.

Roll Threaded Screws
Solid & Tubular Rivets
Nuts, Bolts, etc., in all metals
Small Pressings
Auto and Capstan Turned Parts

SPECIALISTS IN COLD FORGING

**LINREAD LTD., STERLING WORKS, COX STREET,
BIRMINGHAM, 3.   'PHONE: CENTRAL 6121-2-3**

HURRICANE
SPITFIRE
MOSQUITO
BEAUFIGHTER
WHITLEY
WELLINGTON
HALIFAX
LANCASTER

THE STANDARD POWER UNIT

The MERLIN Engine in its various marques has been the standard power unit for all British fighting machines since the beginning of the war..... To call it the best engine in the world is merely to recognise the simple facts regarding its performance and reliability in service.

Extract from "THE MOTOR."

ROLLS-ROYCE
"Merlin" AERO ENGINES

You are invited to inspect the Merlin Aero Engine on view at our Showrooms—15 Conduit St. London W.1.

The **KEYNOTE** *of*
BOULTON PAUL TURRETS

RELIABILITY

SINCE the days of the "trusty sword," the fighting man has set the highest value on reliability.

Boulton Paul armament has achieved an enviable reputation for reliability which, in a complex weapon like a gun turret, is founded on the engineering quality of its component parts.

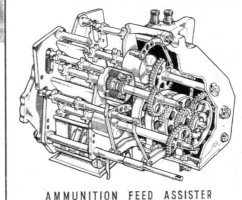

AMMUNITION FEED ASSISTER

Boulton Paul
AIRCRAFT LTD

BPA

DESIGNERS AND MANUFACTURERS OF AIRCRAFT AND ARMAMENT

LOOKING FORWARD TO LOOKING BACK!

With calm assurance he looks forward to the ever nearing days of Peace, when with pride and satisfaction he will look back upon the grim days of 1940, the stirring events of '41 and '42, the glorious achievements of '43.

And in his heart he will pay tribute to the "kite" that pulled him through, to the unfailing performance of his engines which in the tightest corner never failed him . . . all those factors which contribute to the safety of our Airmen and the supremacy of British Aircraft.

Millions of flying hours are safe-guarded by

TECALEMIT
full flow
OIL FILTERS

AVIATION DEPARTMENT

TECALEMIT LIMITED

GREAT WEST ROAD. BRENTFORD MIDDX.

Phone: EALing 6661 (16 lines)

HYDRAULIC & MECHANICAL, DESIGNING & MANUFACTURING ENGINEERS

It's that little Man Again

(With abject apologies to Uncle Tom Handley and all.)

Pray silence for that sunniest of satraps . . . that commander of calories . . . the Warden of Upper Warming'em . . . and Burgrave of Basking-in-the-Plane . . . **UNCLE TOM !**

Well, flyers, talking of hot spots in high spots, I'll give you the 'gen' . . .

(Gin? I don't mind if I do. Skin off your nose!)

Warmth round your toes! As I was saying . . . Ah! there's the 'phone . . . Hullo . . .

布图一裳重今個走領指逄巷入計港通

Oh, yes, for everyone in the plane.

照點保人案玉那散香国古事善一回枣

No, we shan't fly over Flushing! That was Hi-Fli-Kumfi, asking if we fitted central heating in planes. Yes, that's a problem that we solved Fumf and for all.

(Well, for ever more)

Same thing, Sam. Yes, under control of the little man from Johnsons, warm air is fed through the plane in light alloy ducting . . .

(Don't forget the cover, sir)

. . . Ah, yes ; covered with asbestos supplied by Bell's Asbestos & Engineering, Ltd., keeping everyone cosy and cheery.

(I've brought something for you, sir)

Ah, that is kind of you, Mrs. Mop! What is it? A natty numnah for navigators?

(No, sir. It's a posh pullover with plane piping for peppy pilots.)

Sorry, Mrs. Mop. They're not needed if there's

(Cabin Heating I said Heating)

by

G. JOHNSON BROS.

103-149, CORNWALL ROAD, SOUTH TOTTENHAM, LONDON, N.15

Telephone : Stamford Hill 6601-2-3-4.

Telegrams : "Metalitis, Southtot, London."

VICTORY
IS IN THE AIR

The Stygian darkness of the night is o'er
And high above the sounds of waking life
There comes the deep reverberating roar
Of Victors homing from the strife.

Symbolic dawn of better things to come,
Of freedom's triumph and of prospect fair
Of peace and goodwill, happiness and home....
For Victory is in the air

HERE'S TO 1944

TECALEMIT LIMITED GREAT WEST ROAD, BRENTFORD, MIDDX. Phone: EALing 6661 (16 lines) HYDRAULIC & MECHANICAL, DESIGNING & MANUFACTURING ENGINEERS

Tracing Your Family History?

Read *Your* Family HISTORY

ESSENTIAL ADVICE FROM THE EXPERTS

FREE COPY!

Your Family History is the only magazine that is put together by expert genealogists. Our editorial team, led by Dr Nick Barratt, is passionate about family history, and our networks of specialists are here to give essential advice, helping readers to find their ancestors and solve those difficult questions.

In each issue we feature a **Beginner's Guide** covering the basics for those just getting started, a **How To** … section to help you to dig deeper into your family tree and the opportunity to **Ask The Experts** about your tricky research problems. We also include a **Spotlight** on a different county each month and a **What's On** guide to the best family history courses and events, plus much more.

Receive a free copy of *Your Family History* magazine and gain essential advice and all the latest news. To request a free copy of a recent back issue, simply e-mail your name and address to marketing@your-familyhistory.com or call 01226 734302*.

Your Family History is in all good newsagents and also available on subscription for six or twelve issues. For more details on how to take out a subscription, call 01778 392013 or visit **www.your-familyhistory.co.uk**.

Alternatively read issue 31 online completely free using this QR code

*Free copy is restricted to one per household and available while stocks last.

www.your-familyhistory.com

PHL

54060000244201

THE
**PAUL HAMLYN
LIBRARY**

DONATED BY

THE PAUL HAMLYN

FOUNDATION

TO THE

BRITISH MUSEUM

opened December 2000